# THE CIVILIZATION OF FRANCE

# THE CIVILIZATION
# OF FRANCE

AN INTRODUCTION

BY

ERNST ROBERT CURTIUS

TRANSLATED BY
OLIVE WYON

**BOOKS FOR LIBRARIES PRESS**
FREEPORT, NEW YORK

First Published 1932
Reprinted 1971

INTERNATIONAL STANDARD BOOK NUMBER:
0-8369-5648-6


LIBRARY OF CONGRESS CATALOG CARD NUMBER:
70-148877


PRINTED IN THE UNITED STATES OF AMERICA

# PREFACE

THE present work owes its inception to the suggestion of the publisher, who invited me to compose a counterpart to the book on England by Dibelius. The general course of my scientific work on the one hand, however, and the peculiar conditions of French national existence on the other, led me to propose a different method for the work on France. France is a living unity, which is determined quite as strongly by matters of general culture as of politics. It is impossible to understand France from the political point of view without some knowledge of her cultural outlook, and vice versa. For this reason it seemed desirable to suggest an interpretation of modern France in the form of an introduction to her culture, her politics and her economic life.

Since the two latter spheres lie entirely outside the scope of my scientific studies I would not have undertaken this piece of work had it not been for the fact that at that moment I found—in the person of my colleague at Heidelberg, Dr. Arnold Bergsträsser (Privat-Dozent)—a man who was ready to undertake the interpretation of the spheres of politics and economics. It is obvious that a division of labour of this kind is not ideal. In this instance, however, the close personal connexion between the two authors seemed to guarantee a certain measure of unity of view-point. I had to remove to Bonn, however, and our personal intercourse was thus unfortunately interrupted.

On the aim of my own contribution to this work, which I here present to the public, I would make the following remarks: this book does not aim at giving a comprehensive picture of French civilization and culture;[1] it simply seeks

[1] As is done, for instance, in the *Handbuch der Frankreichkunde*, issued by Dr. Hartig and Dr. Schellberg.

7

to give an explanation of its values and systems of ideology; thus it is not a description but a structural analysis. It is in this sense that this book is intended to be an "introduction" to the *understanding* of French civilization.

The way in which I regard the ideological research comes out clearly in the first section. The final ideal of such an analysis of civilization would constitute a complete doctrine of the French outlook on the world, and of the view which France takes of her own position within it, in the sense in which Max Scheler[1] has described this aim of research. In this first sketch this ideal could not be realized. It was therefore impossible to avoid a certain inequality of treatment. Hence this work must be regarded both as fragmentary and experimental.

I hope that my work will be of service to the study of civilization which occupies such a prominent place at the present time in the curriculum of the school and the university. This work is, however, no mere school text-book in the ordinary sense of the word; it is meant for all who take an interest in France and her civilization.

The intelligent reader will immediately notice that there was little material already in existence in harmony with my own point of view upon which I could draw. The best all-round interpretations of French Civilization are (in my opinion) the brilliant essays by Keyserling (*Das Spektrum Europas*) and Sieburg (*Gott in Frankreich?*).

ERNST ROBERT CURTIUS

Bonn, *Easter* 1930

---

[1] In his works: *Nation und Weltanschauung* (1923) and *Die Wissensformen und die Gesellschaft* (1926).

# TABLE OF CONTENTS

# I

## THE CONCEPTION OF CIVILIZATION

WHEN Frenchmen or Germans make a sincere effort to understand each other from the psychological point of view, the whole attempt is often defeated by the emergence of profound, and seemingly insoluble, misunderstanding. The reason for this is clear: each group—whether consciously or unconsciously—tests the foreign civilization by the system of values current in its own.

Some typical examples will make this clear. The German, practical and orderly, often misses both these qualities when he is in France. He imagines that the French also must feel this lack. They, however, are not in the least conscious of any defect; again the German is surprised and possibly annoyed. The Frenchman knows that "somehow or other" things get done, and that in one way or another the matter will be despatched. He prefers to comfort himself with the thought of this "somehow or other", than try to introduce a discipline and order to which the temperament of his fellow-countrymen would never submit. He leaves to us Germans the glory of our good organization; he admits it, but he regards it as an advantage which his country does not need, and which he does not want, because, to him, whether rightly or wrongly, this good organization savours of the barracks. An elastic technique suits the organism of France better than a rigid system; France flourishes in a régime of disorder and slovenliness which we would not tolerate, and it fares every whit as well as Germany, with its system of bureaucratic and scientific order. These differences are due to temperament, and arise from a different outlook on life.

Here is another example, just as elementary. We Germans tend to value a man according to his achievement. We value the work for its own sake. We admire it according to the thoroughness and precision with which it is done.

France does not regard work in this light at all; therefore she does not understand it in us. On the French side the reproach is often made that the Germans work too hard. The Frenchman asks himself: Why do they do this? Can there be some conspiracy behind all this? We also, however, easily fall into a similar error. To us it seems that an existence which fails to see its essential task in terms of labour has a certain lack of dignity. On the other hand, the Frenchmen thinks it is undignified to disturb the balance between work and leisure. Even if in a very humble way, he desires to take some pleasure in life for its own sake. Without doubt, for him joy in existence does possess a value of its own. He estimates people less by their achievements than by what they are, and his test of the worth of the State is the way in which it ministers to the happiness of the community: "Le but de la société est le bonheur commun", says the *Declaration of the Rights of Humanity* of 1795. Modern French theorists of a conservative tendency also adhere to this leading idea.[1]

In the thought of political science also, these opposing methods of valuation appear. To the official representatives of contemporary France, for instance, the ideal form of the State is that of the democratic Republic, which is entirely divorced from religion. From this standpoint they consider the history of Germany defective. They consider that its defect is this: we have had no Revolution, or at least only an interior one—that is, the Reformation. To them this phenomenon appears either reactionary or tragic. They pity us for it, not realizing that our view of our own history, our conception of freedom, and our view of the State differ entirely from the French view. We, for our part, tend to equate the democratic republican consciousness of France with the rhetorical phraseology in which it is often expressed; but in so doing we overlook the fact that it is deeply rooted in the life of the nation.

[1] Cf. Henri Chardon, Conseiller d'État de la République française: *L'Organisation de la République pour la Paix* (1927).

It is not necessary to multiply instances to show how great is the difference between the German and the French estimate of the values of civilization. The difference, however, extends to all the realms of culture and civilization, and indeed, right into the conception of the essence of civilization (*Kultur*) itself.

We do not understand a foreign civilization if we only know its isolated elements. We need to know its inner form of development, and its own conception of itself. The German and the French conceptions of civilization differ fundamentally. If this fact is disregarded or overlooked we fall into a fundamental error, which inevitably gives rise to countless others.

This question is one of far more than theoretical concern. On the contrary, during the War the misunderstanding of mutual ideals of civilization in France and in Germany gave rise to an interminable controversy which also expressed itself politically in propaganda among the neutral nations, and in the official cultural policy of both nations. The difference between both conceptions came to a head in the antithesis: *Kultur* and *Civilisation*. In the war literature of Germany and of France this contrast was often discussed. But it was not a creation of the War. It has deep historical roots which branch out in many directions.

In our classical epoch Wilhelm von Humboldt gave this definition of civilization: "Civilization (*Zivilisation*) is the humanizing of the nations in their external organization, and in the spirit and temper to which this is related; to this elevation of the social situation culture (*Kultur*) adds science and art". This was the conception of German Neo-Humanism. Civilization includes the socializing and moralizing of humanity; but beyond that there rises, as an independent phenomenon, the realm of the creative spirit; to it alone can the name "culture" (*Kultur*) be applied.

This conception reflects the situation of Germany about the year 1800: behind the unhappy and hopeless conditions in social life, and in the State, there was a small community of elect souls, bound together by poetry and philosophy.

This conception of civilization, which dates from the German Classical epoch, was then opposed by Nietzsche. He evolved a new scale of values of the prophetic type, in which the dionysiac and the tragic were opposed to the values of the German Classical school. For him civilization is an ideal of the herd-man. The great elements of *Kultur* are based upon the dominion of the freest and most daring natures. *Kultur* and civilization are wholly different in aim.

To sum up: on the German as well as the French side both these words and conceptions were set in opposition to each other. In both countries this was admitted, but the estimate formed in each nation was exactly the opposite. We rate *Kultur* higher than *civilisation*. France places *civilisation* in a higher category than *Kultur*.[1]

To the Frenchman the word *civilisation* is both the palladium of his national idea, and the guarantee of all human solidarity. Every Frenchman understands this word. It inflames the masses, and under certain circumstances it has a sacredness which exalts it to the religious sphere.

Those who desire to understand this feeling should seek out those parts of France where the primitive sense of awe, which belongs to the earliest stage in human history, has been preserved.

On French soil there are places which seem to be impregnated with the mystery of eternity. I think of the desolate Breton heath of Carnac, where the unhewn gigantic blocks of the Menhirs seem to grow out of the earth, and in their ordered rows seem to proclaim the first glimmering of a sense of number and of law. Still more im-

---

[1] This is why all German criticism of civilization which is based on the thoughts of Nietzsche, all German sociology which takes into account the distinction between *Kultur* and *Civilisation*, is not understood in France.

pressive, perhaps, is the impression made upon the traveller
by the landscape of Périgord, with its meadows and its hills.
There, in the lovely winding valley of the Vézère, is a
wealth of magnificent testimony to primitive times. In
every grey wall of rock there is the dark mouth of a cave;
if we follow the winding course of its labyrinth of corridors
we reach a place where we can gaze upon some of those
magic animal-pictures of the older Stone Age, which have
been discovered by the labours of research of the nineteenth
century.

These prehistoric grottoes of Les Eyzies carry us back
into the dim past, tens of thousands of years ago. With
reverent wonder we gaze out into the immeasurable
distances of the past and the future. We know that still
those Menhirs and these walls of rock will stand, long after
the pomp of Paris, and Rome the Eternal City, have disappeared from the face of the earth. Nature will outlast
humanity. But the traces which have been left by man,
both by his hand and by his spirit, upon one little space of
world history seem infinitely great and venerable. The
polished pebble which I hold in my hand is the witness of
the Prometheus fate of humanity. This stone axe, this reindeer picture cut in the face of the rock—they are the work
of the same forces which built the pyramids of Egypt,
made the frieze of the gods of Greece, as well as the Gothic
cathedrals, and the steel-works of Westfalia. The creative
energy which works through all the ages and spheres of
humanity is one and the same. It has founded the realm
of humanity in the struggle with the forces of Nature. The
struggle of the cave-man with the mammoth is carried on
to-day by the inventor of machines, and the aviator in his
long-distance flight over the ocean. Hunter and herdsman,
peasant and founder of a State, inventor, technician, re-
search-worker, artist, poet—all are working together to
build up humanity. All those who have offered their
strength and their courage for this *opus magnum* are links in
a chain, are the servants of one idea. Only a few have their

names inscribed in the great Book of Remembrance. When we honour these we honour along with them all those nameless ones upon whose service our own lives are based.

Thoughts such as these arise within us at those places in which the primitive history of humanity speaks to us through hieroglyphics. Then, when we come out of the Grottoes of Font-de-Gaume or of Laugerie-Basse, and wend our way back to the little village of Les Eyzies—when we stand before the memorial tablet to the soldiers who fell in the World War, and read the inscription: "À tous ceux qui sont morts pour la civilisation"—this word *civilisation* gains a fullness of tone, a dignity and consecration which we had not hitherto dreamed that it possessed.

In Germany you will not find the word *Kultur* upon any War Memorial. Our people do not understand this word, and we cannot render it into German. It belongs to the sphere in which highly educated and cultivated people move. It does not speak to the heart. France alone, of all nations, is able to express with this word *Civilisation* its most sacred treasures.

It was not always so. This is the fairly recent result of a long and complicated historical process. In order to understand it we must go back to the Ancient World.

When the Ancient poets celebrate the greatness of man they usually enumerate all his capacities and arts. "πᾶσαι τέχναι βροτοῖσιν ἐκ Προμηθέως"—all the arts came to mortals through Prometheus—thus sang Aeschylus of the fettered Titan. He names the building of houses and working in wood, astronomy and mantic divination, seafaring and knowledge of healing, number and writing. All these he has granted to men, and in so doing he has turned helpless children into reasonable beings. In a similar enumeration the famous Chorus of Antigone celebrates the greatness of man, save that here Sophocles extols the *Polis* as the supreme value and final form of all the achievements of civilization: that is, the civil and religious order of the ancient urban community.

The ancient idea of civilization is based upon the summing up of all the blessings of civilization in one conception of value, and upon the binding of this total idea to the *Polis*, or, to use the Latin word, to the *Civitas*. It is the idea of a humanity which has adopted a moral code set over against an existence which is bound up with natural conditions, that is, with barbarism. All that raises man above the barbarism of his origin, all that makes him lord of the elements, all this is civilization (*Kultur*). And all this is equally important and valuable. It makes no difference whether we are concerned with food, housing, agriculture, writing, counting, justice or morals. The fundamental forms of the external arrangement of life in this conception of civilization take no less room than do the elements of the knowledge of nature, or the institutions of corporate human life. Satisfaction of material needs, technical ability, and also the social order and the achievement of knowledge, are all necessary parts of this conception of civilization.

Now this ancient conception of civilization belongs to the racial and intellectual inheritance of Rome, out of which France has arisen. Gallo-Roman life forms the basis of French civilization. The vital substance of late antiquity is continued in France. It reveals its presence through all the centuries of its history, and even to-day it stamps its features clearly upon many features of French intellectual life. France carries forward the ancient idea of civilization into the modern world, not, however, because she has deliberately accepted it, but because it is born in her. It is a primary formal category of the French nature.

But this form has only reached its own self-presentation through the process of national history. France had first of all to exist as a State and a nation before she could understand her significance as a civilized community. This feeling did not arise before the time of the Capetians. For the kingdom of the Franks was a world-empire, not yet national in form, like its model, the Roman Empire.

The Roman idea of Imperial unity, however, remained

B

the driving force in the great historical structures which grew out of the Empire: in the Papacy, the Holy Roman Empire and the French Monarchy.

In Germany we are accustomed to study this development preferably from the view-point of the Papacy and the Empire and the struggle between these two universal powers. But the interweaving of universal and national forces in France has been no less significant for the growth of the modern world.

What form did this process take in France? If we compare the German and the French historical development we can say this: in Germany, the relation between the universal and the national idea is one of conflict, while in France it is one of union. In the history of Germany it is the explosive factor, in the history of France it is the element of fusion. After centuries of passionate struggle we (Germans) entered the new world of modern times with a decadent universal monarchy which was alien to the spirit of the people, with a body of territorial princes continually at war with each other, with a German form of religion which had shaken off the yoke of Rome, but which also divided the nation beyond recall. Neither from the point of view of the State, nor as a nation, were we united in spirit. We wanted something too great for us and we failed. We were on the eve of the seventeenth century, which was to bring us the greatest catastrophe in our history. The French, on the other hand, entered into the modern era with a mighty national State, which compelled all forces to unite, and also overcame the crisis caused by the Wars of Religion. France was then on the threshold of the century in which she was to attain the sunlit heights of her power and civilization.

Crudely expressed, this statement does bring out the striking difference between the German and the French course of historical development. This, however, might lead us to suppose that in France the universal was entirely swallowed up in the national idea. But this is not true. The facts of the situation, which are very remarkable, are these: in their mutual fusion both forces have received an increase of energy. All the claims made by the universal idea are imported into the national idea. It is precisely because France fulfils her national ideal that she believes that she can realise a universal value. In the development of her life as a nation there is produced a new Universalism, whose claims go out to challenge those of the other historical forces. This might also be expressed thus: As a nation France has annexed the universal ideas which were an offshoot from the inheritance of Rome. At the same time she has annexed the Rome-idea itself, and has adopted the claims of Rome as her own.

In so doing she has set herself in opposition to the universal Rome-idea of the Middle Ages as we find it expressed in Dante.

According to the thought of Dante the significance of Rome in the history of the world had been transferred to the Papacy and the Empire, to the Cross and the Eagle. The temporal and spiritual welfare of humanity depended upon the right order being maintained between these two powers. But France could not be fitted in to this view of world history. The French Monarchy, by its very existence, disturbed this order which was based on metaphysics, and it injured it also by irreverent violence, since it rose in rebellion against Pope and Emperor. For this reason France appears in the Divine Comedy as the evil principle *par excellence*, and Dante puts these words into the mouth of Hugh Capet:

> Io fui radice della mala pianta
> Che la terra cristiana tutta aduggia.
> (I was the root of that evil tree
> Which overshadows the whole of Christendom
> With its sinister shade.)

In the Christian world-era Dante is the great herald of the Rome-idea. Hence he felt he must oppose the new power which shattered this idea.

The Emperors of our old Empire were able to feel themselves the preservers and renewers of the *Imperium*. Their work has been shattered, and the Roman element in the German nation is only a great memory. The idea of Rome had a different effect in Italy. Rome continued to exist through the ages. Above the Rome of the ancients there arose the ecclesiastical Rome of the Popes. This again was pushed aside to make room for the Terza Roma of the Savoy Monarchy. And to-day the Fascist State, in conscious connexion with the greatness of Rome in the Ancient World, is seeking to erect a fourth Rome. Thus on the soil of Italy Rome as an idea, and as a dominating force, again renews her strength under the same name. She maintains her own identity.

France does not wish to be Rome, she wishes to be herself. She thinks with gratitude of her eminent mother. She is proud of her Latin character, without intending to be narrowed or confined by it. She preserves respect for her Gallic origin and wishes to preserve the value of the Frankish and Norman elements in the national life. Even for that reason she cannot wholly identify herself with Rome as Italy has done. The consciousness of Rome only awakened in France during those periods when her Latin heritage threatened to be injured or lost by barbarism. Otherwise France produces all her own ideologies from within. But these ideologies display a curious structural relationship with those of ancient Rome. Thus to a certain extent Rome was replaced by France, and for that very reason France cannot admit, or will only admit very slightly, the claims of other historical powers which do appeal, or have appealed, to Rome. Thus in the soul of the French nation the Rome-idea has had a very curious effect: it is a sort of complex, combining attraction and repulsion at one and the same time. It is an important factor in the subconsciousness of the nation.

What, then, are the main stages in the conscious development of the civilization of France?

The first high-water mark of French civilization falls in the period between 1050 and 1150. It was at this time that Gothic architecture, the heroic sagas and the Crusading spirit were growing up on the soil of France. And this Crusading spirit is the first form of the French conception of herself, the first incarnation of the idea of a national mission of France. *Gesta Dei per Francos*—this is the descriptive title which the monk Guibert de Nogent gives to his history of the First Crusade. The Franks are the chosen instrument of God. This was the idea which inspired the people, and led them to offer themselves. Thus, as early as the eleventh century we see that there is already a vital mystical conception of the nation. The clerks seized hold of this, transformed it into poetry, and created a symbol for it in the Legend of Charlemagne. For at that time, under the influence of the Spanish campaigns against the Moors, inspired by Cluny, and in connexion with the great pilgrim roads and places of pilgrimage, there arose that picture of Charlemagne which the Song of Roland and kindred epics show us: the picture of the white-bearded Emperor, who, as the champion of God, rides through the world with his peers, who makes pilgrimage to the Holy Land, and with his Franks conquers many lands in order to bring them to God as an offering, and "holy Christendom to raise". According to the view of that day the Crusades were only the renewed acceptance of that mission which Charlemagne had undertaken for France and for the world.

And this is precisely the characteristic element in that first self-formation of the French national consciousness. The national aim is wider than itself. France fights for Christendom.

It is clear that France then felt compelled to go further, and evolved the theory that she was the possessor of special religious privilege. France has never been content to be merely one among several Christian nations. Under many forms she has always claimed a special position within the

Roman Church. From the very beginning the French Monarchy possessed religious features, and in this it differs entirely from all the other monarchical institutions of the modern world. Gallicanism, which appeared again and again from the Middle Ages down to most recent times, would have been impossible without this religious sanction of the Monarchy.

The maintenance of the religious prerogative of France was, however, definitely more than a political theory. It penetrated deeply into the life of the nation, and led to an absolute fusion of the State and religion. Thus there arose in France a mystical Nationalism. Its greatest symbol is the figure of the Maid of Orleans. It is from her that the saying comes: "Ceux qui font la guerre au saint royaume de France, font la guerre au roi Jésus". The spirit which those words reveal shows the most complete break with the religious universalism which, at least in idea and intention, constitutes the greatness of the Middle Ages. Its place has been taken by a hybrid mysticism which turns national sentiment into a cult and identifies it with the Catholic Faith.

France alone, of all Christian nations, has achieved an emotional fusion of this kind. And this Nationalistic Catholicism has recently again increased in power. The cult of the Sacred Heart, and the reverence paid to the Maid of Orleans, who was canonized in 1920, gives it its colour at the present time. It is one of the strong elements in the *Action Française*.

It would of course be quite untrue and most unjust to say that this mystical Nationalism represents French Catholicism as a whole. France has given to the universal Church an infinite wealth of piety, loving service, holiness, and a sublime life of faith. These are blessings which far transcend all national frontiers, and which spring out of a truly ecumenical spirit. But this does not in the least alter the fact that at all periods in France that narrow and largely disfigured form of religiosity has existed, of which I have just spoken, and that this complete fusion of the national Mythos and the Catholic Faith, this mystical dogma of the nation, is a specifically French phenomenon.

To-day, however, Gallicanism has no meaning, because the modern French State has severed the cords which bound it with the Church in the centuries under the Monarchy. But long before the great Revolution the medieval idea of a special mission—of the *Gesta Dei per Francos*—had become dim. France's conception of herself had taken other forms.

If for us Germans the modern world began when Luther nailed his theses on the door of the Church at Wittenberg, for France the corresponding date would be the year 1494, when Charles VIII. undertook his Italian campaign. For this was the signal for the entrance of the Renaissance into France. The historical particulars of the epoch do not concern us here. But it is of the deepest interest to observe that here, once again, a universal idea is made national. By "nationalization" I do not mean the transformation of that which has been adopted from the point of view of the national spirit—which indeed would not be in any way a merely French peculiarity—but the tendency to exalt this national form into something of universal significance. When it came into contact with the genius of the Renaissance the French spirit reacted with the desire to produce and display something more valuable and to set it up as a standard against the new culture and art of Italy. The sixteenth century, torn by the struggle with the Hapsburgs, and by the horrors of the Wars of Religion, was not favourable to these aspirations. But although few great artistic creations were achieved, the intellectual movement of the period was all the more characteristic.

The monarchy was invested with a new form of romanticism. Scholars developed the theory that the French king ought to have the Imperial dignity, and that Italy legally formed part of the French kingdom. They declared that the time had now arrived for France to take over the intellectual guidance of Europe, which had previously been exercised by Greece, Rome and Italy.

France now wished to cut Italy out of the picture; at the same time, however, she also wished to emancipate herself from the ancient world. The national self-consciousness could not tolerate the idea that France had taken over her culture from Rome. Therefore she decided to revise history in a drastic manner. Scholars proclaimed that the Greek and Roman authors were liars and deceivers. They are said to have claimed that they invented the arts and sciences in order to take away their glory from the ancient Gauls. In France, in very early days, there had been a highly developed civilization, which taught Greece a good deal. Thus instead of the supposed Graeco-Roman legend of history there arose a Gallic legend. Francus, a son of Hector, is said to have been the ancestor of the Capetian dynasty and the founder of Paris.[1] As descendants of Hector the French are the aristocracy of humanity, whereas Aeneas and the Romans were traitors, deceivers and usurpers. It is obvious that once again the national feeling of France was protesting against the predominance of Rome.

From the standpoint of critical historical research, of course, this peculiar blend of fantasies has value only as a curiosity, but it throws a great deal of light on the psychology of the nation. For the first time there is here formulated the self-consciousness of French civilization. It appears in close connexion with the national idea and with the claim for national importance. France ascribes to herself the supreme place in civilization, and then makes that the basis of her national glory.

The period of Louis XIV. fulfilled all that the sixteenth century had desired: the development of the Monarchy, the system of administration, political predominance, religious unity, and finally, the national intellectual culture. That

[1] This was all evolved out of the Frankish Trojan legend of the seventh century. Cf. G. Heeger, *Schulprogramm*, Landau (1890).

which the sixteenth century had aspired after—a French system of civilization as ancient as classical antiquity, setting an equally high standard—was now realized.

And it was precisely this fulfilment which carried the development further. A period which feels itself to be classical does not need any further models. It has attained its majority. The self-consciousness of the French Classical school therefore was completed in the break with antiquity. The external form in which all this was achieved was the long-drawn-out controversy which, in the history of literature, is called "La Querelle des Anciens et des Modernes."[1] This controversy over the question whether contemporary writers were of equal rank with the ancient authors, whether they were even superior to them or not, has a far greater significance than one might imagine at first. It means the emancipation of modern civilization from tradition and authority. In place of these forces there enters in the spirit of critical rationalism and the idea of progress. This spirit draws its arguments from the Cartesian philosophy, and from natural science.

This stage was reached as early as 1700, but the result was that the foundations were undermined upon which the imposing building of the *grand siècle* had been erected. It was based upon the undisputed authority of three powers: the Monarchy, the Church and the classical tradition. In the figure of Bossuet we see the complete incarnation and balance of all three.

In the eighteenth century this balance was lost. The classical form lived on, it is true, and produced a number of brilliant works. But the content had entirely changed. The recognition of the institutions of Church and State had been replaced by the spirit of criticism. The most brilliant and comprehensive minds of the century, Voltaire and Diderot, forged the weapons of the Enlightenment. The monarchy lost touch with the intellectual movement, and at the same time severed its relation with the religious

[1] Cf. the excellent account by Herbert Gillot, Paris (1914).

idea. Literature became cosmopolitan and basked in the sunshine of the favour of foreign monarchs. Thus the individual factors of the national existence separated in different directions.

The Revolution was the great historical event which drew them all together again. Whatever we may think about the Revolution, for France it possesses the supreme significance of a new creation of the nation, and of the idea of a national mission. In the Coalition wars the modern national consciousness of France arose. And this time, too, it coined a universal formula for its national aims, and this was: Civilization.

The word was new. It only appeared towards the close of the eighteenth century;[1] it did not at once find acceptance. It could not compete with the inspiring formula, *Liberté*, *Égalité*, *Fraternité*, with the *Marseillaise* and the *Chant du Départ*. But when Bonaparte subdued the Revolution, when Napoleon overthrew the Republic, it then offered itself as the inevitable watchword for politico-militaristic mass propaganda. In the Army Orders of the First Consul and of the Emperor it was used by preference. This word had the immeasurable advantage of incorporating the intellectual impulse of the period of the Revolution without recalling its political aim.

As a word it was still indefinite, and possessed no content. But it was sufficiently comprehensive to be able to absorb the whole intellectual movement of the nineteenth century in France.

In this process two lines of development must be kept distinct; the historico-political and the natural-science-technical movements.

Out of the confusion of the Revolution and of the Napoleonic era a new social class arose; in July 1830 it be-

[1] Cf. on this point Joachim Moras: *Ursprung und Entwicklung des Zivilizationsbegriffs in Frankreich* (1756–1830), Heidelberger Dissertation (1929). See also my further remarks on this subject in the *Wechsslerfestschrift* (1929).

came supreme. This new class was the *bourgeoisie*. Between the two extremes—reaction, and the Radicalism of the Left —it sought to preserve the *juste milieu* of moderate progress. Its doctrine was a Liberalism based on the English pattern. Its political leader and representative was Guizot, a Protestant. Like so many Liberal politicians of the nineteenth century he entered politics after an academic career. It was he who developed the historical philosophy of bourgeois Liberalism by means of the guiding principle of the conception of civilization. His *Histoire de la Civilisation en Europe* of 1828, and his *Histoire de la Civilisation en France* of 1830 formulated this ideology with lasting effect.

Guizot identified *civilisation* with social and intellectual progress. It is an essentially European phenomenon, since it presupposes the tendency toward freedom which is lacking in Asia. But even though all great nations of Europe have a share in the process of civilization, Guizot believes that, as an historian, he may be permitted to hold the view that in this respect France is in the van. He admits that now and then it has been surpassed; in art by Italy, and in politics by England. But an advantage of that kind only acted as an incentive to France to try to win back the ground she had lost. The civilizing forces in other countries have always had to pass through France first of all in order to receive her definite impress. He bases this theory on the fact of the three essential qualities of the spirit of France: clarity, sociability and sympathy. Thus, according to Guizot, France is the heart of Civilization.

Three main ideas, which had not emerged in the eighteenth century, were incorporated by Guizot into the French philosophy of history of the nineteenth century: world history is the history of civilization; civilization is the development of freedom; France is the leader in the march of civilization.

We find the same ideas in Guizot's younger contemporary Michelet. But how differently they are represented in the mirror of this genius! Michelet carried into history all the glow of a passionate nature, on fire with the desire to awaken the picture of the past to new life. Against this background he set the glowing vision of the meaning of the present. Guizot used the language of abstract argument; Michelet expressed his message in the language of mythical-Messianic vision. To him history is an everlasting struggle between man and nature, spirit and matter, freedom and Fate. The subjugation of the elements, the achievement of free individuality, the spiritualization of the religious conceptions of Christianity, and finally the liberation of the nations from the domination of priests and kings, are stages in this conflict. In 1789 and 1830 France gained liberty for all the peoples of the world. This marked the close of the Christian era. For the new social world which is now arising France will find the word of salvation. Therefore to her belongs the "Pontificate of the new Civilization".

The very language he uses betrays the fact that here a religious passion feeds the enthusiasm for civilization. It seems as though through Michelet's prophecy the eternal genius of France were again expressed, which must ever measure itself against Rome. "Rome", says Michelet, "was the centre of the immense drama whose course is guided by France. If we stand on the summit of the Capitol, at one glance, like Janus, we behold the Old World, which here comes to an end, and the modern world, which henceforth our own country leads on along the mysterious road of the future."

These words were written in 1831. The finest minds in France were then full of Messianic ideas. The political upheaval had stirred the soul of the nation to its depths.

The July Monarchy was not only an era of commonplace, utilitarian bourgeoisie, it was also the epoch of visionary syntheses, of romantic epics of humanity, of Utopias, and of the founding of new religious movements. It was at that time that Auguste Comte moved forward from scientific Positivism to the mysticism of a "religion of Humanity".

At that time the intellectual legacy of Saint-Simon became the heart of a movement in which wild extravagance and far-sighted economic ideas were combined. Saint-Simonism was also a religion, and proclaimed a new form of Christianity. The programme of this school of thought included the famous theory of the "rehabilitation of the flesh", dress reform, and also the organization of banks and of railways. The stamp of the new movement was an enthusiastic social eudaemonism. It also proclaimed the dawn of a new era. But it saw salvation not in politics but in industry, and it clothed this word with a romantic halo.

Saint-Simonism likewise represents the phase of intoxicating ecstasy in which the new age of natural science and technical capacity first discovered its possibilities. And the Saint-Simonists also naturally used the great word which was in the air, and proclaimed the new civilization. They also claimed the leadership for France, and glorified the French people as the truly priestly people: "peuple vraiment prêtre et digne d'initier tous les peoples à la communion universelle".

Thus France as a whole was inebriated with the idea that she was called to be a pioneer to the rest of the world. Philosophy of history and natural science, politics and social reform, all meet at this point. Further, through the lips of a Victor Hugo literature proclaimed that it would undertake the high calling of giving its artistic consecration to the ideal of civilization. About the middle of the nineteenth century this ideal became a phrase. It was absorbed by the nameless spirit of the age, and this is the strongest proof of its influence. The masses of the people absorbed this idea of civilization. The nation as a whole was aflame with the ideas of progress and civilization. France believed that the nineteenth century, standing on the shoulders of the eighteenth, and carrying forward the work of the latter, would finally overcome the last traces of barbarism, and usher in a peaceful, humane and moral permanent condition of human existence. This, in any case, was

the view of most of the intellectual leaders of the nation.
And it was then—in the midst of all these high hopes and
ideals—that the unexpected happened: the outbreak of
war. The effect was terrific. Men were stunned, bewildered.
As in 1814 and 1815, Paris, the "City of Light", again saw
foreign troops marching through her streets. The bloody
civil war of the Commune broke out under the eyes of the
victors. The best minds in the nation were filled with disappointment, anger and resignation. It seemed as though
the age of Barbarism had returned. Like the Romans of the
declining Empire the French felt as though they were given
over to the invasions of the German hordes. This experience and the deep impression it made, has often been described in French literature.

It is noteworthy that the events of the day were regarded
as a tragedy for civilization also by those who had been
severest in their criticism of the optimism of progress of the
nineteenth century. In them too there flamed out, indig-
nantly, the ancient Latin sentiment of civilization. Thus
Flaubert writes in March 1871: "Quelle barbarie! Quelle
reculade! Je n'étais guère 'progressiste' et humanitaire ce-
pendant! N'importe, j'avais des illusions! Et je ne croyais
pas voir arriver la fin du monde. Car c'est cela! Nous
assistons à la fin du monde latin."

The defeat, however, became the occasion for national
self-examination and self-testing. The question was raised:
To what should the national failure be ascribed? The
Empire— Democracy— Catholicism— Materialism?   all
these causes were suggested. In this connexion the problem
of civilization again arose. The Third Republic, which in
the seventies was still weak and immature, needed a cultural
as well as a political programme. It must be based on
reason, and useful for education. It must be able to produce a sense of citizenship, and yet be strong enough to
hold its own against the combined forces of the Catholic
Church and of political reaction. All these requirements
were fulfilled in the philosophy of Charles Renouvier

(1815–1903), the founder of French Neo-Kantianism or Neo-Criticism (*Néo-criticisme*). The philosophy of Renouvier became the system upon which the political science and the official metaphysic of the Third Republic was based. This vigorous thinker, whom Taine called a "republican Kant", had already (1869) published his *Science de la Morale*, an ethic which was based upon the ideal of righteousness, liberated from Christianity, and which has exercised a strong influence upon the modern system of French education. In 1872 he founded the *Critique philosophique, scientifique, littéraire*, the organ in which he discussed the questions of the day.

Renouvier believed that France's defeat was due to her own fault. She had forgotten her ideals of freedom, and she was backward in the pursuit of science. She must learn from the victors. Renouvier gives the following reasons for the superiority of the "Germanic race": Protestantism, the spirit of discipline and obedience; the drawbacks of the "Germanic civilization" are the "cult of power and of Destiny". France needs a new ideal, based upon morality and reason. This ideal can be found—if it is rightly understood—in the idea of civilization.

Renouvier criticized Guizot very severely, calling him a champion of compromise and of an emasculated Liberalism. He defines civilization as "the life of the *cité libre*, and the government of men by themselves, autonomous law, the State as a voluntary, or at least a partially voluntary, union".

These ideas were absorbed into the official doctrine of the French State. They formed a curious blend of Kantian philosophy and the watchwords of 1789. The idea of civilization, renewed in this sense, now became the official ideology of history of the Third Republic. It influenced the education of the State. It was accepted by the French bourgeoisie and also by Socialism. Charles Andler, the excellent Paris Germanist, contended even in 1912 that instead of a metaphysical world-outlook in the German sense the French spirit represents a theory of the destiny of civilization. The work of a "view of civilization" of this kind was, in his opinion, from the eighteenth century onwards, the philosophical mission of France.

The idea of civilization makes it possible to order the whole of the national history in the light of a clearly perceived illuminating human aim. It is then possible to present the Crusades and the development of the nation, the classic period of the monarchy, and the heroic epic of the Revolution, as well as progress in science and social welfare, art and democracy, as stages in the realization of this idea. The World Exhibitions of 1889 and 1900 seemed to show forth visibly that all the peoples of the earth were bringing their gifts to the altar of French civilization.

However, the official ideology of the Third Republic weakened gravely at the moment when this Republic had won a complete victory over its opponents. And this was the case after the Dreyfus Affair had been settled, and the final separation between Church and State.

From that date—perhaps about 1906—the French intelligentsia turned away from the ideologies of the Republic, that is, from democracy, Parliamentarianism and *l'Idée laïque*. The ideas of the Enlightenment have lost their attractive power. In their place there has arisen an organic habit of thought, which appeals to the soil and the life of the people, to tradition and to authority. With alluring romanticism Barrès teaches this doctrine, while it is proclaimed in classic Latin style by Maurras. It inspires the young. Youth desires to be modern. Modern? This means to-day the return to the historic inheritance of the nation. In the formula of Barrès: *la Terre et les Morts*. In the formula of Maurras: the fleur-de-lys of royal France. All the formulas of the dominant system are rejected. All—save one: the idea of civilization.

Naturally, on the lips of the "moderns" this word has a different content from that which it possesses in the schoolbooks of the Republic, of this Republic which has been made by Freemasons, Jews and Protestants. These "moderns" go back to the true ancestors, to Hellas and to Rome, to the ancient development of Provence, based on the *ordo Romanus* of the Church, and the French order of the classical method. *Civilisation*—since the disastrous year of 1789 this has been the confused Utopia of freedom for the modern world on the verge of decay. But now the same word means the remembrance of our origins. It means an ancient inheritance and a holy tradition. It is the flame upon the ancestral altar; reverence for Rome and Latin permanence, which shields the fatherland against the modern barbarism of the *furor Teutonicus*.

This conception likewise completes the cycle of ideas. Once more the French idea of civilization takes up that of the ancient world. It is an old venerable history which is incorporated for the Frenchman in the word *civilisation*. We have touched on the chief stages in its development. The historical point of view which we have gained through this study will now serve us for the purpose of systematic analysis.

From the eleventh century, as we have seen, France has felt the need to sum up her national existence in an idea. She felt she must have a picture, a formula, a word, in which she could be presented. This sense of the need for a presentation and conception of herself is an integral element in the French spirit. No other modern nation knows it in the same measure. England has never felt this need at all. In Germany it only appeared during the nineteenth century, but it expressed itself in the form of a problem, not as a settled solution.

We must go back to the ancient world before we can find analogies with this essential trait in the French character. The genius of Rome has indeed found a magnificent form of self-expression in the poetry of Virgil. The Georgics are dedicated to the praise of the soil of Italy, the *Aeneid* ascribes the founding of Rome to the Divine Will, and interprets its mission in the light of a cosmic process. In

c

Virgil the idea of Rome is a religious idea of salvation, and attains its highest point in the Saviour-prophecy of the fourth Eclogue. At this point it was closely connected with Israel's faith in its Divine vocation. We know how the thought of Christian antiquity has fused both these ideas, the Roman and the Jewish, into a synthesis of world history.

When the France of the Crusades regards herself as the chosen people, and the instrument of the Divine Will, it seems probable that this is due to the renewed reception and assimilation of those ancient popular ideas. But even if this interpretation is not justifiable, seeing that the mystery of the soul of a people is ultimately impenetrable: the situation which we have described, the French impulse to an ideal self-presentation, reveals itself very clearly all down the centuries.

These self-projections change their content in the course of history. But although they change they still form part of a theory which always remains the same, and belongs to the constant element in the French nature. This means, therefore, that the French idea of civilization must be regarded as the ultimate, and (for the moment) final expression of national self-interpretation. Only so can one understand it and do it justice.

How then is this structural theory constituted? The first thing which strikes us when we begin to analyse the theory is the fact that the national idea and the idea of civilization completely coincide. France recognizes no difference between the State as a political entity and the State as a cultural entity. In experience France finds it impossible to separate the concepts of the State, the nation and civilization. There is therefore no French consciousness of the State. Most certainly there is no ultra-glorification of the State. Indeed, the shoe is rather on the other foot. The Frenchman always regards the State with suspicion, and is always ready to reject its advances. Even the word *l'État* has in French a depreciatory accent. The expression *l'État français* is only used as a technical term in law. "The Republic" and "republican"—these words sound too much like official rhetoric, and recall too many political controversies to be able to unite all Frenchmen in one genuine strong sentiment. France feels herself to be, and loves herself as, a nation. Under the shadow of this word there are no controversies. Among us, unfortunately, it is still the case that "national" sounds somewhat differently from "German". A corresponding phenomenon in France would be unthinkable. The words "French" and "national" mean and express exactly the same thing, and this is the reason why the word "Nationalism", which arose during the period of the Dreyfus Affair, is more intelligible and convincing in France than it is with us.

The word "nation", however, means to the French not only the living community formed by history, language and the State, but also the connexion with the idea of civilization. Of course for us too the nation is the civilized community, but the borders of the German civilized community have never agreed with those of the national state, and to-day this is less true than ever. German civilization has never acknowledged itself as a national body. And further, German civilization is precisely a *German* civilization, and describes itself as such. This method of expressing is indeed itself a reason for the conflict between the idea of *civilisation* and that of *Kultur*. For when we speak of *deutscher Kultur* and the Frenchman translates this into *culture allemande*, in his mind this seems like a negation of the idea of "civilization" altogether. *Kultur* must be something essentially universal; it must have a pan-human content. How then, thinks the Frenchman, can one proclaim and propagate a national "culture"? For French sentiment this is a contradiction—indeed it is a challenge. When France identifies herself with her idea of civilization she never speaks of "French civilization" but of *civilisation* in general.

In so doing the French national consciousness broadens out into the universal. It attains the dignity of a human value. France feels herself as a nation, and, at the same time, as a nation she is the bearer of this universal idea.

It is this connexion between national feeling and the idea of civilization which explains the conception of France as the supreme representative of civilization.

I would like to state most definitely that the cultivated minds in the France of the present day have overcome this idea of France as the supreme representative of civilization. It is of course true that this idea still appears in popular forms of public opinion; but in the intellectual class of leaders it only occurs now among those of the extreme Right. In saying this I am thinking of a critic like Massis, who sees in France the bulwark of the Western spirit over against Germany, Russia and Asia.

But even when the idea of a supreme place in the civilization of the world has been renounced, there still exists an essential difference, which divides the French view from our own. The French mind holds firmly to the idea that, at bottom, human nature always and everywhere is the same. It believes in standards which are valid for all, and it believes that civilization itself is a norm of this kind. The conception of civilization is indeed only significant if all men can share it and understand it in the same sense. This faith in the idea of humanity gives to the French conception of civilization its sentiment, its energy and its glow, but it is also the cause of its limitations.

This becomes very evident when man is defined as a reasonable being. Rationalism of Cartesian origin is still, at the present day, one of the most living elements in the French conception of civilization. When, for instance, we read that the famous historian Gabriel Hanotaux says that true civilization is that which "drinks from the pure fountain of Reason", we see clearly that this is something which, from the French point of view, will inevitably bind all men together, whereas to us this idea seems strange and remote. Only recently Léon Brunschvicg, the most influential representative of French philosophy at the present time, declared, that its main idea was "l'idée tout à la fois positive et généreuse d'une raison qui a résolu fermement de n'être que raisonnable". And he adds that the thinkers who followed Kant are just as unreasonable (*déraisonnable*) as the pre-Cartesian Scholastic thinkers. This naïve rationalism is a very characteristic example of the way in which an apparently supra-national idea can in France be strongly bounded and conditioned by the national idea.

But it is very difficult for the average Frenchman to see this. And if we see it quite clearly we ought not on that account to draw the erroneous conclusion that France does not, *optima fide*, think in a universal manner. Among us the opinion is frequently expressed that the French do not really take their conviction that France is working for the service of humanity quite seriously; that indeed this "service of humanity" is only nationalistic civilization in a disguised form. People who talk like this do not understand France, and they do her an injustice. To a great extent France still lives under the influence of the ideas of the Enlightenment, which never impressed us very profoundly, whereas in the land of Reason they still possess their full power over the hearts and minds of men.

Yes, and over the hearts and minds not only of the educated upper class, but over those of the people as a whole. For this is a further characteristic of the French idea of civilization: it permeates all classes of the nation. Through the development of the last hundred years it has become thoroughly democratic. When the Frenchman in a small provincial town or remote village reads in his newspaper about a new invention, and is assured that it means progress for civilization, he knows exactly what is meant. He knows also that the furtherance of civilization is the aim of human society; that this great work of humanity is not achieved by statesmen and generals, but by scholars, writers and artists; that its aim is the improvement of conditions of life among men, and that the blessings of civilization are for all.

The Press and the school spread these ideas among the people at large. The instruction in history in particular does this with very great effect. The history books are often written by excellent historians. They are written in an attractive, clear style, adapted to the understanding of children. The State is not glorified, but it is tested by moral standards. After an account of the reign of Louis XIV., for instance, something like this will be added: "During this epoch France misused her power; she menaced and terrified the whole world, and the whole world declared itself against her. This always happens when one State tries to impose laws on another." Similar judgments are passed on the horrors of the Reign of Terror, and on the War Party of 1870.

The importance of intellectual culture is also strongly emphasized in the teaching of history. The pupil in the elementary school learns that Corneille and Racine have written beautiful tragedies, that Voltaire and Rousseau desired reforms, that Pasteur was a benefactor to humanity; that the Republic teaches everything at its universities which men have learned from the beginning of the world, and that even poor children, if they are clever and industrious, can have a chance of studying at the university by means of the system of free places. An outline of History of this kind, written by Lavisse, closes with these words: "France et Humanité ne sont deux mots qui s'opposent l'un à l'autre; ils sont conjoints et inséparables. Notre patrie est la plus humaine des patries!" This little book is circulated by the million; and this is only one of the thousand channels through which the ideals of French culture penetrate into the life of the people. The educational system of the French Republic, which is based upon the education laws of 1882, and thus will soon have been in existence for half a century, represents a system of national propaganda of civilization with which there can be no comparison elsewhere. It has created the unity of the national spirit.

But the fact that the French idea of civilization has been democratized has still another, and a deeper reason. It is universal not only in the sense that it unites the nation and humanity, and that within the nation it includes all classes, but also because it covers the whole of existence. In this respect it is the continuation of the ancient idea of civilization. It has the same breadth of view which extends from material things up to ideal standards, from the technical to the moral. We may indeed assert that in France civilization begins with food. Gastronomy is part of civilization. So is fashion. Politeness forms part of it. In short, all forms of life share in the glory of civilization. And these forms of life are not the privilege of the educated class—they touch everyone, and everyone, at least to some modest extent, can have a share in them. The intellectual ideal of democracy is supported and completed by democracy in everyday life, which affects the ordinary conventions and standards of decency and refinement. For instance, the traveller who happens to be in a little provincial town of 5000 inhabitants on a market day, and who decides to stay there for the midday meal, will receive a very visible impression of this spirit. A mass of people fills the crowded dining-room of the hotel. Most of the people are peasants and tradesmen; but tourists are there also who have come by car in order to see the old cathedral. One's place is assigned, and the meal begins. To all the same menu is given. But this menu has six courses. It is constructed according to the classic rules of tradition. These are as fixed and unalterable as those of grammar. And the peasant or the manual labourer takes it all as much as a matter of course as does the elegant Parisian lady at the next table.

Not only meals, however, but the ordering of the day, conversation, correspondence and sociability are all regulated: all functions of life are subordinated to an aesthetic order. The name for this is: *les manières*. "Manners," in the French sense of the word, should mean not only the rules of external behaviour, but the expression of aesthetic-moral cultivation. According to the classical conception they form part of morality. Joubert, one of the finest moralists of France, defines politeness as the flower of humanity, and adds: "Qui n'est pas assez poli, n'est pas assez humain". The system of these aesthetically regulated forms of life is so important for the significance of the content of the idea of civilization that it is often absolutely identified with it. Civilization then means the taming of raw nature, the refinement of customs, the humanizing of barbarism. In this sense civilization is a social fact. It means the collective level of pleasing forms of life attained by a whole society.

The broad range of the French idea of civilization explains further how it is that modern technical development has been able to find room within it. The transformation of forms of existence through the powers of steam and of electricity, the industrialization and mechanization of modern life: this great process of upheaval was incorporated organically into the ideal of civilization. For civilization means not only the subjugation of raw nature but also the betterment of human conditions. To a very great extent the misunderstanding which exists between the German and French idea of civilization is based upon the fact that by civilization we mean exclusively, or almost exclusively, these new achievements of the machine-age. If the idea is thus restricted of course there must be opposition to the idea of civilization itself. Civilization then becomes the materially mechanized existence, the hostile force which menaces the sphere of the soul, of art, of the intellect. Of course the dangers of mechanization have also been felt in France, and attention has been drawn to them, and indeed much earlier than among us. In France also individual thinkers, for this very reason, have attacked the idea of civilization itself. But these protests remained isolated. No one can eradicate the idea of civilization from the consciousness of France; its roots have struck too deeply into the soil.

It is indeed the universal idea pure and simple. We have

analysed the different aspects of this universality: connexion with the national consciousness, with the conception of humanity, with the people as a whole, with all the spheres of human life. But in addition to all these this universality has also a dimension in time. The French feeling for civilization is also the consciousness of continuity.

Civilization is progress, and the perfecting of the forms of life, certainly. But to a still greater extent it means the preservation and increase of an inheritance. Charles Maurras defines civilization as the social situation in which the individual who comes into the world finds present incomparably more than he brings with him. "La civilisation", he says, "est d'abord un capital. Elle est ensuite un capital transmis." To us *Kultur* signifies the ideal total conception of all the creative deeds of the intellect. To the French it means the cultivation and the transmission of a treasure. We conceive the law of evolution in civilization as though it were a series of symbolical systems of which each replaces the preceding one. The French do not admit that the structure of history can be broken up like this. To them the movement of civilization consists in the accumulation of the blessings of civilization. As Gaul received the whole of the civilization of late antiquity from Rome, and handed it on to the new Frankish-Roman nation, so France carries the blessing of its civilization through the ages.

I have tried to bring out the essential features of the French idea of civilization as clearly and definitely as possible. This could not be done without a certain measure of artificial simplification.

It is certain that among the younger men the best minds in France are no longer satisfied with the traditional ideals, and that they are resolved that they will not allow themselves to be hampered by them. This change is not yet clearly defined because France is the land of gerontocracy (government by old men), and because psychological changes there are far more gradual than they are among us.

But between the generation of those who were born about the year 1900 and their predecessors there does exist a very tangible difference of attitude. Economic and political problems, as well as problems of ideals, everywhere demand new solutions. The old ideas must be thought out afresh, even the conservative ideas of tradition.

In a book which has roused a good deal of interest (1926) Lucien Romier has critically examined the relation between "nation et civilisation". He stands for the European solidarity of civilization, which, he points out, has lasted for a thousand years, and has only been shattered by the "political materialism" of modern national States. For Romier *notre civilisation* does not mean French, but European, civilization. His programme, however—which we do not need to examine here in detail—betrays romantic and conservative methods of thought, and therefore it can scarcely be fair to the present situation. But it is interesting because it resolutely severs the idea of civilization from the national idea—a daring, and, for French sentiment, probably not an entirely painless operation. We record it as a sign that France is beginning to examine her idea of civilization and to formulate it anew.

The same thing is also taking place in Germany. It is to be hoped that this self-examination will ultimately end the controversy between *Kultur* and *civilisation* for good and all; and, still more, that in the intellectual élite of both countries it will further the understanding of the neighbouring civilization.

# II

## THE NATURAL BASIS

THE French conception of civilization is closely connected
with the relation of the French people to the soil of France.
It has been said that this idea is a fruit of the soil like
French wines. At bottom it is connected with the cultivation of the soil, with the humanizing of Nature. This also
is the root of the feeling of the Frenchman for his land.
Love to the homeland characterizes French national feeling from the very outset. It is the attachment of a settled
people to its own land. It is of course true that in the fifth,
fourth and third centuries before our era the Celts carried
on extensive campaigns of conquest over almost the whole
of Europe, and even into Asia Minor, but the Gauls have
preserved no memories of these times. In the intellectual
inheritance which the French received from their Gallic
ancestors, we can find no trace of that primitive era—
nothing which can be compared with the heroic epics of
the Germanic tribes and their wanderings. The soul of
France knows nothing of *Wanderlust*; it has no longing for
that which is distant and remote. She is tied to the ancient
inheritance of the soil, bound like the peasant with the
spirit of a serf. What the Frenchman loves in his land is the
cultivated soil, the earth which nourishes him. A modern
Catholic poet, François Mauriac, says that "Cybele has
more worshippers in France than Christ". The religion of
the earth is the ancient French religion of the peasant. The
feeling of the French for Nature is rather the earth-piety of
the agricultural labourer and gardener than the urge towards the elemental forces which the man of the Germanic
type seeks in Nature. "Man socializes Nature", says Comte.
That is quite in accord with the French way of thinking.
The Frenchman desires to be lord of Nature, and to subdue
her destructive powers. He loves a defined pattern, a careful design in the order of the fields, the fruit orchards and

43

the groves. But he has no desire to lose himself in the infinity of Nature—whether in vast forests or in the waves of the sea.

The cultivated soil of his land is sacred to the Frenchman. When an enemy touches this soil he feels it a desecration. The bitter hatred of France against the German intruder in the great wars was due in no small measure to this feeling, which belongs to a more primitive stratum of the French soul than the consciousness of the State. Sometimes when Germans and Frenchmen met in a friendly way after the World War moments of tension would arise: this would happen when a German was describing his experiences in the War if it came out that he had fought on a section of the Front where the Frenchman to whom he was speaking had rights and a sense of home. The Frenchman could not bear to be reminded of this; to him it was a humiliation, whereas to the German it was all part of the custom of War.

When the cry goes forth for the *défense du sol* (the defence of the land) France is moved to her depths. It was this which made it possible in 1870 for Gambetta to raise a military levy *en masse* and to make such a stout resistance. When, in 1873, Germany withdrew her army of occupation, President Thiers was honoured by the French as the "Liberator of the soil"—a claim to honour which is typical of the French point of view. "The nation is a territory", said Maurice Barrès at a later date, and he made an attempt to base an idealistic nationalism upon the cult of the soil of France.

This close connexion between feeling for the soil and love of country has always determined the national consciousness of France. As early as the beginning of the twelfth century the writer of the Song of Roland exalts his homeland in these words: "Thou land of France art a land exceeding fair". From the time of the Middle Ages its inhabitants have called France a "fair" land, a "lovely" country, "the fairest kingdom under heaven". Thus to the

French the soil of their country is not only the land consecrated by their ancestors, their mother, by whom they
are nourished, but it is also a privileged section of the
globe, a chosen land of beauty, grace and fertility.

The educational system of the Third Republic turns this
feeling to good account. One of the first things impressed
upon the pupil in the primary school is the fact that his
country is very beautiful. On the cover of his history book
he sees a wreath of fruit and flowers with the inscription:
"Child, upon the cover of this book you see the flowers and
fruits of France. Out of this book you are going to learn
the history of France. You ought to love France, because
her natural aspect is so fair, and because her history has
made her great."

School geography appeals to the aesthetic sentiment.
The pupil learns from the explanations in his atlas that the
outline of France can be defined as a hexagon, divided into
two equal parts by the meridian of Paris. Thus his fatherland has a harmonious, almost geometrical shape.[1] Nature
has favoured it with a pleasing form and an advantageous
position. It is at an equal distance from the North Pole and
from the Equator. In its configuration of the soil ranges of
hills of a moderate elevation predominate: the different
"regions" are nowhere separated by physical obstacles,
and they form an organic unity. It is the Garden of the
World. It includes all the beauties of the earth: the orange
groves and cypress plantations of the Mediterranean coast,
the heaths and rocky coasts of the North, the snow peaks
of the Alps, the pine forests of the Vosges, the volcanoes
of the Auvergne, and, finally, the royal grace of Paris. The
French boy is taught that to learn to know France is to
know beauty.

---

[1] So far as I know, France alone, of all modern countries, has a
myth of centrality. At Bruère in Département Cher a Roman mile-
stone is described as the "Centre géographique de la France". This
recalls the *umbilicus urbis Romae*. Cf. on this point *Larousse Mensuel*
(1923), 174, and Valery Larbaud's charming book *Allen* (1929).

The idea that France is specially favoured by Nature, even from the geographical point of view, goes back to ancient days. The geographer Strabo, in his description of the world, spoke in a famous passage of the "relation of the land to the rivers and the sea", "the ease with which the needs of human life were supplied in friendly contact with others, and the advantages which spring out of all this". It was his opinion that in the very shape of the land it was possible to trace a "work of Providence", and the influence of a "reasonable agency". Modern French science has devoted special attention to the connexion between geography and history.

The immediate stimulus to this study came from the great historian Michelet. He formulated the axiom: "L'histoire est d'abord toute géographie". He introduces the second volume of his history of France (1833) with a very able sketch of a "Tableau de la France", a spirited geographical and psychological description of France, steeped in intuitive vision. After Michelet had created this precedent the newer comprehensive surveys of the history of France have included a detailed geographical introduction. The point of view of modern French geographers, however, created by Vidal de la Blache, now differs in one important respect from the older views. France is no longer regarded as a geographical harmony, created by Providence. People still speak to-day, it is true, of the "elegance of the formation of the land, and of the lines of the rivers" (Brunhes), but at the same time stress is laid on the fact that France is not a geophysical unity delimited by Nature. The regions which are included politically in the State of France were not originally a homogeneous whole, neither from the point of view of geology or climate, nor in relation to its fauna, flora and population. In all these respects France belongs partly to the basin of the Mediterranean, partly to Central Europe, partly to the seagirt region of Western Europe. It is not possible to claim that the geographical character of France can be understood from within, from a French centre of radiation. The hands of men have modelled Nature. She creates, as a modern student says, a geographical personality out of a piece of the earth's surface. To-day France is a "geographical personality" of this kind, but this personality is a result of history. In France the relations between man and the earth are older and more lasting than in other places. The settlements are to a large measure fixed. From time immemorial the same places have been inhabited.

Modern French geographical research has created the conception of "human geography", or *géographie humaine*. The French freely admit that they have received stimulus from the anthropo-geography of Ratzel, but the French and the German conceptions of the influence of humanity upon the earth, and vice versa, are characteristically different. German *Anthropo-geographie* tends to explain history and culture from the geographical conditions, that is, men are interpreted in the light of Nature. The French *géographie humaine*, on the other hand, seeks to see in the formation of the land the conscious influence of man. Against the determinism of Ratzel it sets the idea of "possibilities". That is: existing geographical facts do not represent the coercive side of Nature, but a wealth of possibilities between which, man, the creator of history, makes his choice. This theory reveals the tendency of the French mind to emphasize free human activity over against the forces of Nature and of Destiny. Whereas Michelet bases history upon geography, the *géographie humaine* of the present day is an "historical discipline", a " renewed history".[1]

To a very great extent French ways of living, and the character of the people, have been determined by the geographical character of the country. It includes and

---

[1] Lucien Febvre, *La Terre et l'évolution humaine* (1922). There is an amusing article on the geographical ignorance of the French public in the *Mercure de France* of the 15*th November* 1925, by A. Chaboseau. Cf. also *Revue Universitaire* (1928), 226. Geography as an idea for comedy: Jules Romains, *Donogoo-Tonka.*

combines within its borders the North and the South. In the *côte d'azur* France possesses her own Riviera. The Northern wistfulness of Brittany and the sunshine and happiness of southern shores are united within one physical scene, and in one State. The Northerner can satisfy his longing for the Mediterranean within France, and the Southerner can learn to know the paler colours and the more wistful moods of the North. Therefore France is able to regard herself as the land of reconciliation, of adjustment, of the golden mean. It is the place where discords are resolved in harmony, in moderation, in which they find their final balance. Typical French taste considers the loud excitement of the South and the formless energy of the North to be extremes, both of which are equally immoderate.

To sum up: even as a place to live in, and as a mere piece of soil, the French have surrounded the geographical fact of the State of France with a delicate veil of idealism. A popular mysticism of the soil of France actually exists. To extol one's own land as the most beautiful and beloved country on the face of the earth is only the natural expression of love of country. But when, above and beyond all this, the French discover in their land—in the formation of the soil, and in its river-system—geometrical regularity, or aesthetic elegance, or providential guidance, we can only describe such views as idealistic. In France, however, they are never considered idealistic. The more naturally and simply they are accepted, the more vigorously do they nourish patriotism, and the consciousness of belonging to a chosen nation. The idea that France is a "central nation" is also, of course, an idealistic notion. Every telegraph pole stands between two neighbouring poles, and so every country lies between two other neighbouring countries. Thus the land of Spain, which lies on the extreme edge of Europe, is conceived as a central country, and a bridge between Europe and Africa. The conception of France as a "central" country, beloved of gods and men, is, as are so many other constituent parts of the French consciousness, of ancient origin. The idea that the mean between two extremes is everywhere the good is indeed a thought which recurs continually in ancient philosophy. Even in the Ancient World this idea was applied to geography. To the Roman authors Italy was the central, the fortunate[1] land. Then the French claimed this privilege for their own land. Ronsard's poem in praise of France is quite in the spirit of the Ancient World:

> . . . sans voguer ailleurs, toutes commodités
> Se produisent ici, blés, vins, forêts et prés;
> Aussi le trop de chaud n'offense nos contrées,
> Ni le trop de froideur, ni le vent ruineux,
> Ni le trac écaillé des dragons venimeux,
> Ni rochers infertils, ni sablons inutiles.

To the French the conception of being the central nation has an entirely different meaning from that it has for us Germans; when we regard ourselves as the nation which occupies the central position in Europe we mean by that that we are in the centre between two opposing forces; we mean, therefore, that we are related to all, and that we occupy an all-reconciling position; for us, therefore, the centre is a metaphysical category. To France it means—quite in the sense of the Ancient World—something aesthetic and ethical: moderation and balance. In France the ideology of the central land is transmuted from the physical and climatic into the intellectual and political sphere. "La grandeur de la France", said Renan, "est de renfermer des pôles opposés."

Historically and actually, the most influential geographical ideal is that of the "natural frontiers" of France and of the claims to which this idea has given rise. This conception is of ancient origin. Caesar says: "Germani trans Rhenum incolunt", and thus defines the Rhine as the frontier of Gaul. Even in those days this did not exactly correspond with the actual situation, for we know that the

---

[1] Virgil, *Georgica*, ii. 135 ff.

D

Rhine from above Strassburg to its mouth—with perhaps the exception of some short stretches of country—was already in Germanic hands when Caesar came to Gaul. However that may be, it made it possible for France to appeal to the famous passage in Caesar, and to regard the Rhine as the frontier of Gaul, and at the same time of the Roman Empire as well. Learned antiquaries—and especially those who exaggerate the importance of the Celtic inheritance—have constantly revived this point of view. Later it became an important pillar in the French policy of expansion. It is, however, possible to explain the fact that the phrase, "the natural frontiers of France", inflamed the masses, and could be grasped by the people as a whole without any knowledge either of Caesar or of Richelieu. The reason lies in the power which the ideology of geography and of natural law exerts over the spirit of the French people as a whole. The French mind requires a clearly defined picture of France, almost geometrical in shape: a glance at the map is likewise an insight into the destiny and the privileges of France.

Modern French geography is beginning to criticize this conception of the frontier. The idea that rivers form natural frontiers has dominated men's minds in France for centuries. To-day it is being revised. "Limite, les fleuves?"—so declares Lucien Febvre[1] in a statement which is so important from the political point of view that I quote it word for word : "Mais dans la phrase fameuse de César sur le Rhin qui divise la Gaule de la Germanie, qui fera la part de la vérité, psychologique ou politique? La question du Rhin est bien trop grosse and trop ardue pour que nous fassions autre chose que rappeler son existence; il faudrait, pour l'exposer, tout un volume; mais combien de formations de 'vals', dans l'histoire, à cheval sur les deux rives d'un fleuve ou d'une rivière; combien de sociétés fluviales ayant leur vie propre et leur caractère particulier, alimentées par le fleuve, tirant de lui leur subsistance et leur raison

[1] *La Terre et l'évolution humaine* (1922), 370.

d'être? . . . La notion de frontière linéaire est attaquée et cède. . . . La notion de cadre prédestiné disparaît. Il n'y a plus rien de donné tout fait à l'homme par la nature, d'imposé à la politique par la géographie". Such statements show how science, by means of subtle analysis, is undermining the foundations of the popular geographico-political idealism. In the general consciousness of the nation at large, however, this idealism is still a vital force.

Further, it is out of these geographical conditions and out of this idealism that there arises that feeling of self-sufficiency, that consciousness of self-determination, which is so characteristic of the French spirit. In the history of the soul of Germany, in our art and our poetry, there emerges again and again the longing for the South. We feel the need to complete ourselves with this attractive other, whether by travelling in Italy, or by the struggle for Greek completeness. When we look at French civilization as a whole these features emerge also, it is true, but they play a subordinate part. It is typical of French feeling, and can be traced through the centuries, that the attraction of Italy and of Greece is acknowledged, it is true, but that, ultimately, the French temperament yields to the stronger attraction of the homeland. The spirit of France feels no need to go outside its own borders. To it France is an epitome of the world, a complete microcosm. The Frenchman sits in the centre of the world, and there he remains. To him the most beautiful and harmonious impressions of foreign lands do not weigh for an instant in the balance against the harmonious beauty of his native land and the mildness of its atmosphere. He is not a great traveller. At the height of the Renaissance Joachim du Bellay wrote:

> Heureux qui, comme Ulysse, a fait un beau voyage,
> Ou comme celui-là qui conquit la toison
> Et puis est retourné, plein d'usage et raison,
> Vivre entre ses parents le reste de son âge!
> Quand reverrai-je, hélas, de mon petit village
> Fumer la cheminée: et en quelle saison

Reverrai-je le clos de ma pauvre maison
Qui m'est une province, et beaucoup davantage?

Ronsard expresses the opinion that it is only fishes, birds and the animals of the forest which continually change the place of their abode,

Mais l'homme bien rassis en sa terre demeure,

and Rivarol has said: "Le Français, visité par toutes les nations, peut se croire dispensé de voyager chez elles comme d'apprendre leurs langues, puisqu'il retrouve partout la sienne. . . . Quand on compare un peuple du Midi à un people du Nord, on n'a que des extrêmes à rapprocher; mais la France, sous un ciel tempéré, changeante dans ses manières et ne pouvant se fixer elle-même, parvient pourtant à fixer tous les goûts".

This trait in the French character contains the danger of self-absorption. Sometimes France appears almost like a provincial form of existence, apart from the life of Europe as a whole and from that of the world at large. Now and again even French people feel this. Paul Morand, one of the most interesting figures in the post-War literature of France, who was the first to give an artistic presentation of the vision of the world of to-day with its crises and the blending of continents and cultures old and new, writes: "The other countries are only parts of a continent, of the world; France is a closed vessel, a complete existence, in which Europe is interested but which does not interest itself in Europe". And in another passage: "The world tour is not a French custom; thirteen journeys round the world had been undertaken by the great nations of Europe before any Frenchman had undertaken this adventure. It was not until the year 1714 that a smuggler named *La Barbinais le gentil*, driven by the truly national desire to deceive the treasury, ventured on this enterprise. He made the journey round the world against the grain. His frigate was called *La Boudeuse*".

Even the world crisis of the present day has not appreciably widened the horizon of the French people. "Even though the average Frenchman gets enthusiastic about general conceptions", wrote Henri Bidou in 1926, "in reality he lives in a very small circle of ideas. He knows the conditions in his own town well, those of his country very little. Of the events which take place beyond the frontiers of France he has only meagre and erroneous ideas. The period of the War left French journalists with the habit of regarding the whole world from the point of view of its relation to France; and when a revolution breaks out in China, at once people inquire: which side is favourable towards France? To the Frenchman the world is a great indeterminate sphere in whose centre lies Paris—just as the ancients used to think of a crystal firmament which served as a vault to the earth".

French students at German universities sometimes express their surprise that people in Germany "go out walking such a lot!" And to them it seems that the Germans go for walks without an object! In France expeditions are undertaken in order to "see" something, but it is not customary to wander about without an aim. There is nothing of the nomad about the Frenchman. These psychological differences extend even into habits of thought. There is much truth in the observation of Léon Daudet: "L'intelligence du Français instruit est celle d'un sédentaire qui cherche, par l'acuité de sa vision, à augmenter l'étendue de ses connaissances. L'intelligence d'un Allemand de même niveau est celle d'un nomade qui cherche à obtenir le même resultat par les déplacements brusques de points de vue." [1]

The one thing which counterbalances this tendency of the French to settle down is the attraction exerted by Paris. In Italy, Milan and Rome compete for the first place, and alongside of them Turin, Florence, Venice and Naples lead a very distinctive existence. In England, Oxford and Cambridge, not London, are the home of the national intellectual tradition. Among us decentralization has gone

[1] *Action française* (21st April 1927).

further still. The man who only knows Berlin knows very little of Germany, but he who knows Paris knows the most important part of France. Paris and the provinces—these are the two poles in the national life of France.

To-day Greater Paris, with more than four million inhabitants, includes more than a tenth of the whole population of France. The process of the growth of cities during the nineteenth century in France has worked out especially to the advantage of Paris. According to the statistics of the year 1921 there were then in France only sixteen large towns (with over 100,000 inhabitants) against forty-three in England and forty-seven in Germany, and of these sixteen, apart from Paris, only two (Marseilles and Lyons) have over 500,000, and only two others (Lille and Bordeaux) over 200,000.

"The Provinces" is the collective name for everything which is not Paris. News from places like Bordeaux, Marseilles and Lyons appears in the Paris press under the heading: The Provinces. Paris, the provinces, and foreign countries form for the French the three concentric zones of the planet.

As early as the seventeenth century *La province* had a collective meaning. In one of La Fontaine's Fables a poet asks a fellow-poet:

> Dois-je dans la province établir mon séjour,
> Prendre emploi dans l'armée ou bien charge à la cour?

The use of the word "province" in the general sense (often with the sense of something which is old-fashioned or out of date) is a precipitate of ancient and complicated historical conditions. Originally "Provinces" were the feudal territories which the Capetian Kings, in the course of centuries, brought under their authority. These provinces formed political and social unities (older than the Monarchy) which were based on the life of the people. They had their traditions, rights, customs and usages. The central authority of the Monarchy had to struggle long against these local authorities before it could establish itself. This was effected by dividing the territory of the State into districts for financial administration (*généralités*) which, in part, included several provinces, and, in part, were carved out of the whole territory of an ancient province; also by weakening the "estates of the province". At the end of the *Ancien Régime* France was divided into *généralités* or *intendances* for local administration; into administrative regions (*parlements, bailliages, sénéchaussées*); into ecclesiastical provinces and dioceses; and, finally, for the military administration, into *Gouvernements*. All these divisions, however, crossed and recrossed each other, and formed no unified structure. The administration spoke no longer of *Provinces*. But the spirit of the old provinces was still alive, especially in those *intendances* which covered the same ground as the old provinces.

When the Constituent Assembly met it was felt that there was an urgent need to create a new, unified order of the country; the Assembly felt that it was necessary to be able to look at France as a whole, in order to make the business of the elections less difficult, to reform the administration, and to make it possible to secure a real representation of the nation. The first proposal, which suggested a division of the land into eighty equally large regular squares, was most characteristic. The decree of the 15th of January 1790 finally created eighty-three *Départements*, which were named exclusively after distinctive features in physical geography, in order to exclude all historical recollections. This system of division and this nomenclature has persisted ever since. It is a great difficulty to the French schoolboy, who has to learn all these *Départements* by heart, with their capital towns.

This arrangement suggests very little of the natural and historical development of the country. Still, it has gained a psychological reality which must strike every observer who travels in the French provinces. A period of nearly one hundred and fifty years since the *Départements* have existed has sufficed to give to them an historical physiognomy and a living consciousness of their own. The *Département* is the small *patrie* within the greater *patrie*. The inhabitant of the Orne feels that he differs from the inhabitant of the Calvados or the dweller in the Charente. In many *Départements* there are scientific societies which collect material relating to the geography, history, folklore and literature of the district.[1] Thus, for instance, there is a "Société des lettres, sciences et arts de l'Aveyron", and in the capital of the department, in Rodez, one can find special works like the "Précis géographique du département de l'Aveyron", or an "Esquisse générale sur le passé et sur la situation actuelle du département de l'Aveyron". This example is characteristic, because before the Revolution Rodez was the chief town of the province of Rouergue. Even at the present day the inhabitant of L'Aveyron feels himself to be a "Rouergat"; at the same time, however, we can see this: over the ancient collective personality of the Rouergue there has been superimposed a new one, that of the Aveyron; out of an administrative district there has grown a historic and psychological living unity. To know France really one would need to have a clearly defined picture of the scenery, history and political distinctiveness of each *Département*. The collective reality of France is, as it were, pigeon-holed in various drawers. The distinctiveness and actual existence of the *Département* is so strong because each *Département* is entirely independent of every other, and dependent on Paris alone. This is the reason why a *Département* is a much more definite and self-sufficing unity than an administrative district in Prussia or Bavaria.

In spite of this, however, the division into departments has not been able to erase the memory of the old French provinces, or to annihilate their distinctive life. Even to-day people still use the old historic names for individual parts of the country which were in use before the Revolution. These

[1] For Provincial Academies, cf. C. M. Savarit, *Revue des Deux Mondes* (15th October 1928).

names fall into different categories.[1] The first includes the old administrative and political divisions. Several of them are names of great dominions like Brittany, Normandy, Burgundy and Lorraine. These are, in the real sense of the word, "Provinces", that is, the military *gouvernements* of the seventeenth and eighteenth centuries. At the close of the *Ancien Régime* there were thirty-seven of these "Provinces". They were of very unequal extent, and they correspond to great feudal dominions. A second category includes regions of less size which used to be counties, such as the Gatinais, Valois, Vexin, Velay, etc. Finally, there are the traditional names of "lands" which never formed political districts, but which have always been regarded as geophysical unities. Such, for example, are the Beauce, the Brie, the Sologne. The name "France" has had a very complicated history. Originally it denoted the land of the Franks, between the Loire and the Rhine. There lay the residences of the Merovingians: Orleans, Paris, Soissons, Reims, Metz. Under the Carolingians the name was confined to the central territory, which, on the west (between the Loire and the Seine), was bordered by Neustria, and on the east by Austria. At the early period of the Capet Monarchy the region over which the royal house was supreme was called by the same name. Only towards the close of the Middle Ages—first of all in 1429—does the name *Île de France* occur. This region, which is surrounded by rivers, was called an "island". France was defined as the corner which is bounded by the Marne and the Seine in the south, and by the Oise in the west. The *Île de France* and "France" meant the same thing.

Speaking generally, there is a good deal of confusion at the present time in the French way of speaking about geographical matters. The names of the "provinces" which are of historical and political origin, and the traditional names of the "lands" which represent a clearly defined type of configuration of the country, and of its culture, are

[1] Cf. L. Gallois, *Régions naturelles et noms de pays* (1909).

mixed together pell-mell. This confusion is further increased by the fact that geographers have recently begun
to speak of "regions". In a school atlas, which is in accordance with the new educational policy of 1923, France is
divided into eleven regions: Massif Central; Région de
l'Ouest; Région de l'Est; Région du Nord; Bassin pari-
sien; Région des Pyrénées; Bassin de la Garonne; Région
du Jura; Région des Alpes; Vallée de la Saône et du
Rhône; Région de la Méditerranée. On the other hand,
the geographer of the Sorbonne, E. de Martonne, speaks
of fourteen geographical regions[1] which only partly cover
the same ground as those which have just been named:
Région parisienne et bassin de Paris; Picardie et Champagne; Lorraine, les Vosges et l'Alsace; Bretagne; Limousin; Auvergne; les Causses; les Cévennes, le Jura; les Alpes
de Savoie et le Dauphiné; la Provence; le bassin d'Aquitaine; les Pyrénées. Finally, we must mention the interesting attempt of Jean Brunhes to classify the old French
provinces—not in the sense of unities, but as existing elements in the structure of France—in a system which would
take into account both the geographical and the historical
factors.[2] Brunhes distinguishes six groups:

I. *Kernel provinces* (political and economic points of attraction or centralization): (*a*) Île de France; (*b*) Guyenne
and Gascogne; (*c*) Lyonnais, Forez and Beaujolais; (*d*)
Touraine, Maine and Anjou. Finally, Brunhes adds to
these kernel provinces, Alsace—a stupid and forced attempt, which shows only too clearly its political tendency.

II. *Connecting provinces* which lie between the great river-
basins. Their historical rôle has been one of exchange and
of reconciliation, whether in the intellectual and religious,
or in the political and economic sphere. These are: (*a*)

---

[1] *Les régions géographiques de la France* (1921).
[2] Jean Brunhes, *Géographie humaine de la France*, in the first
volume of the *Histoire de la Nation française* (1920), published by G.
Hanotaux.

Poitou, Saintonge and Angoumois; (*b*) Languedoc; (*c*) Burgundy; (*d*) Champagne; (*e*) Picardy.

III. *Former political kernel provinces* whose importance has now declined: (*a*) Auvergne; (*b*) Berry; (*c*) Bourbonnais; (*d*) Orléanais and Chartrain.

IV. *Provinces which, owing to their geographical position, lie off the main line of communications*, which, therefore, have only played a small part in the political development of the country (districts in the *Massif Central* and its southern branches): (*a*) Limousin and Marche; (*b*) Périgord; (*c*) Quercy; (*d*) Rouergue; (*e*) Gévaudan; (*f*) Velay; (*g*) Vivarais.

V. *Frontier provinces*, the regions in which France has transformed her "natural" frontiers into political ones: (*a*) Dauphiné and Briançonnais; (*b*) Roussillon and Cerdagne; (*c*) Foix, Andorra, Bigorre; (*d*) Béarn, Navarre, Basque country; (*e*) Flanders; (*f*) Lorraine, the three Bishoprics, the Barrois; (*g*) Franche-Comté of Burgundy; (*h*) Savoy.

VI. *Provinces on the sea coast* in which immigrants from abroad have settled, which, however, have been mainly formed into provinces by political history: (*a*) Provence; (*b*) Brittany; (*c*) Normandy.

This attempt to organize the historico-geographical elements of France in "families" according to the function of each, gives a good idea of the wealth and variety of the structure of France.

Possibly geography will soon be unified by a uniform organization of France in "regions". The problem of the "regions" also touches political, economic and cultural questions and problems; it is very closely connected with the tendencies towards Regionalism which will be discussed in the following pages. At any rate, it is an important fact that in science, education, literature, and indeed in the whole intellectual movement, the mind of France sees beyond the theoretical conception of a State cut up into ninety administrative districts, and is animated by the

desire to attain a living view of a country which is organically
united into a whole by Nature and by history. The feeling
for life, the national and cultural consciousness of the
France of the present day, receives through this development a new and wholesome nourishment. It means the
solution of the abstract conception of the State which belongs to the period of the Revolution and to that which
succeeded it. Doubtless the World War hastened this development. In the daily military despatches the names used
were not those of the *Départements* but the old names like
Flanders, Artois, Champagne, Woevre, Argonne. Even
under French rule Alsace will still remain Alsace, and
its division into *Départements* will remain confined to the
language used in administrative affairs.

The provinces and districts of France still present at the
present day a picture of the greatest variety: in climate,
scenery, habits and customs, as well as in the economic,
religious and political spheres. In spite of this, "the provinces" as a whole constitute a unity whenever they are
regarded in relation to the capital. The relation between
Paris and the provinces has a twofold aspect: that of contrast and that of agreement.

The opposition between Paris and the provinces has
played a great part in the later history of France. The
"Commune de Paris" in the Revolution was always the
element which tended more and more towards the Left
and towards the Terror, and it worked upon the feelings of
the Assembly, which represented the nation as a whole,
and was more inclined towards moderation, by fanning
the flames of mob frenzy. The Paris Jacobins undermined
the Gironde, and the endeavour to form "one indivisible"
Republic, by their accusation of "Federalism". This
opposition between the Parisians and the *Départementaux*
broke out again and again during the Revolutions of the
nineteenth century. It was not in the Chamber but in the
Hotel de Ville that on the 4th of September 1870 the
Republic was proclaimed. At that time it was the urgent

tradition of the great Revolution which determined the course of affairs. After the fall of the Second Empire, the nation, represented by its spokesman Thiers, wished to conclude peace immediately. But Paris demanded and forced the rest of the country to consent to that resistance which was to prove so fatal to her fortunes. As Marshal Foch has said: it was the fault of Gambetta that although he established national armies he was unable to lead a national war, that he was unable to free himself from the idea that the destiny of the nation was bound up with that of the capital. When, however, peace had to be concluded, Paris, embittered and disillusioned, launched violent reproaches at the "country folk" (*ruraux*), the "enemies of the Republic", the "men of Versailles", and the conflict led to the bloody civil war between the *Commune* of Paris and the country.

The predominance of Paris had been firmly established by the administrative centralization of the Revolution and of Napoleon I. But again and again the cry has been raised for decentralization: now by the Catholic-Conservative sociologists, now by individualistic revolutionaries, now by specialists in the science of administration, now by Romantic Nationalists. All those who have strengthened the historical traditions of France over against the abstract rationalism of the Republican State machine, and who wish to renew the life of the nation from these sources of energy, have championed regionalism in some form or another. The strongest influence in this direction has been exercised, I suppose, by Maurice Barrés (*Les Déracinés*, 1897). He spoke for Lorraine, but he awakened echoes in Provence, whose nationality and speech had found a worthy poet and renewer in Mistral; in Brittany with its ancient rigid unique character; and soon in all parts of the country. A regionalistic renaissance began at the opening of the twentieth century, and organized itself in unions which sought for legal reforms, and which after the World War have taken up their activity with a renewed intensity.[1] The entrance of Alsace-Lorraine into the French Republic has strengthened these efforts.

In a French school-book of the post-War period one finds this sentence: "La France est un État fortement centralisé, en voie de décentralisation". These attempts to decentralize are still too new and indefinite to have altered the outward appearance of France yet in any essential particulars. Probably they will bear fruit in many directions. In many parts of the country it is evident that local energies are being renewed, and are bearing fruit both in the technical and economic sphere, and also in the intellectual and artistic sphere. The increase in motor traffic also, which is aided by the excellent system of roads[2] has opened up remote regions and brought them into touch with the rest of the country (in 1913 there were in France 100,000 motors; in 1925 there were 750,000; and in 1927, 976,000). Many an ancient little country town which has been cut off from contact with the outer world since the beginning of the railway era is now once more drawn into touch with the modern world. Places of productive intellectual work and intellectual exchange of ideas, like the "Entretiens d'Été" of Pontigny or the Dramatic School of Jacques Copeau, take place in the idyllic setting of some country district. A healthy, active and energetic traditionalism is stirring in the provincial universities or in young newspapers which appear far away from Paris. The provincial Press is hardly known outside France, and even in Paris it is scarcely read, yet it exercises a great influence in the country regions, especially in politics, and increasingly it is regarded as most important. An instance of this kind, how-

[1] Hedwig Hintze, "Der moderne französische Regionalismus und seine Wurzeln", *Preussische Jahrbücher* (1925); also, Otto Grautoff, "Das geistige Leben in den französischen Provinzen," *Preussische Jahrbücher* (1925). H. Hauser, *Le Problème régionaliste* (1925) in the Carnegie Series. Camille Vallaux, "Les Aspirations régionalistes et la géographie" (*Mercure de France*, 1st August 1928).

[2] To every 100 square km. there are in France 115 km. of roads; England, 110; Germany, 68; U.S.A., 62; Italy, 23.

ever, reveals very clearly the limits of decentralization in France, and in what way it differs from that of Germany. In a South German town it is not at all uncommon in a well-kept inn to find no Berlin newspaper, whereas papers from Frankfurt, Munich or Stuttgart will be lying about. A similar phenomenon in France would be unthinkable. In the most remote corner one is sure to find one or another of the great Paris papers. Every provincial reads his own local paper, but he also reads a Paris paper which accords with his political and general point of view. He must know what is happening in Paris. Even if he seldom goes to Paris he desires to follow Parisian life from a distance, and to enter into it as far as he can. Whatever is the talk of Paris is also the subject of conversation in the Café du Commerce at Landerneau-les-Vaches. It will always be the ambition of the provinces to imitate Paris. They want to possess the wares, fashions and public gardens "à l'instar de Paris", as the expression goes, though it sounds half-educated and almost comic.

In spite of the regionalistic awakening, between the capital and the provinces there is a settled stable relation which nothing can or will alter. Paris may possibly be prevented from absorbing all the energies of the provinces, but she will not be prevented from attracting to herself all their best powers. The difference in *tempo* between the rush and noise of Paris and the quiet life of the provinces is just the same as it was a hundred years ago. In one short hour's run by motor-car from the Place de l'Opéra one can reach the ancient town of Senlis, which lies under the protective shadow of a cathedral of the twelfth century, and preserves the ruins of the wall of a royal castle in which the Merovingians held court, and which even then was built upon Roman foundations. The winding alleys, the silent houses, the wealth of medieval churches, all create an atmosphere, in which one sees once more the provincial towns of Balzac's works. When the Sunday visitors have vanished this town returns to the slow rhythm of its ancient unchanging life. But apart from the industrial districts, it is like this all over the country districts in France. The character of French existence is determined by this balance between provincial stability and the dynamic force of the capital. Most Parisians have their home somewhere in the country, their *pays*, perhaps an old house belonging to their family, perhaps a little retreat which they have created for themselves. There are their roots. Thence they draw the best of their vital energy and their connexion with the life of the people. Life in a little grey and ancient town, whose pointed roofs cluster round a weather-beaten cathedral, has been wonderfully described and with great artistic power by Proust in the Combray of his great novel.

In the country the family is still supreme, whereas in Paris it has long lost its significance. There (in the country) a man is valued for his family, according to whether he belongs to a respected, ancient, settled clan. Life passes in labour and in the observance of the traditional customs. Nothing breaks the even course of daily life save events in the family—whether of joy or sorrow. Everyone watches everyone else. The dominion of custom is strong. Even in large country towns everything is closed at midnight, and in the smaller towns the Café shuts its doors as early as eleven o'clock. Those who choose to fashion their lives as they will are regarded with disfavour. People who do not behave as they should are boycotted socially. In this atmosphere flourish the secret dramas which go down to the grave in secret; the terrible passions which the modern inhabitant of European cities scarcely knows any longer; the energies of hatred or ambition which are nursed and tended for years; the consuming longing of a youth which believes that all fulfilment lies in the remote region of Paris. From this psychology and sociology of the provinces French literature draws ever new energies, and a recent novel like *Leviathan* by Julian Green (1929) describes for us this form of French existence with exactly the same traits as those in *Madame Bovary* or *Eugénie Grandet*.

But this quiet provincial life which scarcely changes also conserves values for which the inhabitant of the great capital city will always long from time to time: it preserves historical tradition. It shows unchanged the genuine, original countenance of France, which in Paris, among the whirling changes of fashion, and the crises of people and events, is so difficult to recognize. The country regions are still wedded to the soil, to the seasons and the centuries. And they preserve a costly possession which the overwrought people of the Americanized present need more than ever: solitude. There is a solitude in the French countryside which can scarcely be found any longer in Germany with its dense population. If we desire to get away from the noise and bustle of life, and to break down the bridges which connect us with the rush of the present day, then we must go to France. Even in the larger country towns there is an atmosphere of meditative repose and satisfying comfort which removes one to another age. The declining population means that most people live in old houses. There are few new buildings to be seen. The old churches, town halls and castles are sufficient for the requirements of the present day. Farmhouses can be seen which have scarcely changed at all since the seventeenth century, or even since the close of the Middle Ages. There are regions in which life has gone backwards, regions over which there broods a stillness as of death. Then the solitude can become sad or even uncanny. It seems as though time had been drawn back and reshaped into the past. France then appears as the primitive, ancient, mature, mysterious land which it is; the land which has taken on its present form as the result of destinies and forces operating for thousands of years. The Menhirs of Brittany, the cave dwellings of the valleys of the lower Seine and of the Loire, the prehistoric grottoes of Périgord, intensify this impression by imparting the eerie sense of remote distances in the past which lie beyond the power of thought.

Southern France as well as Northern Spain is the oldest

E

centre of civilization in the world. "Here is the place, where, so far as we know at present, men for the first time became creators." [1] With the reindeer hunter of the Stone Age who decorated the cave of Cro-Magnon with frescoes, art entered into the development of humanity. Even in those prehistoric days various races dwelt and mingled on the soil of France. Since then countless races have followed upon the same soil: Ligurians, Iberians, Celts, Romans, Germanic tribes—and also Greeks from Asia Minor, Saracens and Normans have helped to form the type of the French people. The unity of French nationality is not that of race but of nation. We know how uncertain is our present knowledge on the subject of race and to what controversies it gives rise. But even if as a science it could attain firmly established conclusions and overcome all political and ethnic prejudice still it would not arouse so much interest in France as among us. It is true that France also has had her historians who have used the conception of race in their work. In the Romantic Movement the attempt was made to interpret the political history of France and England, and especially the Revolution of 1789, as a struggle for power between a conquering race and those who have been conquered. But these theories were shortlived. It is contrary to the spirit of France to explain history in the light of a kind of natural Determinism—whether it be that of climate, soil or race—Gobineau's theory of race was unregarded. None can deny that much in the history of France would be illuminated for us if, with any certainty, we could establish the influence of the race element. But there is a complete lack of this certainty. It is better to admit the existence of this gap in our knowledge than to attempt to fill it with images and fantasies which are the fruit of our own desires. It is impossible to determine to what extent France owes something to the admixture of Germanic blood. I say deliberately "determine"—for one

[1] Herbert Kühn, *Kunst und Kultur der Vorzeit Europas. Das Paläolithikum* (1929).

may guess or imagine a great deal. From the German as
well as from the French side this question has often been
discussed, but almost always with political preconceptions
and prejudices. We must also remember that the Germanic
strain was very varied; we have only to remind ourselves
of the differences between the Franks and the Normans.
There is no doubt that the influence of the Normans was
far stronger than that of the Franks. On Gallic soil the
Franks very speedily became Romanized. The Normans,
on the other hand, for a long time led an independent
existence, in which their own legal and State forms were
retained. Their urge towards activity drew them towards
Italy and England; it also gave the strongest impulse to
the First Crusade. According to the conclusions of the
most recent research, it was in Normandy that the foundation of Gothic architecture was laid in the eleventh century. It obtained its full development and completion,
however, in the Île de France.

Purely for psychological reasons, however, the race
question plays a very unimportant part in France. The
Frenchman has no race-consciousness and no race-instinct.
For example, he is unable to understand the instinctive repulsion felt by Germans and Anglo-Saxons towards the
coloured races. This lack of psychological understanding
itself must surely be derived from physiological causes too
obscure to fathom. In any case, however, the lack of this
sense of racial difference is a feature in the French consciousness which strikes the foreign observer, and which
we must take into account in the endeavour to understand
the national ideology of France. A publicist of the Left,
Jean Finot, some decades ago wrote a book upon *Race Prejudice*, in order to prove how absurd race doctrines are if
pushed to an extreme, because they are an obstacle to the
humanitarian, rationalistic conception of civilization: the
ideal of the Enlightenment, of Reason and Humanity, does
not allow the conception of varying race values. But not
less noteworthy is the fact that the historians and ideo-

logists of the Right, Conservatives and Royalists, do not wish
to admit the race conception. To them race seems something far smaller than nation. They regard the varied
admixture of blood, the crossing of races, as an advantage
to France. They regard it as the glory of France that she
has been able to fuse the most varied number of races, to
give them one Faith, and to inspire them with a united
national will. We must also take this factor into account
when trying to judge the question of the results of the
decline in the population. The decline in the French share
in the population of the world is shown by the following
figures: About 1770 the relation of the population of
France to that of the rest of the civilized world was 1:4; in
1850 it was 1:10; in 1914, 1:25; and, according to the latest
accounts, to-day it is probably 1:50. The number of births
over deaths has steadily fallen since the War: in 1924 there
were 72,216, in 1925 only 60,064. During 1923 only thirty-
eight *Départements* showed a surplus of deaths over births;
to-day there are forty-six, thus more than half. Only the
industrial regions in the North and North-East, and a few
of the fertile agricultural districts, still show a definite surplus of births over deaths. But the rich river valleys of the
Garonne, the Rhone, the Loire and the Seine are beginning to be depopulated.[1] The reasons for the decline in the
population are of course very complicated, but it seems
probable that the most important factor is the rationaliza-
tion of the French consciousness; by this I mean not only
the fear of risks, but also the fact that love, marriage and
the procreation of children have become spiritually separated, and dissociated from each other. Efforts of the most
varied social and political kind have been made to stem
the current of *dénatalité*. But these efforts have not been
successful. Perhaps there has not yet been time to allow
these measures to become effective. The social consequences
of the decline reveal themselves in the loss of the value of
the land itself, in the depopulation of the countryside, and

[1] Hans Harmsen, *Bevölkerungsprobleme Frankreichs* (1927).

finally, in the lack of industrial workers, which can only be made up by using a large number of foreign labourers. How strongly this immigrant movement is growing is revealed by the following figures: in 1851 for every 10,000 of the population there were 106 foreigners; in 1872 there were 209, in 1901, 267, and in 1921, 396. These immigrants do not only go into industry, they also slip into the depopulated rural regions. In 1925 official statistics estimated the number of foreigners at 1,639,600, but people who know declare that these figures are deceptive, and that there are at least six millions.[1] If that is so it would mean that at least a seventh of the whole population to-day already consists of foreigners. What the ultimate effect will be it is impossible to foretell. But those who expect that it will cause a weakening, or even a breakdown, of the French State and a diminution of the extension of the cultural influence of France are certainly quite mistaken. In every century France has attracted crowds of foreigners and has assimilated them. Even to-day this power of assimilation to the soil and the civilization of France is unbroken. France shapes her inhabitants in her own image, and these in their turn carry forward the existence and the unique character of France down the ages.

To the Frenchman France seems like a work of art, formed by human hands, and by the human spirit, out of the stuff of Nature. As the French soil has slowly taken on the features of a "geographical personality", so France also regards herself in her historical process as a person. Michelet coined the famous phrase: "L'Angleterre est un empire; l'Allemagne un pays, une race; la France est une personne. La personnalité, l'unité, c'est par là que l'être se place haut dans l'échelle des êtres". But even this personalism of the national and cultural consciousness of France is nourished by the soil of France, by the patient work of cultivation carried on from generation to generation.

[1] E. Gascoin, *Revue Universelle* (1st May 1924).

# III

## THE HISTORICAL BASIS

IT is, of course, impossible to study the basis of French civilization in the form of a condensed survey of French history. Two things only are attempted in this chapter; some of the chief factors in the development of France as a nation are presented in some detail, and some light is cast upon the relation of the French to their own history.

Germany and France arose out of the same political system. Both are offshoots of the Carolingian Empire. It was only after this Empire had fallen that Germany and France existed as separate states. For both peoples the Partition Treaty of Verdun in 843 marked the birth of their independent political development; it was also the beginning of that conflict between France and Germany which has endured for more than a thousand years, a struggle of vital importance in the history of the world as a whole.

It is a curious and remarkable phenomenon: for a short time both countries formed a unity and a living community, but after that, through one crisis after another, they were continual rivals. But although the independent history of Germany and France only arose after the fall of the Carolingian Empire, we must not forget the importance of the centuries between Caesar and Charlemagne; they were vital in their influence on the separate development of the German and the French political systems at a later date. In these eight centuries the foundation was laid for the whole of the later process of development. Gallo-Romans and Germans lived together for a time, it is true, but their previous experience had been very different.

The difference, briefly stated, is this: the history of Germany begins with resistance to Rome; the history of France begins with submission to Rome. In the dawn of our historical epoch there stands the figure of Arminius the

Cheruscan. We call him Hermann the Liberator. To us the battle in the Teutoburger Wald is the symbol of our liberation from the Roman yoke. But in France the whole course of events was entirely different. In the eight years of war from 58 to 51 B.C. Caesar subdued the whole of Gaul. Here also, it is true, an attempt was made to free the country. Under the leadership of Vercingetorix, in the year 52, there was a general rising of the Gauls. But Vercingetorix was shut up in Alesia, forced to surrender, and was executed at Rome. This defeat meant the suppression of the nationality of Gaul. French history begins with Romanization, with the loss of national freedom, and of her own independent culture. This fact produced a peculiar discord which still affects the spirit of the French nation at the present day. The figure of Vercingetorix remains a great historical memory; it remains the symbol of the hereditary Gallic nationality. Even Napoleon III. had a gigantic statue set up at Alesia in memory of Vercingetorix. Few Frenchmen, however, would really wish that Vercingetorix had conquered. In French opinion the rebellion of Vercingetorix certainly constitutes a claim to glory, but the Frenchman admits that his defeat was necessary, and indeed salutary. Roman civilization, the Roman idea of the State, were historical forces of the highest significance. Through the process of Romanization they were assimilated by Gaul. It was to the Roman conquest that she owed her civilization.[1] Gaul would have been Germanized if she had not been Romanized. Gaul "shared five centuries of her history with Rome" (Bainville). She gave up her Celtic language, with the exception of the few meagre relics which still form part of the vocabulary of the French at the present time. She gave up her Celtic religion, with the exception of certain undercurrents which are difficult to discover, but which sometimes emerge in the continuance of very ancient customs and superstitions. In France

[1] Cf. the observations of E. Bickel in the *Bonner Jahrbüchern*, 1928, 1 ff.

it is customary to regard the *esprit gaulois* as a Gallic inheritance: this is the spirit which takes pleasure in treating delicate matters in a witty or amusing way, combined with hostile mockery of authority, ecclesiastical or secular. Gallic also is said to be the desire for change, the search for novelties, the tendency to oscillate between sudden enthusiasm and slackness, the impulse to initiate: all elements which represent a temperamental basis rather than essential features of the spirit and the mind, or cultural values. But the Roman speech, the Roman language and culture, the art of the drama and of rhetoric, the sense of and faith in the State—all this Gaul received from her conquerors. For the conversion of Gaul to Roman Christianity constituted a second process of Romanization, and meant a fresh intellectual separation from the Germanic Barbarians.

About the year 1500 there arose a school of thought in French history and literature which exalted Gaul at the expense of Rome. "Celtomania" is the name given to the ideas of this school. In the sixteenth century several writers even advanced the fantastic theory that Gaul was the instructress of Athens and Rome. Later authors were more modest. The best scholar in Gallic and Gallo-Roman history at the present time, Camille Jullian, however, reveals in his work a curious discord. He sketches a brilliant picture of pre-Roman Gallic culture. He attributes the abiding impulse of France towards unity to Gallic roots, and in the Druid assemblies on the banks of the Loire he sees the first sign of the will to the *union sacrée*. He attributes to the Gaul the desire for logical clarity, and a versatile and precise intelligence, marked only by two defects: a power of imagination which pictures the thing desired as though it were already attained, and a joy in brilliant empty eloquence which paralyses action. With regret he notes that the Gauls wasted their talents in a sterile imitation of the pattern set by the Romans, instead of expressing their ideas in terms of their own spiritual and intellectual inheritance. They forgot their history and denied their own past. At the same time, however, Jullian vigorously rejects the assertion that France is the pupil and heir of the "Latin genius". Both ethnically and in their own souls he declares that the "thirty millions" of Gauls were unchanged from the time of Caesar to that of Clovis, and even later. Even at the present time, he says, France is right in cultivating reverence for Roman poetry and wisdom, but she ought to separate "Latin education" (which Jullian feels he must accept) from the received opinion on the Roman Empire; in his judgment the latter was "a menace to humanity". When Caesar subdued Gaul "he laid the foundations of a decadence which ended in a catastrophe."[1] It is impossible to discuss here the curious and contradictory ideas of this eminent scholar; they may, however, be regarded as an interesting psychological symptom of an inward conflict which the French spirit absorbed into itself at the very beginnings of its history. This theory may not be of great importance, but it cannot be overlooked.

The conquest of Gaul by the Romans was the first, and therefore the most important event in the history of France; the invasion of the Franks under Clovis was the second. Both events have one common factor: in each case Gaul was conquered by an alien people. The differences, however, are far greater than this resemblance. Both from the political and from the cultural point of view Rome was superior to Gaul. With the Franks the situation was exactly reversed: they had nothing to set over against the Gallo-Roman culture, so they had to assimilate it themselves.[2] Clovis did conquer the last Roman governor certainly, but he took over this rôle himself. He received from the Eastern Roman Emperor Anastasius the title of a Consul, he put on the purple tunic, and to the Gallo-Romans he was able to appear as the representative of the Empire. The stamp of the political thought of Rome was imprinted upon his

[1] Cf. C. Jullian: *De la Gaule à la France* (1923).
[2] For the relation between the Franks and the Gallo-Romans cf. Albert Hauck: *Kirchengeschichte Deutschlands*, i. 167 ff.

system of government. A second factor must be mentioned
which was equally important. Under the influence of the
Gallo-Roman clergy, perhaps also under the influence of
the historical example of the Emperor Constantine, Clovis,
together with his people, accepted the Christian faith in its
orthodox Roman form. He was baptized at Reims with
three thousand Franks by Bishop Remigius. Henceforth a
double bond united Clovis with Rome. "By baptism Clovis
became a comrade of the Romans, and his policy influenced
that of his descendants. Merovingians and Carolingians
maintained it firmly. As he pushed forward into the old
Roman lands he also extended his power over the Germanic tribes."[1]

The conquest of Caesar meant the Romanization of
Gaul, and the conquest of Clovis led to the Romanization
of the Franks. In both instances the higher civilization conquered. Only in the Roman conquest victory was on the
side of the conquerors, while in the Frankish conquest it
was on the side of the vanquished.

The historical position of Charlemagne is more complicated than that of Clovis. Symbolically this appears in the
fact that both French and Germans claim him as the
founder and first hero of their history. Upon that island in
the Seine which constitutes the historic kernel of Paris, and
is therefore named the Île de la Cité, an equestrian statue
of Charlemagne stands in the open space opposite the
façade of Notre-Dame.

Charlemagne has had a greater influence on the historical imagination of France than on that of Germany.
"The popular poetry of Germany", says Scherer, "ignored
the great Emperor altogether; in the consciousness of the
nation his memory was revered simply as that of a lawgiver; his deeds and his heroes were forgotten. Through the
French *Song of Roland* he came again into prominence, and
enkindled the imagination of Friedrich Barbarossa as a
political example." In France the memory of Charlemagne

[1] Aloys Schulte: *Frankreich und das linke Rheinufer* (1918).

was exalted by the Church, which was thankful for his protection. The aspiring national consciousness, and the newly
awakened spirit of the Crusades, which was aroused in the
conflicts of the eleventh century against the Saracens in
Spain, then created its expression in the *Chansons de geste*,
which celebrate Charlemagne as a divinely endowed champion of legendary fame. At an early date he appears in
legend as a pilgrim to the Holy Sepulchre. In the Abbey of
St. Denis relics used to be shown, which, it was said, Charlemagne had brought to Aix from Jerusalem, and which
Charles the Bald is supposed to have brought to France.
The French kings called Charlemagne their *progéniteur*,
and after the coronation ceremony each king used to send
the shroud of his predecessor to Aix to be placed upon the
tomb of Charlemagne—a custom which was observed until
1775. At the suggestion of Barbarossa the process of canonization was instituted in 1165, and it was successful, but as
it was pronounced by the Anti-Pope Paschalis III. it was
never finally accepted. In France the cult of the great Emperor was encouraged by St. Louis. In the Calendar of the
Saints Charlemagne appears on the 28th of January. This
day was proclaimed a public holiday by the Parliament of
Paris, and this was the custom until the Revolution. From
the sixteenth century Charlemagne was the patron of the
Paris University. "La Saint-Charlemagne" was a school
holiday, and was celebrated until the beginning of the
Third Republic. Thus throughout the centuries the figure
of Charlemagne was a national figure in the historical
memory of the French people.

Nationalistic French historians see in Charlemagne the
renewer of the Roman Empire, which is henceforward a
Christian Empire. According to this conception he owes
his importance in history to the fact that he civilized and
Christianized Germany. He desired a united Christendom.
That was his Roman aim. Hence to these historians he was
a Frenchman (Bainville). But they forget that his mother
tongue was German, that he encouraged the study of that

language, that he called the months by old German names, and that it was he who caused the old songs of the wars of the Germanic kings to be written down.

When French historians annex Charlemagne to France they naturally bring a political bias into their study of history. Their aim is to reduce the significance of the Germans to a minimum. It was not always so. The nobles of the *Ancien Régime* liked to trace their ancestry from the Frankish conquerors, and the Count Boulainvilliers (1658–1722) based upon that a race theory of French history which, as is well known, had a great influence during the Revolution (with polemic intensity), and in the Romantic Movement. The importance of the Germanic element was generally recognized, whether one sympathized with it or not.[1] After the War of 1870 there was a reaction : Fustel de Coulanges, in his *Histoire des institutions politiques de l'ancienne France* (1888 ff.) came to the conclusion that the Frankish "conquest" was a peaceful settlement of Romanized Germans, and that the Franks did not impart anything new or distinctive to the Gallo-Romans.

The desire to diminish the part played by the Germans was increased by the World War. A historian like Hanotaux, the author of the *Histoire de la Nation française* (1920 ff.), declares that the Carolingians were "Belgians", and that the Franks were "Hollanders" or perhaps "Scandinavians".[2] Thus French history has been recently disinfected.

Both historical conceptions, the French and the German, must be overcome by the view that in 800 there was no national consciousness at all, that the separation between Germans and French which gradually became pronounced in the course of history, had not yet taken place. The *regnum Francorum* was not a national structure.

If we compare the history of France with that of Ger-

---

[1] There is a characteristic instance of a friendly attitude towards the Franks among the French nobles in an expression used by Montalembert in the *Journal des Goncourt*, ii. 109 ff.

[2] *Revue Hebdomadaire* (28th June 1924), p. 391.

many we note that one of the most striking differences lies in the fact that France early attained national and political unity, whereas Germany only realized it—and then not completely—in 1871. For the old German Empire, even at its highest points, never possessed that formal unity which was the portion of France. Whence comes this difference in historical development? The Roman idea of unity very early struck deep root in France. But the Merovingians, and then the Carolingians, were only able to realize this idea imperfectly. In the tenth century it seemed as though the national unity were finally shattered. The central power of the Monarchy was weakened. "The people fled from the Imperialism of the Crown to the protection of the territorial lords, which reduced them to a position of dependence" (Schumpeter). A number of small secular and ecclesiastical lords were gaining all the power in their own hands. The feudal system arose, and for centuries it menaced the central authority.

The feudal system is a universal phenomenon in the Germanic-Roman Middle Ages. But in France it became the starting-point of the growth of a new strong central authority; this was not the case in Germany; this is one of the reasons which explains why France was ahead in the development of national unity.

One of the feudal families in France became so strong that it finally attained the royal dignity. This happened in 987, when Hugh Capet was elected king. The throne was vacant by the death of the last French Carolingian, Louis V. Strictly speaking, the history of both countries as independent states does not begin until the Carolingian dynasty has died out (911 in Germany, 987 in France). For until that time the idea of the Great Frankish Empire was still alive, at least as a geographical-cultural sentiment, and "Gaul" was still used as a comprehensive name which covered both France and Germany, both in German Gaul and in French Gaul; in the same sense the name "Frank" was used with the distinction between the Eastern and the Western

Franks.[1] But Hugh Capet is the first French king of whom we know that he did not understand the Frankish tongue. In the true sense of the word he is the first French king.

The kingdom of the Franks became France during the eight centuries of Capetian rule. Hundreds of years elapsed, however, of arduous labour and conflict, before the Capetians secured their dynasty. They were Dukes of the Île de France, and Paris was their capital. But the territory over which they ruled was small: it included about four *Départements* of the France of to-day. The great vassals —the Lords of Burgundy, Flanders, Normandy, Gascony, Toulouse, of Narbonne and Nîmes—and also many smaller and still smaller lords were independent rulers in their own territories. It was not until the twelfth century that the Capetians were able to undertake the lengthy and toilsome task of freeing the royal authority from the fetters of feudalism. They were able to effect this because the ancient Carolingian idea of the Monarchy and of the State—even although it had been limited to a purely abstract legal claim—had never been entirely lost. Further, the Monarchy had the support of the Church, which crowned and anointed the kings; and further still, there was the fact of their central position in the country.

If we are to understand the development of France it is essential to realize the special character of the French Monarchy.

The French Monarchy had indeed an ecclesiastical origin—the baptism and coronation of Clovis. At first, however, it was a secular organization. But in the course of centuries—or, to state it more precisely, from the second half of the ninth century—it was transformed by the influence of the clergy into a sacerdotal and religious dignity, for a thousand years.[2] It is this which distinguishes the

[1] R. Wallach, *Das abendländische Gemeinschaftsbewusstsein im Mittelalter* (1928).

[2] The classic desciption of these conditions is that of Renan, *Revue des Deux Mondes*, vol. 84 (1869), p. 79 ff.

French Monarchy from the other monarchical institutions of Europe. It explains many features in the history of France, in French Catholicism and in French national idealism.

The oil with which Clovis and his successors were anointed in Reims was said to have been brought from heaven by a dove in the *sainte ampoule*. Through the Grace of God (*gratia Dei*, and similar expressions which were used in the eleventh century were originally devotional formulas) the French kings received their dignity. They were the servants and the deputies of God. Through the consecration (*sacre*) the priestly character of the Monarchy was sealed. "Kings and priests", said Louis VII., "are the only ones who are consecrated by the ecclesiastical institution by being anointed with the Holy Oil."

From the hallowed personality of the king there issued priestly healing powers. Until the Revolution the French kings healed scrofula by the laying on of hands. Even Charles X. revived this practice, which, however, at that time—1825—aroused the spirit of mockery.[1]

As a priestly king the French monarch was also under the obligation to secure the practice of the legal order of the Church in his dominions, and to guard the purity of the Faith. The first French king who ordered the burning of heretics was Robert the Pious, under whose rule, in 1022, thirteen Cathari were burned in Orleans.

Under the presidency of the same pious king the Archbishops of Reims, Sens, Tours and Bourges declared at the Synod of Chelles that French bishops had the right to reverse Papal decisions. Such an episode already reveals the germ of the whole of the Gallicanism of the future. The French clergy were more "royal" than "Roman" in their sentiments: they could and did see in the King of Saint Denis their Supreme Head. The title *Rex christianissimus* was borne by the French kings from the time of Louis XI., who received this honour from the Pope for the Revocation of the Pragmatic Sanction of Bourges.

[1] Cf. M. Bloch, *Les Rois thaumaturges* (1927).

One of the dangers which menaced the kingdom of the early Capetians was the growing power of Normandy. This danger became a definite menace when the Normans conquered England in 1066. The Norman dukes were now kings as well. Henceforward the French kingdom was threatened both by Germany and by England. The powerful Norman dynasty of the Plantagenets, which from 1154 ruled over England, Normandy and also over central and south-west France, through the marriage of Henry II. with Eleanor of Aquitaine, was conquered, after a struggle of a century, during the years 1204–1208. It sought to raise its head once more with the aid of the King Otto IV. of Brunswick. But the Allies were beaten in 1214 at the battle of Bouvines. This victory meant for the French Monarchy the final victory over feudal resistance, and the preservation of its authority as a continental power. The South, however, was still independent. Through the Albigensian Crusade it was won for the Crown: by means of abominable horrors, through rivers of blood Southern France was brought under the influence of the Monarchy, and of the Île de France. When Philip Augustus died, in 1223, the power of the Crown was so much strengthened that his son was able to succeed him as his natural successor.

At first the kingdom of the Capetians was an elected Monarchy, but through its own vitality it became an hereditary Monarchy. This development was a fact of great significance for the historical importance and greatness of France.

The first Capetians tried to make the right of free election secure by arranging that the heir to the throne was always "elected" during the lifetime of his father—after the example of the German Emperor. In this way the Crown remained in the hands of the Dukes of France. The last time that the succession was secured in this manner was in 1179, when Louis VII. had his son Philip Augustus elected king. Until that time, therefore, the only "legal ground" of all the Capetians was that of election. But "the strengthening of the Monarchy after the activity of Suger also turned out to the advantage of the Capetian claim to inherit the Crown".[1] This was expressed after the death of Philip Augustus. That the French Crown was hereditary in the male line became part of the legal consciousness. Later this conviction was formally recognized in juridical form.

France owed her early and permanent unity as a State primarily to the hereditary Monarchy. This preserved France from that weakening and destruction of the central authority and of the national unity which was fatal to Germany and to Italy. Another favourable circumstance was the fact that Hugh Capet and his first ten successors always had a direct male heir. From 987 till 1316 they follow in a direct line of descent. Royalist writers see in this an act of Providence; we see in it the irrational factor, the "accident" which is a formal category of history as a whole. This "accident": that for hundreds of years all the Capetians had a son who survived them, cannot be explained by any of the usual historical logical methods as a legal matter. But it is the cause which enabled the hereditary law to be carried out; this explains why the Capetians were able steadily to increase the power of the Monarchy— which, again, is the reason why France became great. Among the Capetians there were also some outstanding rulers. In the form of St. Louis the French kingdom gained a consecration which increased its prestige. His grandson Philip the Fair was so strong that he was able to suppress the Order of the Knights Templars, to force the Papacy to depend upon France, and to strengthen royal absolutism. This royal Gallicanism reminds us of Louis XIV.; in other points too both these reigns resemble each other: both fought against finance magnates in the interior of the country, both struggled for the possession of Flanders, and both strengthened the central authority of the Crown.

Soon after the death of Philip the royal succession passed to the younger line of the Capetian dynasty without con-

[1] Holtzmann, *Französische Verfassungsgeschichte.*

F

flict—to the Valois. It was considered quite natural that women should be ineligible to govern; otherwise if that had been allowed a woman might have brought France with her as part of her dowry in marriage to a foreign ruler. In spite of this, however, the exclusion of women, and also of their male issue, from the right of inheritance in any form was established by law, with the aid of the Crown lawyers and assemblies of notables.[1]

At the same time, however, there arose a crisis which threatened the French Monarchy with utter ruin: this was the Hundred Years' War with England, intensified by the bloody conflicts between the Burgundians and the Armagnacs. In 1431 an English king was crowned King of France in Notre-Dame.[2] But in those years of terror at the beginning of the fifteenth century French patriotism arose. It found moving and inspiring expression in the literature of the day, and it was incarnated in an active and victorious form in the figure of the Maid of Orleans, the peasant girl of Lorraine, who reconquered the land for the King of France. To-day for all French people Jeanne d'Arc is the most living symbol of the national idea. In the reverence which is paid to her differences of party disappear. Her presence at the Coronation of Charles VII. in Reims makes her appear as the instrument of the renewal and establishment of the Monarchy. Her canonization by the Church is the sign and seal that she represents the rôle of France as the champion of the Catholic Faith. But French democracy also appeals to her: the Maid of Orleans represents the people of France which contained the energy needed to cleanse the land from the foreign foe, and to save the existence of the nation.

Once again there occurred a crisis which menaced the unity of the nation and the authority of the dynasty: the

[1] In so doing no one appealed to the *Lex Salica*. This only took place later, cf. Holtzmann, *Französische Verfassungsgeschichte*, 185.

[2] Till 1802, the Peace of Amiens, the English kings also bore the title of Kings of France.

Wars of Religion of the sixteenth century, which lasted for a generation. It was then, however, that Henry IV. and Richelieu completed the work which established the organization of the Monarchy. Under Louis XIV. Royal Absolutism received both its theoretical basis and its magnificent development. Its visible monument is the Palace of Versailles.

Two experiences of his youth were of epoch-making importance for Louis XIV.; the Regency of Mazarin and the Fronde. When, in 1661, he himself took over the reins of government he was resolved that he would not permit any Chief Minister to rule alongside of himself. He was determined to be sole ruler, and this in fact he was. He tolerated no longer any other elements of power in the State. This was why he allowed Fouquet to be condemned, and this is why he broke the final resistance of the nobility and of the Parliament. Thus he became the final creator of the absolute Monarchy. Through his wars he completed the programme of the policy of Richelieu, and the triumph over the Hapsburg Dynasty. By the Revocation of the Edict of Nantes he completed the work of the Counter-Reformation. And, finally, he organized the artistic and intellectual forces of the nation, and in so doing created in all spheres of culture a representative style: representative of the Monarchy, representative of France and representative of a century of civilization in Western Europe.

This style we call French classicism. It is not an imitation, either of the style of antiquity or of the Italian Seicento. Versailles reminds us as little of Palladio and Bernini as Racine reminds us of Sophocles. But all the creations of this classical spirit in architecture, landscape gardening, poetry and eloquence reveal the same law of style: complete and pleasing proportion; the victory of proportion over fantasy, the subduing of the individual to the law of an ideal balance. It was for this very reason that the French classic style was able to be both a national style and a universal style. Thus in it we see once more the peculiar quality of French civilization: the power of realizing the universal in and through the national.

At the height of the period of Louis XIV. Bossuet once said: "Sous Louis XIV la France a appris à se connaître". Never has the significance and importance of this period been better described. The French spirit through the civilization of Versailles came to full self-consciousness. It was not merely posterity which declared that this epoch was classical. The epoch itself felt and knew that it was so, and deliberately willed that it should be so.

During the epoch of Louis XIV. France experienced a development in the State, in the intellectual sphere and in its inner spirit such as no other modern nation has known. It was so deep and thorough that even the shattering experiences of the Revolution and of the nineteenth century were unable to eradicate its influence. Certainly the Revolution, democracy and the Republic have entirely transformed the form and spirit of the State. But the heart of the French conception of the State, unity and centralization, is still essentially one with the inward impulse which the French Monarchy realized through eight hundred years of its history. To-day Louis XIV. means more to the French people than Napoleon. In the France of the present day even to the Republican, even to the Freethinker, the Monarchist-Catholic seventeenth century is absolutely the "great century" *par excellence*. For it has given a permanent form to the national spirit.

Frenchmen of all shades of political opinion therefore regard Louis XIV. as a splendid manifestation of the national genius. Of course in saying this the emphasis may vary greatly. The reactionary historian uses the great king as an illustration of the advantages of the Monarchical system, the Republican points out his bourgeois Ministers, piously reproaches him for his policy of conquest, and represents the Monarchy as the forerunner of the modern democratic national State which finally attained its majority at the Revolution.

As a practical political programme the Royalist Movement of the present day has no significance in France. As an idea, however, it exerts a strong influence over the intellectual élite. It is the French form of Neo-Conservative thought which is so characteristic to-day of large sections of the intellectual youth of Western and Central Europe, and which expresses itself as a Romantic Idealism with "Restoration" as its watchword. In France it has destroyed for ever the official historical legend of the Third Republic. Even those intellectuals who still adhere to the Republic admit objectively the historical importance of the Monarchy. In this way French history has regained that continuity which it possesses in actual fact.

Some of the most characteristic features in the French State, and in French civilization, can be traced back to the Monarchy. As I have already said, these are: Centralization, Gallicanism, Classicism (if by this much-abused word we mean all that is of permanent and living value in the culture of Versailles). Further, the traditional French policy of expansion, and especially its Rhine policy, goes back to the Monarchy and indeed to its earliest days. Fritz Kern, a man who knows the story of the development of France better than anyone else—a story which for us Germans is bound up with so many bitter memories—has shown that both in thought and in their claims the Capetians were kings of the whole of France.[1] "Gradually and definitely, but quite deliberately, France accepted the Royal authority; in so doing, however, she claimed that she was submitting not to a West Frankish king, but to the heir of the Carolingians. His rights do not cease where the Emperors Otto and the Salian rulers placed the frontier, but at the boundary set by Charlemagne. For at that time the French did not exist; as yet there were only Franks. On the other side of the frontier, in Germany, the inhabitants of the land of the West Franks were called 'Karlings', and their land was called 'Karlingen'; this set the seal on the

[1] Fritz Kern, *Die Anfänge der französischen Ausdehnungspolitik* (1910).

idea that the successors of Charlemagne had their seat of authority in Paris; unconsciously this idea supported the French idea of Empire, as though France, with its claim on the whole, preferred to live in its western half, whereas Germany and Lotharingia seemed to be merely parts of, or appendages to this Empire." The abstract, mythical and nebulous legal claims of France were then systematically developed by the Crown lawyers of the later Capetians. This claim was intended to conceal the ambition of the prosperous national State and the dominating policy of the official class. Statecraft utilized it, and the weakness of the decaying Roman Empire favoured the French policy of conquest. Richelieu and Louis XIV., the Revolution and Napoleon, all only continued the "historical Rhine policy of the French" still further, whose impulses and methods during the time of the Peace of Westfalia down to the eve of the Ruhr occupation have been described so vividly by Hermann Oncken.[1]

It is idle to discuss whether the French Rhine policy was necessary; whether it was determined by the accident of history or by geographical or political factors. Those who blame the robberies and scandalous deeds of Louis XIV. should also blame the blinded German princes who, from the days of Charles V. to Napoleon, have betrayed and sold Germany. For many years to come it will be impossible to form an impartial opinion on this most serious, complicated and menacing question, which has been bound up with the course of European history for the past thousand years. To disentangle the actual facts from their setting and examine them scientifically and objectively is, at present, an impossible task; inevitably our judgment must be affected and shaped by our political opinions.

Turning to the interior development of France, the same may be said of an estimate of the French Revolution.

There are two versions of this event: that of the Republicans, and that of the opposition. Between both there lies a

[1] Oncken, *Die historische Rheinpolitik der Franzosen* (1922).

small sphere of objective research, where thinkers are honestly endeavouring to study the question with unbiassed minds. But, so far as public opinion, political discussion and historical works composed by men of letters are concerned, and also in school histories, controversy still rages round the subject of the Revolution. In history there is both a revolutionary and a counter-revolutionary legend. Even scholarly research does not quite escape from the influence of political bias.

The history of the Revolution has always been a political weapon in France. The three accounts which appeared in 1847—those of Lamartine, Michelet, and Louis Blanc—were the storm signals of the February Revolution. They attained their end: they shattered the bourgeois Monarchy.

But the experiment of 1848 failed. France was not yet ripe for the Republic. Still more unfortunate was the experiment of the Second Empire, and that of the Commune. After 1789 France passed from crisis to crisis. The question naturally arose: Does this not point to deep-seated defects in the structure of the State and of society? Where can we find the cause of all this? It was easy to say: "in the Revolution!" On top of that there came the experience of the Commune of 1871 with all its horrors. This explains why in its early years the Third Republic was overwhelmingly conservative and monarchist in its outlook: the restoration of the Monarchy only failed owing to some quite small accidents.

This explains the view of the great Revolution which now took the field. Taine's *Origines de la France contemporaine*, the first volume of which appeared in 1876 in the guise of a positivist analysis of facts, constituted a strong attack upon the achievements of 1793. Polemical bias spoiled both Taine's method and his presentation of the subject. Among the supporters of the Revolution it aroused indignation. After the fall of MacMahon (1879) the Republican system was consolidated. The Third Republic felt the need to connect its ideals more closely with the revolutionary tradition. In 1885 the city of Paris, which had been the foremost factor in the Revolution, founded a Chair at the Sorbonne for the History of the Revolution. The first occupant of the Chair was A. Aulard. From this vantage point until 1922 Aulard lectured on the history of the Revolution. As he said in his Inaugural Lecture, he was a grateful son of the Revolution which had emancipated humanity and science; in order to understand the Revolution one must love it.

Aulard's work of research gave a great impetus to the scientific study of the subject, and added much to the sum of knowledge. He opened up a wealth of new sources which shed new light upon essential points, and he poured out a flood of devastating and convincing criticism on Taine's method.[1] But his own method of presentation— the *Histoire politique de la Révolution française* (1901; in German, 1924) is, at the very least, one-sided, for it regards the events of 1789–99 essentially and solely from the standpoint of the Republican and democratic State; that is, from the point of view of the Third Republic. Aulard seeks to show that the Revolution does not represent a break in the national history; he argues that it only carried through a progressive movement which the defects of the royal policy had hindered. Aulard explains the horrors of the Revolution, not, like Taine, from the psychology of the Jacobins, but as the result of the menace of the foreign enemy. The Reign of Terror is not palliated, but he claims that at least it had one merit: it saved the Revolution, and the country as a whole. Aulard does not glorify the leaders of the Revolution; far from it; he reproaches Marat for his ambition to be dictator and Robespierre for his religious dogmatism. To him both are "reactionaries". Aulard's hero

---

[1] A. Aulard, *Taine historien de la Révolution* (1907). Aulard's own method, however, has also been attacked, and with valid reasons, by Augustine Cochin in his posthumous works, *Les sociétés de pensée et la Démocratie* (1921) and *La Révolution et la Libre-Pensée* (1924). About him cf. A. de Meaux (1929).

is "Danton, the great and the good", whom Robespierre betrayed.

But just as within the National Convention the parties of the Gironde and the Mountain fought against each other, so recently also in the camp of the historians who swear by the Revolution internal strife has arisen. Albert Mathiez, who belongs to a younger generation than Aulard, and who also differs from him politically, has guided the history of the Revolution into new paths.[1] Mathiez also bases his work on a scrupulous examination of the sources, and he also has a political bias. He, however, champions Robespierre, and is against Danton. To him Danton is the traitor, the man of compromise, the defeatist. Robespierre he regards as a great statesman, who wished to carry out the principles of the Revolution to their logical conclusion: to the Socialist Republic, which would have realized not only political but also economic equality.[2] In any case he has proved that Robespierre may be regarded as the forerunner of modern Socialism, even though he were not its prophet. Aulard's conception is that of bourgeois radicalism, while that of Mathiez corresponds to proletarian-socialistic idealism. From this point of view the Revolution was a failure.

But this does not yet exhaust the conflicting ideas about the history of the Revolution. Although the radical and the Socialist historical conceptions attack each other (and their inner opposition is only badly patched up by the theories of the *Radicaux-Socialistes*), they are still one in this: they do stand for the Revolution, which, however, they interpret differently. They have, however, a common opponent: the Counter-Revolution. This camp also is divided within itself. It includes conservatives, clericals, royalists and other varieties. But they all regard the Revolution as a misfortune, and they attack it. This is done comparatively

[1] His main work is *La Révolution française* (1922–27). He has also published a number of isolated studies.

[2] A glorification of Robespierre, based upon Mathiez, is offered by Jean Héritier in the *Revue des Questions historiques* of 1st October 1928.

objectively by Jacques Bainville in his brilliant *Histoire de France* (1924). Like Aulard he tries to show that the Revolution was not a unique phenomenon in French history. From this, however, he draws different conclusions. He points out the analogy between it and the rebellious communes of the twelfth century, the Jacquerie of the fourteenth, the Cabochins of the fifteenth, the Leaguers of the sixteenth, and the Fronde of the seventeenth century. Thus to him the Revolution is "un épisode à sa place dans la suite de nos crises et de nos renaissances, de nos retours à l'ordre et de nos folies". The difference between the crisis of 1789 and those of the earlier centuries lies in this: that this time the leaders of the nation were not equal to their task. He grants that after the death of Louis XIV. the Monarchy was in need of reform. It knew it, and it could have reformed itself. But Louis XVI., actuated by theories which were out-of-date, restored the Parliament, and in so doing he "provoked the Revolution". Even after the episode of Varennes the Monarchy might have been saved. When, on the 16th of July 1791, the Jacobins brought in a proposal to depose the king, La Fayette ordered the troops to fire upon the crowd; if a little more energy had been displayed, he believes that demagogy would have been crushed. But this the Constituent Assembly did not achieve; it had not sufficient energy. It dissolved itself voluntarily, in order to make way for a new assembly (the Legislative) and with this the Revolution entered upon its second decisive stage. Incapable of establishing a republican authority, it was forced to abdicate in favour of a military dictatorship, which ended with the invasion of France. Thus the final result of the Revolution was completely negative.[1]

In 1793 the revolutionary leaders in the intoxicating sense of "freedom", in their fever of transformation, and in their hatred of "tyrants", had despised the old régime. This revolutionary propaganda has been influential even

[1] The most recent work against the Revolution is *La Révolution française*, by Pierre Goxotte, 1928.

down to the present day. It has disfigured and slandered
the past in France to the French themselves. One of the
great official scientific historians of the Third Republic,
Ernest Lavisse, said truly: "C'est une mauvaise condition
que celle de l'historien en France. Il n'a pas de public
pour entendre l'histoire impartiale du passé. L'Angleterre
s'enorgueillit de s'appeler la vieille Angleterre; vieille
France est presque une injure; cela marque la différence."
Nationalistic interpretations of history like that of a Bainville may at least lay claim to the merit that they have
popularized a just appreciation of old France. This is a
real gain, even if some of the criticisms of the method and
of certain details may be justifiable.

Although the presentation, interpretation and estimate
of the Revolution is still dominated in France by the most
violent contrasts, there is far more unity of opinion about
Napoleon. France regards the personality and the work of
Napoleon differently from ourselves. The Caesarist hero
cult, which from time immemorial has characterized the
feeling of so many Germans about the Emperor is alien to
the feeling of the French—at least it is so at the present day.
It is of course true that during the Restoration and the
bourgeois Monarchy there was a popular Bonapartism.
The form of expression taken by this reverence for Napoleon stirred Goethe, then an old man, to express a very
critical opinion about the Emperor: "Since the great man
who threw so much of the world into terror and anguish,
and who was able to dominate so large a part of it, appears
to have expiated all the harm which he had done to it by a
sorrowful, perhaps despicable, close to his life, people do not
get very much agitated about his memory, but—as many
books and writings show—they allow his greatness to be
continually renewed in the memory and imagination of
men. Iron or bronze founders, modellers in clay or wax,
and especially the ever-active lithographer, create one picture of him after another, one event in his life after
another. . . ."

The Bonapartism of those days was the sentiment of the liberal patriotic bourgeoisie, for whom Béranger wrote his poetry. It was the legend of Napoleon as a man of the people.

Alongside of that there was a literary Napoleon-Romanticism created by Hugo, Balzac and Stendhal. Politically this did not signify very much. When in 1851 Napoleon III. assumed the reins of State he was chosen not so much for the glamour which was connected with this great name, as because men felt the need for a settled authority, which would be able to protect property and prevent proletarian outbreaks like that of June 1848. The Second Empire was not inclined to intensify the Napoleon cult. A Bonapartism of the streets, lusting for revenge, flamed up for a short time after 1870, during the Boulanger crisis in Paris. From the literary point of view Barrès has preserved this element in his political novels of the period. Since that time in France "Bonapartism" means a political way of thinking which is conservative, anti-clerical and anti-parliamentarian, and desires a régime of the "strong hand". This, however, has nothing to do with a Napoleon cult. On the whole it may be said that to the republican sentiment of modern France Napoleon was a national disaster. The opinion expressed in the year 1903 by Lieutenant Foch (later on Marshal Foch) in a lecture to officers on the Battle of Laon[1] (March 1814) must be considered representative. He reproached Napoleon with having exhausted the vital energies of the nation by his insatiable ambition. The conqueror in him killed the sovereign. Napoleon had to fall, because the sense of justice in Europe was against him. "Laon est bien la défaite du génie par le Droit révolté. La leçon sera là, même pour nous soldats. C'est la Justice reprenant, quoi qu'on fasse, son cours inévitable dans la pérennité des âges. C'est Valmy recommencé; 1792–1793 retourné contre nous. Oui, enfin, après

[1] First printed in the *Revue de France*, (May 1921). Cf. now R. Recouly, *Le Mémorial de Foch* (1929), 126 ff. "Foch sur Napoléon".

avoir montré à l'Europe les peuples se levant victorieuse-
ment pour sauver leur indépendance, c'est l'Europe que
nous retrouvons victorieuse pour la même cause, avec les
mêmes armes, du génie militaire le plus colossal de l'histoire, coupable d'avoir porté atteinte à ses droits. Décidé-
ment, il n'y a d'opprimés que ceux qui veulent l'être."

Thus, even for a military man, for a Foch, it was against
the moral order of the world that Napoleon dashed himself
to pieces. The breakdown of the Emperor restored Justice.

But this leaves no place for hero-worship, no possibility
for feeling the tragedy of genius. An act of presumption has
been expiated, and that was the end of the matter. To
average French opinion Napoleon remains certainly one
who has contributed to the national glory, and the executor
of the Revolution, who destroyed the Holy Roman Empire,
and removed from the Pope his temporal power, but still,
above all, he remains the man who out of personal ambition threw his country into seas of trouble and brought
heavy sorrows upon her.[1] That France is united in this
opinion can be very naturally explained by the fact that
twice it had to endure the Napoleonic experiment. The
reign of Napoleon III. and its result was the death-blow of
Bonapartism.

On the 1st of March 1871, the National Assembly at
Bordeaux made a statement in which these words occur:
"Elle . . . confirme la déchéance de Napoléon III et de sa
dynastie, déjà prononcée par le suffrage universel, et le
déclare responsable de la ruine, de l'invasion et du démem-
brement de la France". In 1919 France expected to hear a
similar declaration from Germany about Wilhelm II.

From the point of view of world history the period of the
Revolution and the Napoleonic era form a unity. Modern

---

[1] It is important to distinguish public opinion about Napoleon from
the estimate of him formed by his biographers. In both cases in the
course of a century the general attitude has changed greatly. But the
two tendencies do not agree. Cf. Villat, "Où en sont les études
napoléoniennes?" in the *Revue des Cours et Conférences* 26 (1924), i. 158 ff.

France can be interpreted in the light of this quarter of a century, from 1789–1815. This statement cannot be illustrated here in detail. Only a few brief points can be mentioned.

Albert Sorel in his great work, *L'Europe et la Révolution* (1885–1904), has demonstrated the truth of a statement, which since that time has often been repeated—namely, that Republican and Imperial France, under the mask of a supposedly new conception of law, in the form of the sovereignty of the people, continued the foreign policy of the *Ancien Régime* and the empiricism of statecraft: hence the war against Austria and the conquest of the Rhine frontier. This policy, however, clothed itself in a new ethos: in the idealism of revolutionary propaganda, in a crusading enthusiasm for freedom and humanity. Since then in France there has been a fusion of the ideas of republicanism and of nationalism.[1] And according to the situation which prevails at the moment the product of this fusion may be expressed either as a peace-loving radicalism of the Left or as a warlike Nationalism. In my opinion this is the explanation of the polarity between the tendencies of the Nationalists and the tendencies of the Left which has been worked out by sociological analysis.[2] At the present time these two extremes are represented by Poincaré and Briand. These views are not mutually exclusive, but they condition each other.

The ideals of the Third Republic are connected with the tradition of the Revolution, and one cannot positively imagine that this tradition could be broken down. The secularization of the State and of the schools, and, finally, the laws of Separation of 1906 are the results of this ideology. But the remarkable thing about this situation is this: that the Revolution has become a tradition, and hence a conservative element. The official speakers of the Third Republic do exalt the Revolution, it is true, but on no

---

[1] Cf. my book, *Französischer Geist im Neuen Europa* (1928), pp. 221 ff.

[2] Max Clauss, *Das politische Frankreich vor dem Kriege* (1923).

account do they wish to continue it. During the nineteenth
century the motto "continuer l'œuvre de la Révolution"
was still effective and full of meaning. To-day the bourgeois Republic has only one desire: to hold firmly to that
which has been attained, and to secure it against the
radicalism of the Left. The "élan révolutionnaire" exists,
as Thibaudet has said, only in literature. Nothing is more
conservative than the ideal of progress of the Third Republic. The need to stabilize that which exists has to use
the phraseology which is borrowed from the upheaval of
1792. This is revealed very plainly in the embarrassments
of the "radical" party.

It is impossible here to analyse the many and varied
after-effects of the Revolution in modern France (we need
only recall the Dreyfus affair). There is only one point
to which I would still draw attention. That feeling of
democracy in the life of France which strikes every
foreign observer is one of the results of the Revolution. The
theoretical conception of equality has produced a natural
consciousness of equality. The people know that even the
President of the Republic is only a *citoyen*. The new value
set on the people as a whole which is enjoyed to-day constitutes one of the greatest differences from the *Ancien
Régime*. One only needs to read La Bruyère's chapter on
"The Great Ones" in order to gain a vivid impression of
the general position of the people under the Monarchy.
Vauban, in his *Dîme Royale*, urged on his sovereign that
in France the *menu peuple* had always been valued too
little. Since the people became sovereign all has changed.
And, like every sovereign, it has its admirers, and also its
flatterers and its parasites.

The highest and purest form of the praise of the people
is contained in Michelet's book, *Du Peuple*. It appeared in
1846, and it reads as though it were a premonition of 1848.
Michelet makes the people the object of a religious cult; he
exalts their childlikeness and simplicity, and their prophetic spirit. His confession of faith belongs to that extrava-

ganza of Messianism, which in the thirties and forties of last century turned so many of the best heads in France.

But the idealization of the people is still to-day thoroughly typical of the intellectuals of the Left. It forms part of the message of *Laïcisme*. It is alive in groups like the *Union pour la Vérité*, and in personalities like that of Alain. With him it forms part of the doctrine of radicalism.[1] "The people" usually means manual labourers, peasants and the inhabitants of small provincial towns. Alain's friend Jacques is a bootmaker who philosophizes while he plies his hammer. He does not expect anyone to give him an income; he likes work, and he wants to bring up his eight children properly. He knows too that there must be rich people, "mais je ne veux pas qu'ils se disent les maîtres". He knows that he is dependent on his customers, but they ought not to make him conscious of it. "Ce n'est pas l'égalité des fortunes qui me paraît être la première justice, c'est l'égalité dans le ton et les manières, et la liberté des opinions. Je veux des égards, enfin." There is no better definition of the feeling of the democracy of France than in those words.

The "people" are always suspicious of the mighty. Alain desires that those who rule shall regard themselves simply as delegates of the people in control of the government departments. He feels a sense of solidarity: with the people against the aristocracy, the intellectuals, the busybodies who think they can "run" everyone else! He is the "citoyen contre les Pouvoirs". Mistrust of the Government on principle, an instinctive hostility to the authority of the State, are characteristic peculiarities of French feeling; probably they are due to the experiences of the people under the absolute Monarchy, which have not yet been forgotten. Perhaps this also is the source of the emotional content of the word *peuple*, at least as it is often used: the patient acceptance of poverty, and the pride in belonging to the poor little people—very characteristically expressed, for instance by a writer like Péguy or Charles-Louis Philippe.

[1] Alain, *Éléments d'une doctrine radicale* (1925).

In France as well as in Germany the nineteenth century was a flourishing period for the writing of history and for the historical sense. To-day in France the study of history is passing through a crisis.[1] Among the elementary school teachers there is a strong desire to do away with the teaching of history. But among the intellectual leaders also history no longer possesses the spiritual force which it exercised at the time of Michelet, Taine or Sorel. This scepticism about history appears to be in part caused by the opposition between the two national points of view about history which were discussed earlier in this chapter; in part also, however, because Determinism has gone, and from Bergson onwards there is a new sense of the mobility and accidental character of history, and of the impossibility of predicting events. Finally, in France as among us, the experience of the World War has made the younger generation doubtful of the immanent meaning of history and of the use of history for life.

[1] Cf. A. Paul, "La Crise de l'histoire" (*Revue de Synthèse historique*, 38, 113 ff.); A. Chaboseau, "L'Histoire dans l'enseignement" (*Mercure de France* of November 15, 1925); Albert Thibaudet, "Die Geschichte im heutigen französischen Bewusstsein" (*Europäische Revue*, December 1927); Henri Massis, "L'Histoire, philosophie du 19e siècle" (*Les Cours de l'Institut d'Action française*, January 1925).

# IV

## LITERATURE AND INTELLECTUAL LIFE

LITERATURE plays a far larger part in the cultural and national consciousness of France than it does in that of any other nation. In France, and in France alone, can the national literature be regarded as its most representative form of expression. It is—perhaps—possible to understand England from the point of view of politics and ethics: the Empire, the State Church, the sects, "games", social structure, etc. But in any case Shakespeare and Keats are not typical of England. France, however, cannot be understood at all—politically, socially, or even from the purely human point of view—if literature is left out of account; if we fail to grasp the central, uniting part it plays in every sphere of the life of the nation. Further, unless we read the French classics, and read them in the way the French read them, we cannot possibly understand France. All the national ideals of France are coloured and shaped by literary form. In France if a man wishes to be regarded as a politician he must be able to express himself in some form of literature. If he desires to exert influence as a speaker he must have a thorough knowledge of the collective literary treasure of the nation. No man who is not master of the spoken or of the written word can exert any influence in public life. In France the thorough knowledge of the specialist can never atone for a lack of literary culture. It is only in France that we find the type of political writing of which Barrès and Maurras are the representatives at the present day: that type of book which attracts the literary person by its form and the politically-minded person by its formulas. Such books may contain polemics, analysis, doctrine—but one thing they may never be: purely specialist literature. In France politicians may write novels, and novelists may compose political books, without losing the right to be "taken seriously". Chateaubriand was a Cabinet Minister and the inventor of a new prose at one and the same time. Claudel is one of the great French poets of the present day; at the same time he is an Ambassador of the Republic. Some of the most brilliant books of the most recent French literature have been written in the Ministry for Foreign Affairs on the Quai d'Orsay.

In France the close connexion between literature and the State dates from the seventeenth century. Richelieu and Louis XIV. deliberately established this connexion. In the eighteenth century literature was used for the purposes of social criticism and political reform. The Revolution of 1789 was steeped in literature, as were also the Revolutions of 1830 and of 1848. The Second Republic placed Lamartine at the head of the State; the Third Republic made Victor Hugo a Senator and the patron saint of their *laïque* religion. His funeral was transformed into a national celebration; Anatole France, similarly, was buried with all the official honours of the Republic. From Victor Hugo comes the saying, "Literature is civilization". Of France, at least, this is true.

In France literature fulfils the function which among us is divided between philosophy, science, poetry and music. Why have these forms of intellectual and artistic expression no representative value in France? Let us briefly survey their position in the civilization of France. We will begin with philosophy.

Philosophy in France has only become a concern of the whole educated section of the nation when it has appeared not as pure philosophy, but as a wisdom distilled from the experience of life and from knowledge of the world, or as a lever of political emancipation, or as the intellectual forerunner of new social forms, or as the ally of natural science. Scarcely ever, however, has it dominated the minds of the educated classes by the power of metaphysical speculation. The metaphysical passion of the East, of the Greeks and of the Germans, is alien to the French spirit. In Germany intellectual culture may be philosophical, in France it can be literary only. The great French metaphysicians—Male-branche, Maine de Biran, Hamelin, to name only a few—lived in great seclusion, and never came into contact with the intellectual movements of their time. Even Comte only became known to a wider circle a generation after his death. In the realm of philosophy the French, as a nation, have absorbed chiefly the intellectual achievements of the sceptics, of the thinkers of the school of the Enlightenment, of moralists and social philosophers; this selection is typical of the values of French civilization.

It is, however, an undoubted fact that Descartes is the most important factor in the intellectual history of France. Why? There are several reasons. The *Discours de la Méthode* is written in the style which the Frenchman requires in the literary classics. Neither in range nor in intelligibility does he overstep the bounds of that which the cultivated French-man, with his literary tastes, can assimilate. The work of Descartes established and made legitimate the conception that even the philosopher must adapt the expression of his ideas to the habits of thought and speech of the *honnête homme*.

Bergson declares that "la philosophie française s'est toujours réglée sur le principe suivant: il n'y a pas d'idée philosophique, si profonde ou si subtile soit-elle, qui ne puisse et ne doive s'exprimer dans la langue de tout le monde". Bergson considers that this is a particular virtue of French philosophy. But surely this simply means that philosophy has to submit to the dominion of the literary conventions, and to the tyranny of the ordinary healthy human understanding? This process, however, has a bad effect on philosophy. Cramped within the limits of certain forms of speech and expression, not of its own making, philosophy loses much of its force; for all its efforts at independent criticism are checked by an artificial barrier. The final result of this subordination to the literary con-ception is this: that which was conceived as philosophy is consumed purely as literature. Cartesianism also has had to go through this process.

But the literary form of the *Discours de la méthode* only partly explains its influence. There are other reasons—rightly or wrongly—Cartesianism may be reduced to a formula: to the simplest which can be imagined, and one which throws a great deal of light on the national temper. It is regarded as the philosophy of reason, of reason pure and simple. Every Frenchman has the feeling for the *clare et distincte percipere*. It is possible to believe that the Cartesian conception of Reason includes all those tendencies towards *bon sens*, logic, order, clarity, which are so deeply rooted in the French character; once this has been granted these very tendencies are explained and justified from the philosophical point of view. Thus an absolute legend has been formed around Descartes and Cartesianism. The difficult and complex philosophy of this great thinker has been forcibly simplified and toned down till it is represented as a mere catchword, which ultimately does not mean much more than the *clarté française* of which we hear so much. Descartes as the lawgiver of Reason, and the liberator from faith in authority—this is one of the *clichés* which constantly recur in the intellectual conventions of France. In popular presentations of the subject the genius of Descartes is extolled because ultimately he is said to represent the development of that sane human reason which every French peasant possesses. Writers of this kind even claim that the most splendid incarnation of the Cartesian spirit at the present time is that of Marshal Foch—which leads to the natural conclusion that it was the Cartesian Method which secured victory to France in the World War.[1] In ways like these the figure of Descartes has been misrepresented, and his teaching has been obscured; indeed, we may say quite definitely that this popular Cartesianism has become the greatest hindrance to the development of the true philosophical spirit in France. Both abroad and at home it has spread the idea

[1] This is not an invention of my own. I found it in Chevalier's *Descartes*.

that the French mind is purely rationalistic: an idea which everyone who penetrates into the genuine and deep nature of France at once perceives to be false. For this reason to-day all serious thinkers in France are giving their whole attention to the endeavour to reveal afresh the philosophy of Descartes in its pure form, to remove it from the sphere of popular philosophy, and to incorporate it organically into the whole connexion of the great achievements of the thought of France which are so little known. This, however, does not alter the fact that even to-day French philosophy—to an extent unknown in Germany—is still the concern of specialists and of a small group.

There is still another reason why philosophy in France could never form the central point of its intellectual life. It has wrongly allowed itself to be dominated by literary form and average intelligence; it has also surrendered to natural science. When Bergson declares, "La philosophie n'est que le prolongement de la science", he is in the line of ancient tradition. The philosophical spirit of France hesitates to formulate a system. It does not feel the necessity to articulate and construct afresh the whole range of being from the idea of the Logos. The philosophical spirit of France accepts "Reality" without reflection, and makes the effort so to order its ideal synthesis that the usually valid existence of things is respected, so that one can still use the individual materials of the philosophical structure, even when one does not accept the conception as a whole: "Les morceaux en sont toujours bons", as Bergson says. Our German conception is quite different. We believe that the partial view and the view of the whole determine and condition each other, both logically and metaphysically; that "reality" has no independent value and substantial existence of its own; that it can only be understood from the point of view of a super-reality. Finally—from the time of Hegel—we have come to believe that history is as much an object of philosophical consideration as Nature. Hence our philosophy is threatened with the dangers of dominating reality metaphysically, and of idolizing history from the teleological point of view. French philosophy has other habits of thought, and incurs other dangers. It centres on "physics", using this word in its ancient comprehensive sense. In Descartes geometry and metaphysics are so closely connected that it is impossible to decide which is foremost. French philosophy was primarily occupied with "the abstract and concrete sciences of inorganic matter" (as Bergson expresses it)—that is, with mathematics, mechanics, astronomy, physics and chemistry; then it analysed social life; then, through Comte, quite logically it produced a classification of the sciences, which begins with mathematics and ends in sociology. Taine and Renan continued this line of development, and Bergson himself does not, or does not primarily, make the Dionysiac affirmation of the universe, nor is he a rebel against the fetters of the understanding, as he is generally considered amongst us, but a careful thinker, who tries, upon the basis of experience and natural science, to outline a positive metaphysic.

Thus French philosophy easily loses the possibility of moving the spirit in its ultimate depths, because it pays tribute to powers outside philosophy and preserves their "inherited rights": speech, literature, natural science, reasonableness, and, finally, the national habit of mind. It realizes exactly as many philosophical ways of thinking as are possible to unite with the stable forces of civilization. The "philosophical spirit" can only so far be considered an attribute of France as it limits itself to the need for logic and the general conceptual conception of all problems. In this sense Bergson was able to say: "Le besoin de philosopher est universel: il tend à porter toute discussion, même d'affaires, sur le terrain des idées et des principes. Il traduit probablement l'aspiration la plus profonde de l'âme française qui va tout droit à ce qui est général, et, par là, à ce qui est généreux. En ce sens, l'esprit français ne fait qu'un avec l'esprit philosophique."

Both the excellences and the defects of French philo-

sophy are the results of the sense of reality, the desire for
stability, and of the anthropocentric order upon which the
French conception of *civilisation* is based. Its conservative
Humanism could not endure either the Pantheism of a
world-intoxicated ecstasy, nor the transcendental idealism
of the creative spirit, nor the knowledge of salvation which
desires redemption and depreciates the value of the world,
nor the moral criticism of an heroic will to power. A Hegel,
a Schopenhauer, a Nietzsche are unthinkable in France.
They would destroy the garden of civilization and the realm
of humanity. The sense of infinity cannot live freely within
French philosophy. But philosophy can only be supreme
where it can roam freely through unexplored spaces without let or hindrance. This is why philosophy can only play
a secondary part in the intellectual life of France.

What I have just said about philosophy applies equally,
and for similar reasons, to music. In this sphere particularly
we need to free ourselves from some traditional prejudices.

France and music: this is one of those problematical
subjects around which national and psychological mis-
understandings have gathered. Even thirty years ago in
France it used to be admitted without question that Germany was the home of great music. That was one of the
few spheres in which, without envy, the French admitted
our superiority. Since then all this has changed.

Among us, again, the opinion is still widespread that in
France music counts for little or nothing. Those, however,
who know concert programmes, and the taste of the public
outside Germany, and outside Europe, know that German music no longer is supreme, and that French music
has become its rival.

In Germany music has an easy time, perhaps too easy.
Even as early as 1905 Romain Rolland warned us that
musical Germany was in danger of being drowned in a
flood of music.[1] In Germany, at that time—through Stefan
Georg and his group—an attempt was made to evolve a

[1] *Musiciens d'aujourd'hui*, 196.

form of German intellectuality which would emancipate itself from music, and which was even explicitly hostile towards it. Where new intellectual energies and willed tendencies break forth they necessarily direct themselves against that which has been already attained, against the accustomed, the obvious, the universal possession. Thus in Germany it seemed to be a duty to try to free the intellectual life from music.

In France the situation was the very opposite. From time immemorial the traditional system of culture has granted very little room to music, even when it has admitted it at all. This does not mean that France has no honourable place in the history of modern music;[1] we need only recall the French-Flemish art of the Renaissance; Lulli, who came from Florence and settled in Paris, Couperin and Rameau, and the controversies which raged round musical taste in the eighteenth century. During the first thirty years of the nineteenth century, too, music was ardently practised and studied in Paris. The performances of the Symphonies of Beethoven in the Conservatoire gained a position of great importance. After that, however, the tide ebbed. One proof of this lies in the fact that Berlioz complained that he suffered bitterly from the indifference of the public.

After 1870 the tide turned, but progress was slow. Still, a new era had begun. In 1871, under the shadow of defeat, the *Société nationale de Musique* was formed. Its aim was the extension of French music, and its motto *Ars gallica*. Henceforward this became the watchword of the musical movement in France. In 1919 one of its leaders, Vincent d'Indy, was able to crown his life-work with the symphony *De bello gallico*.

But this development did not proceed without set-backs. The national tendency of new French music was checked by the influence of Wagner's music.

[1] Cf. H. J. Moser, "Französische Musik" (in the *Handbuch der Frankreich-Kunde* edited by P. Hartig and W. Schellberg, 1928, i.).

We all know the hostile reception which Wagner received in Paris in 1861, and the unpleasant episode of the *Tannhäuser* performance, which had only one valuable result: Baudelaire's beautiful and noble apology for the German master. Twenty years passed before anyone again ventured to stand up for Wagner in Paris. In 1882 Lamoureux opened his series of Symphony Concerts. They paved the way for the new music. Wagner's art speedily captured the intellectual élite of the youth of France. A *Revue Wagnérienne* was founded in 1885; in its pages every form of art, every kind of intellectual problem, was interpreted from the standpoint of Wagner. Mallarmé celebrated

> Le dieu Richard Wagner irradiant un sacre
> Mal tû par l'encre même en sanglots sibyllins.

Verlaine's poem *Parsifal* also belongs to the same category. Wagner was one of the most potent influences in the whole poetical and intellectual movement of the years 1885 to 1905 known as the school of the Symbolists. The enthusiasm for Wagner also succeeded in interesting the French public, to a hitherto unknown degree, in music in general. For some time too it influenced French composers.

Inevitably there was a reaction. In 1894 the *Schola Cantorum* was founded. Its aims were at first confined to the renewal of ecclesiastical music, along the lines of the liturgical movement, which, in the year 1850, had been inaugurated at the Benedictine monastery of Solesmes, under the guidance of the Abbot Dom Guéranger. Soon, however, its scope became broader. In 1900 an *École Supérieure de la Musique* arose out of this movement as a separate branch of the work. This became the most important centre for modern French music. Its founder, Vincent d'Indy, carried on his work in the spirit of his great teacher, César Franck.

A new period began with Debussy's *Pelléas et Mélisande* (1902). Here, for the first time since *Carmen*, a musical drama had been created, which was nourished entirely on the French instinct for art, while at the same time it founded a new style. It was from this date that France began to count, in quite a new way, in the musical world as a whole.

To-day the most recent French music is ranged against Debussy, as the latter was ranged against Wagner. "Debussy has gone astray, because he escaped the German snare only to fall into the Russian toils. . . . Debussy played in the French style, but he used the Russian pedal. . . . Even *Pelléas* is music of an emotional type. All music of that kind is suspect. Wagner is the type of music to which one can listen emotionally." This is the opinion of Jean Cocteau,[1] the protagonist of the most recent music in France.

This new music bans impressionism and mysticism. Its aim is to be both classical and up-to-date. It still uses Wagner as a foil. "Let us read once more", says Cocteau, "*The Case of Wagner* by Nietzsche. Never have lighter and profounder things been said. When Nietzsche praises *Carmen* he is praising the gaiety which our generation seeks in the music-hall. It is a great pity that Nietzsche enforces his argument with an illustration drawn from a work of art which is artistically inferior to the work of Wagner. The kind of music which is swept away by music of the impressionist type is, for example, a certain American dance which I have seen in the *Casino de Paris*."

We might, however, inquire whether the American trap were not as dangerous to French music as the German or the Russian? In any case, however, the arts in young France are once more in contact with music. In the intellectual world of France to-day music enjoys an importance which, previously, it has scarcely ever known. This, indeed, was one of the characteristic features in Rolland's *Jean-Christophe*. It was a surprise for all readers that a French poet should choose as his hero a German musician; and perhaps the surprise was greater in Germany than in France. For as student, critic and novelist Romain Rolland is indeed one of those who have worked most dis-

[1] In *Le Coq et l'Arlequin*, 1918.

interestedly and influentially for the renewal of the musical sense in France. As a young man he also had experienced the intoxication of Wagner's music. He worked through a whole generation at the attempt to cultivate musical taste in his nation. He hailed the rise of Debussy—certainly without disguising the fact that personally the twilight and aristocratic refined tenderness of this tonal speech was not that which moved him most deeply. He compares Debussy with Racine; but he adds, this is only one side of the French genius. He finds the other in Berlioz and Bizet. In them he finds—*faute de mieux*, as he adds characteristically—the France of the Revolution and of the democratic community. Although he welcomes the rise of French music, still he knows that it is an aristocratic affair of the élite, not a real force in the national existence.

Can it ever develop further? In spite of all self-sacrificing efforts to restore it—of which those of Maurice Bouchor were of the most value—it is difficult to believe it. At one time there used to be French national or folk songs. But they have disappeared, and all efforts to revive them seem at present artificial. Their place is taken by the *Chanson*.

What music means to-day to the cultivated Frenchman has been very aptly described by Jean Schlumberger: "Music, formerly an almost secular method of expression, has become the expression of the inward life. In that which concerns the French mentality, not on the surface, but on its deeper side, a transformation has taken place, which has touched the inmost sides of the character and the disposition. It is quite certain that music is not yet such a popular force as it is in Germany; perhaps it will never become this among us, and it would be childish to over-estimate the influence which it is able to exert during a time in which the minds of men are exercised by the brutal conflicts of politics and economics. Also I say merely that it has developed, and properly speaking, behind the scenes of the world of feeling, as a kind of general capacity for stimulation. This is an important element in the work, which must be achieved slowly, patiently, and almost in secret, in order that the work of statesmen may be productive and permanent." In spite of the renewal of the musical and the philosophical life in France it still remains true to-day that the most characteristic expression of the intellectual life of France is literature; its function is the dominant formative activity, which sets a standard of taste and affects the nation as a whole.

Science also must yield pride of place to literature. Humanistic studies above all have not the position in France which they occupy among us. In France they lack the stimulus which they received in Germany from Humanism and from Protestantism. In Germany, indeed, the union of both these forces prepared the way for the florescence of our Humanistic studies. In France Humanism has expressed itself rather in literary (Ronsard), or philosophical (Montaigne), or in political form than in the historical-philological form. But the event which was of far greater influence and more widespread in its results was the suppression of Protestantism. Amongst ourselves its tendency towards independent private judgment and independent criticism in the great questions of the destiny of individuals and of nations has been to the advantage of the development of the Humanistic studies. In France there never has been, or is, anything of this kind. A Doctor Faust would be as impossible there as a Herder or a Hegel. Thus it comes to pass that in France the Humanistic studies, compared with our development, have flowed partly into the broad bed of literature and of politics, partly into the limited field of specialist research, while some have been led astray by the lure of supposedly natural science methods, or, finally, have been transformed into psychology or sociology. Naturally these are only the broad features of the development, and many exceptions could be mentioned, but they *are* exceptions, and for the most part (think of Renan, for instance) they can be traced back to the fertilizing example of German science. To that we must add another consideration: the sphere of the intellect, if we may use simplified expressions, to the Frenchman is static, while to us it is dynamic. In research the French expend their energy on Nature rather than on the intellect. To them "Science" means originally and essentially natural science. Hence in France it is highly honoured, because it serves the cause of the domination of Nature by man, the emancipation of man from the elements, and the liberation of the intellect from the authority of dogma, society and custom. In France, therefore, the most popular form of science is medicine. We need only recall the pride of the "enlightened" apothecary Homais in *Madame Bovary*! This, of course, was a caricature, but it has a basis in reality. The medical man is *le curé du républicain*. A chemist and doctor like Raspail (1794–1878) was able to play the part of a political "Patriarch of Radicalism", and to prove the truth of this claim by many years of imprisonment, gallantly endured. A Positivist like Littré (1801–1881), who was both a doctor and a philologist, was regarded by the Republicans as a "Sage", who placed the results of his thought at the service of the politicians. From 1900 onwards Pasteur and Curie have been the symbolic figures in whom the genius of science is incarnate. During the last ten or twenty years there has been a great deal of discussion in France about the "value of science". The whole idea was that of the mechanistic natural science which was both the factor of progress and the opponent of the Church. In France the exponent of the national spirit is not the philosopher, nor the musician, nor the scholar, but the man of letters.

The counterpart of the person known amongst us as a *gebildeter Mensch* (educated person) is in France the *lettré*. The *lettré* is the man or woman who is versed in literature. He knows his classics, or pretends to know and admire them. He knows how to produce apt quotations from the great national writers. Once I accompanied a *lettré* to a great government building of several storeys. We had to pass through many passages and ascend many stairs. As we walked along he remarked, "Nourri dans le sérail, j'en connais les détours". We were supposed to know that these lines came from Racine's *Bajazet*. At the present time in France there are many complaints about the decline in literary and humanistic culture. The French may be pessimistic if they choose. From our point of view France is still the land of the Humanist tradition.

There is a classic description of this tradition in Sainte-Beuve's Inaugural Lecture given at the *École Normale* in the year 1858. Anyone who desires to understand French literature should study these pages: "De la Tradition en littérature, et dans quel sens il la faut entendre" (in the fifteenth volume of the *Causeries du Lundi*). Sainte-Beuve compares the Humanist-literary tradition with the great Roman roads which are still visible at the present day, which spanned the whole Empire and led to the Eternal City: "Descendants des Romains, ou du moins enfants d'adoption de la race latine, cette race initiée elle-même au culte du Beau par les Grecs, nous avons à embrasser, à comprendre, à ne jamais déserter l'héritage de ces maîtres et de ces pères illustres, héritage qui, depuis Homère jusqu'au dernier des classiques d'hier, forme le plus clair et le plus solide de notre fonds intellectuel. Cette tradition, elle ne consiste pas seulement dans l'ensemble des œuvres dignes de mémoire que nous rassemblons dans nos bibliothèques et que nous étudions: elle a passé en bonne partie dans nos lois, dans nos institutions, dans nos mœurs, dans notre éducation héréditaire et insensible, dans notre habitude et dans toutes nos origines; elle consiste en un certain principe de raison et de culture qui a pénétré à la longue, pour le modifier, dans le caractère même de cette nation gauloise, et qui est entré des longtemps jusque dans la trempe des esprits."

Sainte-Beuve's conception of tradition has, however, already become historic. It still preserves the unity of style with the late Classicism of the eighteenth century and of the Empire. But the heart of his contention is still valid at the present day. The problem of tradition is expressed differently in the France of the present day, but it is still a vital element in the national life. When France came to itself after the War it began to recall its Graeco-Latin tradition. The *Collection Guillaume Budé*—a new edition of ancient authors with translations—was founded, and in a few years it has achieved a great success.

French Classicism and Humanism are indissolubly connected. In France, quite as much as in Italy, Virgil is one of the ineradicable and fundamental elements of culture. French Humanism passes through Rome to Athens, whereas ours usually leaves Rome out of the picture. Classical and classicist France has generally regarded Hellas with a certain mistrust. It is the mistrust of the Romans towards the Graeculi. Rome stands for law and order, Greece for plays, sophistry or myths. Plato is too near to the Mysteries. It is true that there has been a Platonist tendency in France, but it did not form part of the main stream. Among the French classic writers it is easy to distinguish the "Romans" from the "Greeks". The Romans are Corneille, Bossuet, Montesquieu; the Greeks are Racine, La Fontaine, Fénelon. There has always been a French Hellenism, but it is mostly a psychological and rationalistic Hellenism, to which Pindar and Aeschylus are more remote than Euripides and Aristotle. We (Germans) seek in Greece the mysteries of Orphism, France seeks symmetry in the Parthenon, restraint in Greece, and in Athene wisdom. Even the French who see in Greece the highest revelation of the intellect cannot sacrifice to it the Latin idea. When Charles Maurras asserts that "the Valois and the Parisis were like Attica in its purest form", he also blames those who deny the service which Rome has rendered to the world. Rome has perpetuated Hellenism—but unfortunately also, and that is the reproach of Maurras, Semitism and the poison of Asia.

To be a Hellenist and despise the Romans is an exceptional, not a contradictory attitude. To-day it appears now and again among scholars whose political views lean towards the Left, who see in the Roman idea the support of the idea of authority in Church and State, whereas to them Greece (Archimedes!) means an asylum for free research and independent thought. A popular reconciliation-formula has been given by Victor Hugo with his brilliant simplicity: "La France est de la même qualité de peuple que la Grèce et l'Italie. Elle est athénienne par le beau et romaine par le grand. En outre elle est bonne."

Sociologically the esteem in which literature is held is expressed very clearly. The significance of the French *Académie* is perhaps the most impressive example of this fact. To be received among the forty immortals is the highest honour which can fall to the lot of a Frenchman. Cabinet Ministers, generals, ecclesiastical dignitaries, strive to attain this honour. The *Académie* is the national representative of literature. Through it France has made intellect a national institution. "L'Académie," says Renan (*Essais de morale et de critique*), "comptait à peine quelques années d'existence, et un immense résultat était atteint, l'ennoblissement de l'esprit. Jusque-là, mendiant, parasite ou pédagogue, l'esprit n'avait point eu de forteresse, et avait cherché son asile à l'ombre de l'église et du château féodal. Désormais c'est l'homme d'esprit qui accorde aux gentilhommes le titre de confrère." Since the day when it was founded it is true that the *Académie* has often had to endure attacks of Gallic mockery, and to incur the reproach of rigidity and stagnation, but it still preserves its prestige, and by the election of men of the highest intellectual rank it can always renew its strength. This prestige is greater abroad than it is in France itself, to the extent in which it feels itself bound up with the French idea of civilization. It is greater in the provinces than it is in Paris, where gossip and detraction form part of the necessary stimulus of the literary life. But it still has power to-day to stir the ambition of the best intellects. Reception into the *Académie* secures to the fortunate immortal an increase in power and

independence, which is of great value. The Academician is
courted by all those who have set up as candidates for the
*Académie* themselves, and by the still wider group of those
who hope one day to enter this eminent body. Further, the
*Académie* has an annual sum of 200,000 francs to administer
in literary prizes. But this gives it a far-reaching influence.
Finally, the Academician is an *homme arrivé*. He need take
no more notice of anyone. During the period of his candi-
dature he has to exercise a most careful silence in order not
to hurt the susceptibilities of anyone. Once he is elected he
regains his freedom of opinion and of speech. "The Roman
slave", says Fernand Vandérem,[1] "knew such joys only on
the day of the Saturnalia. The Academician . . . knows this
joy every day of his life." Material advantages also accrue
to the fact of election. As soon as an author can add the
magic words *de l'Académie française* to his name, his royalties
and the editions of his books increase greatly.

As we know, the *Académie* is the creation of the absolute
Monarchy, and the classic epoch of French literature co-
incides with the period of Louis XIV. French classicism
reflects the consciousness of sovereignty possessed by the
French Monarchy. But it was able to outlive it, and for the
past two and a half centuries it has been the most important supporter of the value of the French mind to the world.
The classical literature of France grew out of the intellectual movement of the Italian Renaissance. Corneille,
Racine, La Fontaine, would have been, it is true, great
poets apart from this, but they would not have become
classics, if by a classic literature we mean one which has
been formed on a great model, and upon a system of
aesthetic reason. The French classics were intended to be
rational imitations of the ancients. This leading idea, however, came to them from Italy. Italian Humanism had
worked this out in connexion with the *Poetics* of Aristotle,
in the course of a most active and stimulating controversy,
between 1527 and 1613. But whereas in Italy the poetical

[1] *La Littérature*, Hachette, 1927.

production of the Renaissance arose quite independently of these theories, the rationalistic intellect of France watched over the poetic genius carefully and gave it its laws. From Ronsard to Malherbe and Boileau we see a close connexion between the method and practice of poetry. The French classics were developed through a historical process which lasted for more than a century.[1] Ronsard and his school (about 1550) had laid down the principle of the imitation of antiquity. In a second cycle—about 1630 —the rules of this imitation were constructed into a body of doctrine; the classic doctrine was finally complete. The development was then crowned by the generation of the great classical writers of 1660. These three phases were so detached from each other that each rejected the preceding one because it had reached a higher standpoint. Thus the great classicism of the third phase overcame the doctrinaire spirit of the second, and replaced it by the taste which we call the *Grand goût classique*. The mechanism of work done according to rule had become an organic instinct. The double dependence—on ancient literature and on Italian poetry—had been overcome by the mature independent sense of form of the national genius. The great works of this period are not artificial imitations; they are natural achievements. In them the period of Louis XIV. created a style which is entirely French, which, by means of the theory of imitation has developed into a complete originality. There is now no longer any trace of the humanism of the Italian Cinquecento. The Renaissance has been replaced by a new world-style of classic stamp which France created, and which she evolved at the moment when the classical genius of Italy succumbed to the Baroque. It is characteristic that Bernini's plans for the completion of the Louvre in Paris were not approved. The Colonnade of Perrault was in greater harmony with the taste of the period, and at the present day it still gives a very impressive testimony to the ideals of order, symmetry

[1] Cf. René Bray, *La Formation de la doctrine classique en France* (1927).

and moderation which France evolved at that time. We Germans do not find it easy to enjoy and appreciate Racine. Lessing, and many after him, have blocked the way to the understanding of the French classics. But the architecture of the same epoch can lead us back into the right path. Whoever has grasped the significance of the form of the Hotel Biron in Paris (now the Rodin Museum) will also understand the same achievement of proportion in the classical literature.

That the French classics have created a world style, in contradistinction to all other literature, is due above all to the happy accident that this development took place at the same time as the highest point in the power of the French Monarchy and the prestige of the French State. The king himself took a great personal interest in the whole matter. He took Molière under his wing, and protected him against his enemies. He called Racine to his court, made Bossuet tutor to the Dauphin, and Fénelon tutor to the Duke of Burgundy. *Esther* and *Athalie* were written for the pupils of St. Cyr, the *Discours sur l'histoire universelle* and *Télémaque* for the royal princes. It seemed to be a repetition of the Augustan age: the monarch of a world empire gathering round him a group of eminent men whose brilliance shed a reflected glory upon his person, and upon the system of the State. This comparison occurred forcibly to the people of that day, and was the reason of the "Querelle des Anciens et des Modernes". The fact that there was this strong desire to imitate the great models of antiquity led finally to the production of a literature of similar value. French classical literature had attained its majority. The cultural consciousness of the period claimed that its own value ought to be recognized, and that it possessed a glory of its own. Until the end of the *Ancien Régime* the political predominance of France smoothed the way for the expansion of the classical style in Europe. It was this actual element of power which carried the poetry of Boileau, the tragedy of Racine, Le Nôtre's art of landscape-gardening, the architectural ideas of Versailles, the court ceremonial and the dictionary of the *Académie* into foreign lands. The greatness of the Classical school, however, consists precisely in this: that it is more than, and different from, a French royal style. Racine, Molière, Boileau, La Rochefoucauld, La Bruyère, Madame de La Fayette, and the other founders of this literature, surpassed Lulli and Le Brun. The spirit of the literary art of the epoch survived the forms in which it was then expressed, and its style of decoration. As early as the eighteenth century the connexion between the classical spirit of literature and the Catholic state religion—a connexion which had previously been rather loose—was severed. The connexion with the authority of the Monarchy and the State was severed also. Voltaire was to achieve this separation. Classical literature could now develop the sceptical and freethinking elements of rationalism of which *Frondeurs* like Saint-Évremont, or Cartesians like Fontenelle, had been unofficial representatives in the preceding era. It was now able to combine itself with the English philosophy of the Enlightenment and with the criticism of the day. It was able to prepare the way for the Revolution, and thus enabled Taine to submit the thesis that the *raison oratoire* of the Classical school had been the intellectual agent of the upheaval. It is, of course, true that this classicism of the eighteenth century differed entirely from the classicism of the seventeenth century. But it still preserved the earlier formal traditions. Voltaire's *Mérope* is constructed on the pattern of the tragedies of Racine.

This pseudo-classicism was destroyed by the literary movement of the nineteenth century. But for that very reason the real greatness of the Classical school again became apparent. In France when a literary movement, or an individual author, has reached artistic maturity, almost always his work reveals an aesthetic kinship with the artistic instincts of that period. No French author can ever forget that the Classical school is behind him, and even when he is unconscious of it the fact of this tradition will help to shape his style. The indefinable essence of the classical spirit arises ever anew on the soil of France. In Valéry and Gide the Symbolist school of 1890 attained the clarity of form and the closeness of texture of the Classical school; even in Dadaism its most talented supporters developed along these lines. The persistence of this classical instinct is, naturally, a result of conscious cultivation and tradition. Every Frenchman has passed through the school of this classical literature. The schoolboys of the Third Republic receive the basic elements of language, of artistic and psychological culture from works which were ripened in the sunshine of the Monarchy. This classical literature is not the private preserve of an intellectual élite; it has become a national possession. This was possible, because it was not connected with any particular view of the world, and also because, both in language and in artistic feeling, it is definite, lucid and pleasing.

Since France, as a country, occupies a central position, her literature too may be described as a literature which stands midway between two extremes. It is not characterized by supreme inspiration, nor by the depth of its feeling for life, but by the harmonious balance of intellectual moderation.

Among us neither *Faust* nor *Wilhelm Meister* could become a universal possession of education. But in France, La Fontaine, Racine, Bossuet, Molière, Voltaire, have attained this position.

From the German point of view, certainly, Goethe surpasses every one of these authors. The Englishman, also, will never understand that the French prefer their Racine to his Shakespeare. But the question: Who is greater, Racine or Shakespeare, Poussin or Rembrandt, is unfruitful. The values of French literature do not lie in the absolute greatness of individual personalities, but in the elevation of the collective level, and in the inward continuity of the intellectual tradition. It is characteristic that to the question: "Who was the greatest Frenchman?" no one can find an answer. France has produced no Dante, no Shakespeare, no Cervantes, no Goethe. Instead of this, however, she possesses a literature which forms an unbroken and vital unity, and which in its wholeness represents a personality of an incomparable kind.

In our intellectual system of values the idea of genius is supreme. We expect genius to renew for us the face of the world, or to create a spiritual world of its own. The French mind has different values. It rates balance higher than force, and perfection higher than originality. France has produced great poets, but the greatness of its literature is not based upon poetry but upon prose. Rivarol, the most profound and most brilliant spirit of old France in its decline, once said, "C'est la prose, qui donne l'empire à une langue; la poésie n'est qu'un objet de luxe". This is a political point of view; it is, however, only the political aspect of a fundamental intellectual attitude. The wonderful verse of Racine is as near to prose as poetry can be without giving up the attempt to be poetry. In France it is impossible to imagine a purely lyrical poet being admitted to that narrow select circle of eminent names in which the nation contemplates the highest elements in its intellectual wealth. "Le lyrisme est un accident chez nous", says G. Lanson, "la création en a été tardive et laborieuse; la source du lyrisme s'ouvre, en somme, assez rarement dans l'âme française". Flaubert wrote in 1852: "Il faut déguiser la poésie en France, on la déteste" (16th December 1852 to Louise Colet). And Baudelaire: "La France éprouve une horreur congénitale de la poésie". And earlier still André Chénier: "De toutes les nations de l'Europe, les français sont ceux qui aiment le moins la poésie et qui s'y connaissent le moins".

The fact which impresses critics most of all is the non-lyrical character of the literature of France. There was, indeed, once on French soil a flowering of lyrical poetry in which the tenderest poetical flame burnt steadily: the Provençal poetry of the twelfth and thirteenth centuries. The

Northern French lyrics of the Middle Ages were formed on that model, although they did not attain the same heights of magic and primitive charm. But the art of the troubadours was only able to flourish in the midst of that Southern French culture which was destroyed by the Albigensian Crusade, the Inquisition and the reforming activity of the Dominicans. This work of destruction is one of the sacrifices which France has offered for the sake of her political and intellectual unity.

The French tendency to scepticism and mockery, to that view of reality which is free from all illusions, has always been a hindrance to the development of the poetical faculty. To mistake well-turned verse for poetry is a danger which lies in the very character of French literature. The historical reason for this lies in the system of French classicism. The aesthetic doctrine of the Classical school, namely, dealt only with poetry, that is, with the species of literature for which the ancient literatures used verse. So it came to pass that in France the idea of poetry became an artistic conception which was purely formal and defined, and based entirely upon the classical model. This explains the fact that frequently rhymed speech is mistaken for poetry. For all ages this mistake was sanctioned by Boileau. Boileau belongs to the impeccable French tradition, and his position is equally impregnable.

Several times youthful rebels have ventured to try to shake his authority, but almost always they ended by making an apology. Sainte-Beuve is a typical example of this change of front. Boileau is always "saved", however artificial the method of rescue may be. Prosaic correctness is covered by his name. By many who swear by him he is less read than praised, but he remains a symbol of the classical tradition. He remains also a symbol of excellent craftsmanship and artistic proportion. Flaubert, when he was growing old, used to refresh his mind with Boileau, when the young naturalistic school sought to annex him. A Romantic like Delacroix could write: "Boileau est un homme qu'il faut avoir sous son chevet, il délecte et purifie; il fait aimer le beau et l'honnêteté, tandis que nos modernes n'exhalent que d'âcres parfums, mortels le plus souvent pour l'âme, et faussent l'imagination par des spectacles de fantaisie."[1]

Boileau's greatest opponent was Victor Hugo. But if Boileau kills poetry by his "reasonable smoothness" (Remy de Gourmont), Hugo endangers it by his swollen rhetoric. André Gide once gave this reply to the question: Who is the greatest French poet? "Victor Hugo, hélas!" Victor Hugo certainly stands alone by virtue of his forceful speech, the wealth of his images, his sparkling antitheses, and the furious force and eloquence of his language. He intoxicates and captivates. But this language, which flows along so majestically, is speech, not song. No literature can produce poems which can compare with this for rhetorical effect. The peculiar quality of Hugo and his greatness—the element which secures him an immortal place in the heart of his nation, is his brilliant capacity of expressing the feelings of the people as a whole. He is the "sounding echo" of the masses, giving audible expression to the spirit of the people in its political and social agitation. His verses vibrate with the beat of the drums and the sound of trumpets. He is the singer of the people. He is at his happiest when he exalts Paris, or sings the epic of the Revolution and of the Empire, or the social visions of the future of the nation and of humanity. There is no detraction from his fame in the statement that the purely lyrical quality which distinguishes the language of Goethe or Keats is almost entirely absent from the poetry of Victor Hugo.

Purely lyrical poetry in the great style is very rare in France before Baudelaire. The appearance of the *Fleurs du Mal* (1857) was therefore one of the greatest and most remarkable events in the literature of France. By his contemporaries he was scarcely understood. It was only the Symbolist movement which began to give honour to Baudelaire. For many years, however, in the criticism of the

[1] Eugéne Delacroix, *Œuvres littéraires*, i. 96.

*Académie* he was only considered a writer of the second rank. It is only to-day that this opposition seems to have been broken down. Baudelaire's poetry has captivated the literary public in even wider circles. To-day the main question is, as Léon Daudet has recently expressed it: "Victor Hugo or Baudelaire?" This question represents a revision of aesthetic values which is of great importance for a true estimate of French literature.

The case of Baudelaire has a still more far-reaching significance. Since Baudelaire there has been a modernist movement in French literature. In France, Classicism, Romanticism, Naturalism, all have this in common: they are all immediately accessible to the normal consciousness of the enlightened European. One can enter these literary regions on the ordinary level. It is possible to define them, and to explain them exhaustively.

With Baudelaire the situation was altered. Here we enter a world which can no longer be grasped by reason. It is only possible to understand it at all if one has a feeling for the mystery of poetry, a sense which the average man may lack just as much as the feeling for music, or the capacity for mystical experience. After Baudelaire came Mallarmé and Valéry, Rimbaud and Claudel, and the younger and most recent poets who have broken down the firm structure of the rational theory of the universe. Quite recently there have been great discussions in France about the conception of *poésie pure*. Henri Brémond, that sensitive psychologist and the historian of French mysticism, whom the *Académie* claimed as one of its own elect some years ago, has made a brilliant plea for "pure poetry". But the very fact that he makes this plea shows how new and unusual the view of pure poetry is to the French mind.

This whole development means a far-reaching change within the literature of France. There are in France to-day two literatures, alongside of each other, and one above the other: the traditional one which is accessible to every educated reader, and that of "modernism" in which a new form of consciousness is foreshadowed. The latter is the laughing-stock of popular journalists, who feel that they are the official representatives of the French *bon sens*. Probably both forms of literature will continue to exist.

In France, literature of the rationalistic kind will never cease to call forth the admiration of the best intellects. For it possesses aesthetic values which will outlast changes in forms of consciousness. Perhaps only a Frenchman can appreciate them fully. A passage from a letter of Flaubert will make this clear: "Nous nous étonnons des bonshommes du siècle de Louis XIV, mais ils n'étaient pas des hommes d'énorme génie; on n'a aucun de ces ébahissements, en les lisant, qui vous fassent croire en eux à une nature plus qu'humaine, comme à la lecture d'Homère, de Rabelais, de Shakespeare surtout; non! mais quelle conscience! Comme ils se sont efforcés de trouver pour leurs pensées des expressions justes! Quel travail! Quelles ratures! Comme ils se consultaient les uns les autres, comme ils savaient le latin! Comme ils lisaient lentement! Aussi toute leur idée y est, la forme est pleine, bourrée et garnie de choses jusqu'à la faire craquer. Or il n'y a pas de degrés: ce qui est bon vaut ce qui est bon. La Fontaine vivra autant que le Dante, et Boileau que Bossuet ou même Hugo" (1853). Those who are not French would feel it impossible to place La Fontaine alongside of Dante. But Flaubert's way of thinking will always remain a living opinion in France. Gide, in his African diary (1927) makes the following entry: "Achevé la lecture complète des Fables de La Fontaine. Aucune littérature a-t-elle offert jamais rien de plus exquis, de plus sage, de plus parfait?"

In the intellectual as well as in the social sphere France is both the land of daring innovations and of tenacious conservatism. In France an artist who discovers a new world of beauty will easily find a small group of admirers and disciples, but only very late in life will he gain admittance to the pantheon of taste in which the generally recognized possessions of the national intellectual wealth are preserved. So long as he does not possess the official sanction which is conferred by the salons, by criticism, and by the Academy, he will never be considered complete. Stendhal, Balzac, Flaubert, Mallarmé, the Impressionists —all went through this process. This is the reason why so many French artists and poets have first of all found sympathy and understanding in foreign lands, whereas at home their claim to fame was only acknowledged very hesitatingly. The final judgment on the worth of an author is delivered in France only fifty years after his death. Official taste tends to be still more reserved when foreign countries are lavish in their praise. The protectors of the French tradition usually arise and stigmatize the new tendency in art as "non-French". This means that the aesthetic controversy is carried out into the political arena. Because artistic taste in France is regarded as a national possession, it must be preserved from becoming falsified, or foreign in its form. When the national tradition in taste is based upon the standard of the Classical school, naturally everything which is non-Classical is an alien importation, poisonous and harmful. At the present day several critics still argue heatedly about this question: Can we say that Rousseau, or the Romantic movement, or the Symbolist movement were good? Can they be regarded as French? From the sixteenth century onwards the influence of foreign literature has made itself felt again and again, at certain periods, in France. But just as regularly reaction has followed, a "nationalising" of taste, a defensive reaction, whether it was directed against Spain, Italy, England, Germany or Russia. The assimilation of a foreign intellectual world is never carried through completely. Controversy still ranges round Shakespeare and Goethe. In France there will always be critics who will express loudly their distaste for the tiresome foreigner, like the old Sarcey when he exclaimed: "Assez de Shakespeare, assez d'Ibsen, assez de Tolstoi, assez de Maeterlinck, Rentrons en France, que diable!"

The greatest creations of the literature of France, classical tragedy and the modern novel, have this in common (which further, is a specific peculiarity of the French intellect): both are an analysis of the passions. While German literature tends to become metaphysical, that of France is psychological. From Montaigne to Racine, from Balzac to Proust, this quality is revealed with an ever-renewed delicacy. French literature is an inexhaustible discourse upon man. It is a course of instruction in the knowledge of humanity.

French literature has no myths; in this it resembles the literature of Rome which has no epic of gods or heroes. The Greek Olympus is interpreted in France in an allegorical or psychological sense. In general mythology is not missed. The Classical genius of France can say with Martial:

> Quid te vana iuvant miserae ludibria chartae?
> Hoc lege quod possit dicere vita: "Meum est".
> Non hic Centauros, non Gorgonas Harpyiasque
> Invenies: hominem pagina nostra sapit.

Indeed, all aspects of French literature reveal "man", express that of which life can say: *Meum est*. The feeling for the reality of the human heart, the revelation of its tragic or grotesque secrets, constitutes its greatness. What are the conflicts which move humanity? Thus ask Corneille, Racine, Pascal. What is hidden in the remote corners of the soul? So ask Montaigne, La Rochefouchauld, La Bruyère. Desire for power, ambition, physical passions—French Classicism has subjected this play of forces to an analysis which will always remain valid. Its psychology is a realism free from all illusions. French literature has in its memoirs, collections of letters, maxims and aphorisms a characteristic mass of material with which no other literature can compare. It is inexhaustible. It will always exercise the greatest attraction for those whose lives are concerned mainly with love or politics, for those who have more to do with persons than with dead things, who influence men, and who must learn to know men. The French psycho-

logists from Montaigne to Proust are men of the world who
know it through and through. They present love as a myth
nor do they enter into metaphysical speculation about it;
but they ask: How does love arise, how does she find her
realization, why does she pass away, how does she drift into
error? Is there anywhere else save in France a psychology
of love like that which we find in *Adolphe*, in the *Chartreuse
de Parme*, in the *Éducation sentimentale*? This could only arise
in a country in which love is regarded as the obvious and
chief concern of humanity, in which the language has
created such untranslatable expressions like *faire l'amour* or
—if we go into a higher sphere—like *aimer d'amour*. It is
only in French society that psychology and the life of love
are woven into an almost indissoluble unity. Only a type
of humanity which is preoccupied with the desires and the
results of love could produce such a psychological literature. The love proclaimed by Dante can lift us to the stars,
Romeo and Juliet can flood us with poetry; but with
Racine we say: "That is exactly right".

In our literature there is a great deal of theology,
whether it be that of Lessing, Herder, Goethe, or of Hölderlin. In France theology is, and remains, the province of the
Church alone. A free religiosity, a personal synthesis of
religious and secular experience, can scarcely flourish there
at all.

It is of course true that theology, that the deepest and
most intimate experience of Christianity, the most spiritual
form of mysticism, can be expressed in literary form. Pascal,
Bossuet, Fénelon, only to name these three, prove this
completely. But theology, like all other forms of the intellect and of science, will only become part of the intellectual
possession of the educated section of the nation by way of
literature. This, again, is a characteristic feature of French
literature. Science does not penetrate directly into the
consciousness of the educated people, but only after it has
declared itself in an exemplary literary form. One function
of French literature is the "popularization" of knowledge,

or to put it differently: the de-specialization of science. In France great thinkers and research workers have often been great writers as well: Descartes, Montesquieu, Buffon, Michelet, Taine, Renan, Bergson. Philosophers who wrote badly like Comte, had to wait half a century for official recognition. Characteristic of France also is the type of writer who himself is not a creative scholar but who can mediate to the literary public the results of a certain science. Thus in the period of Louis XIV. Fontenelle made astronomy accessible to the Court, and Voltaire made a survey of world history for Madame du Châtelet. The Frenchman will allow himself to be instructed in all forms of knowledge if the literary form is good. In France, in the ranks of the intellectual types, the writer ranks higher than the scholar. For the intellectual life of France the literary circles mean far more than the universities. Everything can be said, and, if it is well said, it will find a hearing. And what has once been well said will live on imperishably in the memory of the nation.

The intellectual tradition of France is incarnate in the whole body and series of its classical works. Only he who accepts this tradition, assimilates it, and comes to terms with it, can hope, for his part, to represent the spirit of his nation. In France anyone who wishes to educate in matters literary and intellectual, who desires to have readers, listeners and disciples, must complete this whole process. He must know how to value and balance the Classical and the Romantic schools, scepticism and spirituality, the heroic sentiment and the pert mockery, the profane and the sublime, in this tradition. Charles du Bos said once: "Il existe un grand dialogue dont il nous faut souhaiter qu'il dure aussi longtemps que notre race, car il s'en dégage la musique la plus compréhensive et la plus solennelle que le génie français ait fait rendre à l'instrument qui lui est propre: le dialogue Montaigne-Pascal. Un Français est profond dans la mesure où, à son rang, il sait maintenir ce dialogue vivant en lui."

The German would decide either for Montaigne or for Pascal. The Frenchman will feel that he cannot sacrifice either to the other. In the whole company of the great authors he sees reflected the wholeness of the worlds of intellect and spirit. He comes to regard literature with a respect bordering on reverence. In France alone is there a *religion des Lettres*: the surrender of the whole intellectual existence and of all the powers of faith to literature, to its tradition, its cultivation and its admiration. Only a French poet—Mallarmé—could write: "Tout existe pour aboutir à un livre". In France, as Thibaudet has said, there exists a "mysticism of books"; and in this minds can meet and make friends which are otherwise separated by all the conflicts of politics, aesthetics and general outlook on life. It is, of course, true, that every day these conflicts—in every French newspaper—break into the sphere of literature. But it is still true that in France—and nowhere to the extent in which it is so in France—there is a superior sphere which rises above these conflicts. This is the sphere of "pure criticism"—this word is used in the same sense as the expression *poésie pure*. In it discussion is replaced by dialogue. It will never wholly refrain from pronouncing an opinion, but it does not condemn, and it does not argue. It contemplates in the mirror of the written word the complicated course of human affairs. It has become a final form of wisdom. It is one of the purest expressions of the French mind.

## V

## RELIGION

It is not easy to estimate the position of religion within the general structure of French civilization. Even a cursory glance at history, and at the life of France at the present day, reveals the existence of two points of view. These views are absolutely hostile to each other, yet both can support their claims with solid arguments.

France calls herself the eldest daughter of the Church. The Cluny Reform was her gift to the medieval Church. It was she who summoned Christendom to the adventure of the Crusades. She reveres as her patron saint and liberator the Maid of Orleans, whom the Church has canonized. With fanatical ardour she extirpated the heresies of the Middle Ages and the Reformation of the sixteenth century. In Modern Catholicism she occupies a very important, if not actually a leading position. The conclusion seems clear: the Catholic religion belongs to the very essence, to the indestructible existence, of France. Between France and Catholicism there exists a vital bond of union of a special —many would say a supernatural[1]—kind.

One of the most influential Catholic intellectual leaders of modern France, the Dominican Lacordaire (1802–1861), declared that it was the destiny of the French nation to be the special ally of the Church. He laid stress on the fact that France had opposed the three great enemies of the true faith—Arianism, Islam and Lutheranism—and that through Pippin and Charlemagne it had founded the ecclesiastical State.

According to Lacordaire, in France love of the Church

---

[1] Lucie Christine (see below, p. 153) makes the following entry in her diary on the 28th of September 1884: "Notre-Seigneur m'a parlé de sa Mère dans la sainte communion; 'Vois', m'a-t-il dit, 'combien mon cœur aime la France! Je ne pouvais rien lui donner de plus cher que ma Mère, et je la lui ai donnée.'"

and love of country are both directed towards the same object: thus there arises a "supernatural patriotism".[1] Pius X. recognized the mystical prerogative of France in a phrase which Catholic publicists often quote: "Si le supernaturel vit partout dans le monde, il vit surtout en France."[2]

On the other hand, however, from the time of the Middle Ages onwards, France has been constantly in conflict with the Papacy. For centuries Roman ecclesiasticism and Gallicanism struggled with each other, and this struggle is not yet over. The great Revolution of 1789 meant a collective apostasy from the Church. No other nation has ever made such a violent break with Christianity. France has been the source of the most violent attacks on religion. Through his books Voltaire taught thousands to scoff at all that is sacred, and to renounce their faith entirely. The France of the Third Republic has renewed the fight against the Church on all fronts, and has led an anti-religious campaign which finally achieved its ends in the Law of Separation of 1905. When we look at this aspect of the question it seems as though it would be truer to say: France is godless and sceptical, the land of irreligion.

France, the refuge of the Catholic faith; France, the champion of the emancipated reason,—in the question of the relation of French civilization to religion these are the two contradictory theses which are constantly discussed by ardent supporters on both sides, both in France and abroad. Paul Bourget, the famous Academician, wrote during the World War: "La France reste le grand pays catholique, malgré le gouvernement, ses électeurs, ses codes, ses journaux, malgré tout." This statement has, however, been met by the counter-question: Is it conceivable that France will remain loyal to a point of view which is absolutely opposed to the whole trend of her political and intellectual life?

[1] Lacordaire, *Discours sur la vocation de la nation française* (1851).
[2] Goyau, *Ce que le monde catholique doit à la France* (1918), p. 185.

RELIGION          131

How are we to explain this paradoxical and contradictory situation, which is evident in the sphere of fact as well as in that of opinion? When we turn to the history of France for light, however, we are confronted by a new difficulty: the problem which has just been stated reappears in the written histories themselves. Without exception, all the accounts of the history of religion in France are written from one standpoint or the other, and can therefore only be used with caution. But in spite of this the attempt must be made to reach a just view of the state of affairs by means of a careful comparison of the two points of view.

One point, however, stands out clearly in the situation which I have thus briefly outlined: the religious problem in France takes the form of an alternative between Catholicism and unbelief. This is the one, and only, challenge. There are Protestant churches in France, it is true, and from time to time individual Protestants have taken an effective part in politics or in intellectual life, especially under the Third Republic; but in the religious struggles of modern France Protestantism means practically nothing. When we say that for three hundred years religion in France has been the source of constant and heated conflict, it is always the Roman Catholic form of religion which is meant. This is also true of Italy and of Spain. France, however, differs from these two countries in the passion with which Catholicism is defended on the one hand and attacked on the other—in the intensity of the struggle, and the widespread influence of the religious conflict, which affects every aspect of political and intellectual life. These religious conflicts cut far more deeply into the life of the nation, and cause more division and bitterness than interconfessional difficulties in Germany. In France, at least, the opposition is far more evident. This is due to the fact that the French as a nation, whether Catholics or sceptics, feel it imperative to define their position absolutely clearly on this question. If we were to judge the religious situation in France by its political and intellectual manifestations alone, it would look like a fight to the death between two hostile armies. In the give-and-take of everyday life, however, hostility dies down.

The religious history of France begins with the Celts. Even St. Thomas Aquinas believed that the religious institutions of Gaul, which culminated in the Druid priesthood, provided a specially favourable soil for the development of Christianity, and on this point modern thinkers agree with him. Oriental cults then came into Gaul with the Roman legions, and among them was Christianity. The first Christian communities to witness to their faith were those of Lyons and Vienne. The blood of the one hundred and seventy-seven martyrs who were executed at Lyons (to use the expression of Georges Goyau) "colours the first page of the history of the Church in France". A few years later Bishop Irenaeus ot Lyons defined the true faith, and gave precedence to the Roman Church (*potentior principalitas*). A rich garland of legend used to adorn the story of the Christianization of Gaul. Criticism, however, has plucked it to pieces. It appears that the process of evangelization was slow and gradual. In the third century Toulouse, Vienne, Trier, Reims, Bordeaux, Paris, Bourges, Sens and Cologne became the seat of bishoprics. A Gallo-Roman bishop was present at the Council of Nicea (325). Towards the end of the fourth century the rural population was still, to a large extent, pagan. Their apostle was St. Martin, a Pannonian soldier. He founded the first monastery in France, Ligugé, near Poitiers, and died in 397 as Bishop of Tours. Alongside of St. Denis he figures as the patron saint of the Merovingian Church. To many French Catholics there is something symbolic in the fact that the German offer of an armistice in 1918 was accepted on the 11th of November, the Feast of St. Martin. Paul Claudel has utilized this idea in a poem which celebrates St. Martin, and also pours forth sinister floods of hatred against the Germans.

A century after the death of Martin of Tours Clovis and

his Franks accepted the Catholic faith in Reims. Gallo-Romans and barbarians now possessed a common faith. The Franks revered the saints of Gallo-Roman Christendom: St. Martin of Tours and St. Geneviève (d. 500), the patroness of Paris, whose prayers delivered the city from the invading Huns. For the next few centuries the destinies of the Frankish Church were bound up with that of the Frankish monarchy, and the idea of the Empire: this meant establishment and development under Charlemagne, followed by decline and ruin under the destructive influence of feudalism. The great prelates of the realm were drawn into the struggles for power of the feudal lords, and the inferior clergy also degenerated. The restoration of the discipline and authority of the Church was the work of Cluny (founded in 910). The spirit of Cluny renewed and strengthened the Papacy; also—in the campaigns against the Moors in Spain—it permitted the idea of a religious war to mature, which bore fruit later on in the flaming zeal of the Crusades. A monk named Guibert de Nogent interpreted the religious vocation of France as a national mission from his experience of the first Crusade (about 1120). The title of his work, *Gesta Dei per Francos*, is still often used as a watchword when France wishes to reassert her claim to be the champion of the Catholic faith in the world.

When the zeal and fervour of Cluny were fading Cîteaux (founded 1098) became the germ of a new ascetic piety, through the activity of St. Bernard (1091–1153), who was equally great as a mystic, a founder of monasteries and an ecclesiastical politician. Bernard, whom Dante was to choose as his guide when the sublime vision of Paradise was opening up before him, was the spiritual flame of Western Christianity when it was at its height in the twelfth century. This was the period when France was adorned with the "luminous robe of her cathedrals" (in 1144 Suger consecrated the choir of St. Denis)—whose devotion still testifies so powerfully to the energies of faith which existed in the Middle Ages in France.

France's position as the leading nation in Western
Christendom was then further strengthened by the Paris
University. There Albertus Magnus, the German, had in-
troduced Aristotelianism into the philosophy of the Church.
There his pupil and successor Thomas Aquinas worked.
It was there that the union of the Catholic faith with the
Thomist system was achieved, which from the time of the
Counter-Reformation has become obligatory within the
Church. At the same time the Capetian dynasty produced
in St. Louis a ruler who exercised his royal authority in the
Franciscan spirit, and belonged to the Third Order of St.
Francis, without ever allowing the dignity and independ-
ence of his authority to be subdued by ecclesiastical de-
sires for dominance. Scarcely fifteen years after his death
(1297) Louis was canonized by Boniface VIII.—by the
same Pope who, a few years later, was to be humiliated by
Louis's grandson and successor, Philip the Fair.

Philip the Fair emerged victorious from his struggle
with the Papacy. He had secured the support of the French
clergy, the majority of whom were prepared to cite the
Pope to appear before a General Council on a charge of
heresy. It is at this point that, for the first time in French
history, "Gallicanism" appears as a determining factor:
that is, the successful assertion of French national feeling
against the dominating claims of the Papacy.[1]

At this period Gallicanism was not yet a theological doctrine of the constitution of the Church. The strength of the
opposition lay in the Monarchy; the clergy merely supported the Crown. Gallicanism of this kind was not ecclesiastical but royal. This was the theory of Philip the Fair:
Christ finds in the French kingdom, more than in all
others, a firm foundation for the Christian faith; He knows
that in France He is more loved, feared and honoured than
elsewhere; for this reason He has endowed the French
monarchy with special privileges, and has granted it ex-

[1] Cf. "Théorie du gallicanisme" in G. Hanotaux, *Sur les chemins de l'histoire*, 1924, vol. i.

emption from any other form of domination whatsoever.[1] The Gallicanism of Philip the Fair was further displayed in the abolition of the Order of Templars, and in the removal of the Papacy to Avignon, and thus into the immediate sphere of French influence. The Babylonian Exile (at Avignon) filled the Christendom of the West with wrath and sorrow; it weakened the Papacy, and it increased the abuses in ecclesiastical administration; it nourished ecclesiastical Gallicanism. French clerics developed it into a theory of theology and Church government; it is true that this could never actually be carried out in practice, but for hundreds of years it existed as a claim and an instrument of attack, and at any moment it might make its claims felt. Meanwhile the French monarchy fell from its high estate, from the height of its power, into the distresses and confusions of the Hundred Years' War. The fact that deliverance came through the Maid of Orleans, who was inspired by religion, meant that in a new form, and upon a higher level, the French national idea was fused with the Catholic faith. But the interior life of French Catholicism declined rapidly. The cry for reforms could not be quieted. Meanwhile, over the heads of the faithful, the Curia and the French Crown made a pact: the Concordat of Francis I. stabilized the situation from the point of view of Church government; the inconvenient demands for reform were ignored.

Meanwhile the Reformation spread to France. Lutherans were the first in the field, and the Calvinists followed. It

---

[1] From the reply to the Coronation statement of the Emperor Henry VII.: ". . . altissimus Jesus Christus in regno ipso pre ceteris mundi partibus sancte fidei et religionis christiane stabile fundamentum reperiens sibique et eius vicariis et ministris summam impendi devocionem considerans, sicut se in eo pre ceteris magis amari, timeri et honorari conspexit, sic ipsum pre ceteris regnis et principatibus singulari quadam eminencia prerogativa disposuit honorari, ipsum a cuiusque principis ac domini temporalis superioritate potenter eximens et exempto regem suum solum quodammodo monarcham perpetua stabilitate confirmans."

is estimated that a third of the nation went over to the side of the Reformation about the middle of the sixteenth century. Protestantism penetrated into Parliament, into the ranks of the lower and the upper nobility, and from the year 1560 it became a political movement. It was opposed by a Catholic Party, led by great feudal lords, who were determined to defend the ancient faith either with their sovereign or against him. To the central authority of the Monarchy the attitude of the great feudal lords was as great a danger as political Protestantism. The "Wars of Religion" developed into a political civil war, and even the religious peace of 1598 was a political peace treaty. It enacted that, within certain fixed limits, Protestantism was allowed to exist in France. But the nation as a whole had rejected it. They would not tolerate a Protestant sovereign. After 1600 Protestantism has meant very little in the spiritual history of France. Protestantism and the French spirit are incompatible.

The defeat of the Reformation in France cannot be explained solely from political causes. There are other and deeper reasons which lie in the spirit of the people. About 1530 enthusiasm for the new evangelical Christianity was universal in France. A large number of individual believers and priests hoped for a reform within the Church. But when Calvin went to Geneva, and it became increasingly plain that the Reformation was a schism, this hope was shattered. The fear of breaking with the ancient Church was a religious motive which hindered the expansion of Protestantism. Fear of persecution also played its part. Further, the dogmatic spirit of Calvin alienated from the movement many minds which were attracted, and might have been won, by the idea of religious liberty. In the horrors of the Wars of Religion religious questions ceased to be concerns of the inner life at all. The principles of the faith were swallowed up in the military and political struggle for power. Protestantism was regarded as the principle of anarchy, the cause of all the disturbances from which France was suffering. The religious problem was transformed into a social question: henceforward this way of regarding the matter became the standard point of view in France. We might almost say that through the experiences of the Wars of Religion it has become a typically French point of view. Ultimately, however, these explanations are only different ways of saying the same thing: it is obvious that the religious needs of the French people can only find their fulfilment in Catholicism. The ancient Roman ideas of order and authority, the close union between the idea of the State represented by the Monarchy, and the religious institutions (which lasted for a thousand years), religious wars against unbelievers and heretics,—all the forces of a long history have combined to imprint this form of religion upon the life of France.

If a religious revival were to take place in France it would have to arise out of Catholic piety. And a renewal of this kind has actually taken place. We have only seen the unique significance of this movement since the publication of the monumental work by Henri Bremond, entitled *Histoire littéraire du sentiment religieux en France*.[1] This book supersedes all the older works, and has revealed a rich variety of new points of view.

The origin of this religious awakening can be traced back to the second half of the sixteenth century. At that time, under the influence of Tridentine theology, there took place that fusion of Humanism with the Christian spirit which is described as "spiritual Humanism" (*Humanisme dévot*). The movement began in the Society of Jesus. Its highest and purest representative is St. François de Sales, whose *Introduction à la vie dévote* (1608) is still the devotional book which is read most widely in France at the present day. From the close of the sixteenth century, alongside of spiritual Humanism, a mystical current appeared which rose higher and higher towards the year 1650, and

[1] Eight volumes (1916 ff.). Cf. also my articles in *Hochland* (April 1920, May 1924, October 1928).

then slowly subsided in the second half of the seventeenth century. At first it was under the influence of Spanish mysticism. But with Bérulle, the founder of the Oratorians, it became independent. A mysticism arose which was peculiarly French in spirit and style. It was theocentric, directed the gaze of the soul towards God and the inner life of the Godhead. Its aim was not asceticism but adoration; not self-conquest but the opening up of the soul to the energies of grace. Through the influence of Bérulle the life of the French clergy was renewed; this was the teaching which inspired St. Vincent de Paul, the great apostle of active love to one's neighbour; it reached its highest point in a mysticism of "adherence", which, unlike Protestant piety, did not wish to "feel" or to "know" God (for that would denote an anthropomorphization) but only to "adhere" to Him, to give oneself to Him beyond all speech or feeling. Out of these sources there arose the cult of the Sacred Heart, whose inmost meaning is a concentration of all the powers of worship on the interior aspect of the Person of Christ, although it is precisely this form of devotion which has so often fallen into materialistic ways.

The mysticism of this "French School" should not be confounded with Quietism. It is far removed from all sentimentality or subjectivism of religious experience. It is based wholly on the Church and on dogma. Its leaders, like Bérulle and Olier (the founder of the seminary for priests of Saint Sulpice), regarded the training of the clergy as one of their main tasks. Their spirituality is directed towards the objective content of dogma. Transparency, harmony, moderation breathe through the religious attitude of this mysticism, and give to it something of the classic French style. It worked in quietness, and scarcely came into contact at all with secular history or with purely intellectual movements. Hence, on the whole, little is known of this movement. For this very reason, however, for those who desire to understand the inner piety of Catholic France it is important.

Jansenism is a religious movement of the seventeenth

century in France which is far better known; this, however,
is due to the fact of its close connexion with the general
history of thought. Racine was a disciple—even though an
errant one—of the Jansenists. The great figure of Pascal is
connected with Jansenism. The history of Jansenism has
been classically described by Sainte-Beuve in his *Port-
Royal* (1840–1859), which has only been surpassed by
Bremond. All these circumstances have made Jansenism
appear more important than it really was. It is not true to
assert that the school of Port-Royal was the only refuge of
"spiritual" Christianity in the seventeenth century. The
vital centres of the mystical movement were quite equal to
it in power. Jansenism, it is true, turned its back on mysticism. It fixed its attention on the fact of Original Sin, and
the burden of individual sin. It was a form of Puritanism,
characterized by a bigoted theological temper and a sec-
tarian intellectualism. Port-Royal and its opponents were
drawn into a wordy warfare supported by controversial
pamphlets. The religious vitality of the movement was
dried up by an unending stream of these controversial
tracts. The Jansenist controversy was most unfruitful; it
weakened French Catholicism inwardly, and exposed it to
the attacks of the Enlightenment. But Port-Royal became
the spiritual home of Pascal. His piety bears Jansenist
traits, but it finally outgrew the polemic of the *Provinciales*
and the narrowness of Jansenism. Pascal's *Pensées*, the un-
finished sketch of an Apology for religion which was published in 1670, after his death, is one of the most magnificent and moving documents of the Christian religious life.
The philosophical and religious struggle of a personality
of genius, the inner drama of a soul oscillating between
the human sense of sin and fear and the hope of grace, is
revealed in the *Pensées*. A classic of French literature, a
deeply original thinker, Pascal is at the same time one of
the great religious personalities who have always found an
echo in spiritual natures akin to their own in other churches
and other nations far beyond their own borders.

If, in addition to these high forms of spirituality, we take into consideration the reform of the Religious Orders and of the secular clergy, the great development of practical charity, of evangelization and of missions, we gain an impressive picture of the renewal of French Catholicism at the time of the Counter-Reformation. To French Catholics the seventeenth century is the "century of the Saints". But it was also the period in which the development of the monarchy reached its summit in absolutism. Once again, as in the days of Philip the Fair, Gallicanism had to serve to support the claims of the Monarchy. Louis XIV. regarded himself as the defender of the true faith. He permitted Jansenism and Quietism to be condemned, and made the fateful resolve to break the system which had been in vogue with regard to the treatment of the Protestants from the time of Henri IV. In the year 1685 he ordered the Revocation of the Edict of Nantes, a decision which even Catholic historians condemn to-day.

The public opinion of the day, however, was loud in its applause. Bossuet spoke of it as a miracle. Many Protestants recanted out of fear of the *dragonnades*; but those who remained true were strengthened in their faith and in their resistance by the persecution. The religious unity of France, which Louis XIV. desired to effect, could not be attained by force.

With the eighteenth century the religious life of the Church in France began to slacken. Intellectual leadership went over to the opposite camp. The philosophy of the Enlightenment in its various forms, from Deism to Naturalism and Materialism, dominated the minds of men. Atheism spread among the leading classes of society.

The forms of religion and the State, Catholicism and the Monarchy, were so closely connected that the fall of one power involved the fall of the other. This appeared inevitable. The masses regarded the Church as an instrument of royal authority. The Monarchy itself, by its Gallican claims, had given colour to this point of view. When the

Revolution triumphed, it had to abolish the Catholic
Church as well as the dynasty.[1] From 1793 it worked
fanatically to try to remove all traces of the Christian past
in France. At that time countless treasures of ecclesiastical
art were destroyed by order of the official authorities. In
Chartres a patriot proposed that the Cathedral should be
destroyed; the proposal was only turned down because
people thought that the ruins would block up the streets
and hinder the traffic. Notre Dame in Paris was proclaimed the *Temple of Reason*. Then Robespierre replaced
the worship of Reason by that of the *Être Suprême*. The
"natural religion" of the Enlightenment—freely interpreted in the spirit of Rousseau—was elevated to the rank
of a State religion. But in spite of persecution the Catholic
religion continued to exist. After the devastation of the
Reign of Terror she was able once more to raise her head.
The State permitted the Catholic Church to exist un-
hindered, but she could no longer draw on the revenues of
the State for support. Church and State were separated.
The State, however, required from the priests the oath of
fidelity to the Republican constitution, and this brought
division into the Catholic camp.

Even Napoleon, who had no religious connexions at all,
recognized that, for political reasons, it was necessary to
have an understanding with the Church. Only she could
satisfy men's minds. It was also desirable in order to ease
the minds of those who had bought ecclesiastical property.
The Curia for its part was also concerned to procure for
the French clergy the means of support from the State.
So there came into being the Concordat of 1801, which
regulated the relations between the French State and the
Curia until 1905. It allowed wide powers to the State and
made concessions to Gallicanism. On Easter Sunday 1802

[1] For the "Political and Social Ideas of French Catholicism from
1789–1914" cf. the book by W. Gurian, *M.-Gladbach*, 1929. Also
P. R. Rohden, "Zur Soziologie des politischen Katholizismus in Frankreich," *Archiv für Sozialwissenschaft*, 1929, 468 ff.

the Concordat was celebrated by a Te Deum in Notre Dame, in the presence of Napoleon. Almost at the same time there appeared a book in which—contrary to the whole philosophy of the eighteenth century—the beauties of the Catholic religion were exposed to the gaze of those who had eyes to see: this book was Chateaubriand's *Génie du Christianisme*. But those who were trying to restore Catholicism were confronted by great obstacles during the Imperial era. The inward opposition between Napoleonic absolutism and the Papacy soon led to conflict: the seizure of the Pope, the excommunication of the Emperor, and the struggle for power between the policies of Gallicanism and that of Rome. The fall of the Empire created a new situation.

The Restoration of the Bourbons meant an alliance between the Throne and the Altar. The external power of the Church was strengthened, but it was also bound up with the whole cause of Counter-Revolution. Ecclesiastical and Royal Gallicanism were once more united. Joseph de Maistre's plea for the papal claims for dominion (*Du Pape*, 1819) was ineffective. The secret society of the "Congregation" was the most powerful instrument of the Catholic propaganda, which was supported by political reaction. When, in the July days of 1830, the forces of reaction were defeated, the people of the day believed that Catholicism had been finally defeated also. The rebels profaned Notre Dame, plundered the houses of Religious Orders, and raged against the Church. The masses were hostile to religion, and their intellectual leaders upheld humanitarian, social, democratic, and in any case non-Christian, ideals. But in this crisis French Catholicism discovered new energies. The freedom of religion, of the press, and of teaching, which had been granted to all citizens, was also of service to it. In order to take their place in the life of the nation, however, the Catholics had to recognize Liberalism as the basis of action. Montalembert, then a young man, led the way in this direction. Lamennais stated clearly that he recognized that the times required the separation of the idea of Catholicism both from Gallicanism and from Royalist doctrine. The policy which he outlined in the journal *L'Avenir* (1830–31) was both democratic and ultramontane. Lamennais, however, was condemned by Rome, and he broke with the Church. Liberal Catholicism had suffered its first defeat, but it was not disheartened. Lacordaire took the helm. He made the pulpit of Notre Dame his platform. His eloquence inflamed the younger Liberals and gained the sympathy of the intellectuals for Catholicism. Public opinion became tolerant.

Apart from politics, too, French Catholicism renewed its life under the July Monarchy. Catholic philosophers made great efforts to construct an historical apologetic for the faith. Prosper Guéranger, a Benedictine monk, and a former co-worker of Lamennais, made the Abbey of Solesmes the centre and the starting-point of a liturgical reform by replacing the Gallican Liturgies by those of Rome. Frédéric Ozanam (1813–1853) gathered Catholic students at the universities into a society for charitable activity among the working classes, and thus became the forerunner of "social Catholicism".

The inward renewal which was expressed by all these forms of Catholic life had this result: the Revolution of 1848 was far less hostile to religion than that of 1830. The Trees of Freedom which were planted at that time were dedicated by priests. When, however, soon after the February Revolution the radical revolutionary party of the Left sought to seize the reins of government, Archbishop Affre of Paris fell a victim to their violence. But the victory of the bourgeois revolution in June 1848 again strengthened the position of the Church. Men like Cousin and Thiers felt that an alliance with the Church was the one means of salvation from *démagogie*. Whereas after 1830 the Church emerged from the upheaval with a sense of defeat, after 1848, when she came to take stock of her position, she found that she had gained in power and influence. The Education Act of 1850 (the *loi Falloux*) granted her freedom in education. This political success was the work of Montalembert.

The *coup d'État* of 1851 strengthened the position of the Church. The French bishops hastened to welcome it, and Pius IX. declared that through it Heaven had expiated the guilt of the Church against France. The Empire and Catholicism made common cause. The clergy extolled the Crimean War as a crusade. Only a few leading Catholics like Montalembert either remained loyal to Liberal ideas or returned to them. Its close connexion with the authoritarian régime injured the interests of the Church both among the masses and in intellectual circles. Towards 1860 the word "clerical" began to be used in the sense which it still bears at the present day, and Anti-Clericalism began to emerge. Intellectually, also, opposition was intensified. The habit of thought fostered by the study of natural science and historical criticism (in 1863 Renan's *Vie de Jésus* appeared) shook the foundations of the traditional faith. At the same time there awakened among the faithful the desire for the miraculous. The visions of the Blessed Virgin at Lourdes (1858) found credence in many directions. The ecclesiastical authorities recognized the miracle. The Syllabus of Pius IX. (December 8, 1864) was the final defeat of Liberal Catholicism. The last article in this document condemned the statement: "The Pope can and should come to terms with progress, Liberalism and modern civilization".[1] The last relics of Liberalism and of ecclesiastical Gallicanism were then torn up by the roots by the Vatican. French believers submitted to the decrees of the Vatican. This did not lead to an Old Catholic movement as it did in Germany.

The events of 1870–71, like those of 1848, strengthened Catholicism in France. Among the victims of the Com-

---

[1] "Romanus Pontifex potest ac debet cum progressu, cum liberalismo et cum recenti civilitate sese reconciliare et componere."

mune were some thirty priests, among them the Archbishop Darboy of Paris, who were shot by the rebels. To
the faithful the military defeat and civil war seemed to be a
punishment of Providence. In the National Assembly there
was a strong conservative majority which was friendly to
the Church. It resolved to build the Church of the Sacré-
Cœur in Montmartre. At that time the cult of the Sacred
Heart became both a national and an ultramontane symbol. Social Catholicism also received a new impulse. Two
officers who had returned from a term of imprisonment in
Germany, Count Albert de Mun and Marquis de la Tour
du Pin, organized the Catholic Labour movement under
the motto: Counter-revolution by means of the Syllabus.

This question, however, was insistent: what should be
the attitude of the Catholic towards the new form of the
French State, the democratic Republic? The Republic did
not yet seem secure. Some years elapsed before the danger
of a royalist restoration was overcome. To a large number
of citizens the Republic seemed a violent break with the
French tradition of centuries. The leaders of the Republic
carried forward the work of the Revolution of 1789, and
all the demagogic machinations of the nineteenth century,
with their hostility to the Church. Catholics, therefore, were
faced with this alternative: either they must oppose the
Republic, or, they must accept it, and fill it with the
Christian spirit.

In 1878 Leo XIII. became Pope. He also was steeped in
the spirit of the Syllabus, but he showed a tendency to become reconciled to modern society. The majority of the
French clergy, however, were anti-Republican in spirit.
The French Government made capital out of this fact, in
order to be able to conduct an anti-clerical policy "for the
defence of the Republic". Le cléricalisme, voilà l'ennemi, was
the phrase used by Gambetta. But the astute policy of Leo
XIII. strove for reconciliation. The Republic was established. It had overcome the Boulanger crisis. The Mon-
archists were discouraged.

The signal for reconciliation between the Curia and Republican France was given by the toast proposed by Cardinal Lavigerie at Algiers on the 12th of November 1890. "Quand la volonté d'un peuple," he said, "s'est fermement affirmée sur la forme d'un gouvernement et lorsque, pour arracher un peuple aux abîmes qui le menacent, il faut l'adhésion sans arrière-pensée à cette forme politique, le moment est venu de déclarer l'épreuve faite, et il ne reste plus qu'à sacrifier tout ce qui la conscience et l'honneur permettent, ordonnant à chacun de nous de sacrifier pour le salut de la patrie." These words caused great excitement, and were regarded with violent disapproval by some in the Catholic camp. People did not yet know what line the Pope would take. The Encyclical *Rerum novarum* of the 15th of May 1891 gave directive principles to the Catholic Labour movement and to social Catholicism. It seemed to push the problem of the relation between Church and State into the background. But as early as 1892 the Pope dispelled all uncertainty by the Encyclical *Au milieu des sollicitudes* (16th February 1892), which was published in French. It summoned French Catholics to recognize the constitution of 1875, and thus established the policy of *ralliement*. Naturally this met with some resistance. Royalist Catholics emphasized the fact that in France they were Frenchmen, even though in Rome they were Catholics. They wanted to make a clear distinction between the spiritual and temporal power of the Pope. The Republicans also were not free from misgivings. They feared that this new policy was merely an opportunistic move. They pointed to the increase of Catholic anti-Semitism; Édouard Drumont had become the leader of this movement through his book, *La France juive* (1885), and his paper, *La Libre Parole* (1892). The elections of 1893 were a defeat for the supporters of the *ralliement* policy. The Government, however, was conciliatory. In a speech in the Chamber on the 3rd of March 1894, the Minister Spuller used the famous expression of the *esprit nouveau* which should prevail in the relations be-

tween Church and State. Meanwhile there was the Dreyfus affair; there was a great growth of anti-Semitism on the
one hand, and republican Radicalism on the other. Under
the leadership of Waldeck-Rousseau the Government *bloc*
of the left was formed, and this gave new energy to anti-
Clericalism. When Leo XIII. died in 1903 his policy of conciliation had failed. Only a few Catholics had responded
to the idea of the *ralliement*. The Republic, for its part,
intensified its anti-Catholic legislation. The Ministry of
Combes drove out the Religious Orders. In July 1904 the
French ambassador at the Vatican was recalled. On the
9th of December 1905 the law was passed which decreed
separation between Church and State.

In another place we shall see[1] the part played by *Laïcisme*,
that is, the anti-religious policy of the "secular" State
(*L'idée laïque*) when the Concordat was broken. In the
following paragraphs I will deal only with the religious
development which has taken place since that date.

Even after the separation of Church and State there was
still one tendency within Catholicism which worked for reconciliation between the Church and democracy. This was
the Christian Youth Movement created by Marc Sangnier,
in the nineties, entitled the "Sillon" (the furrow).[2] Its aim
was to realize republican democracy through Catholicism,
because this would increase the responsibility of the individual citizen. The *Sillon* conceived democracy as the political development of a moral idea which can only reach its
goal with the aid of the Christian spirit. The originality of
the *Sillon* consisted in the fact that it desired to be, and in
fact was, "life" and a community of "friendship" which
would feel itself bound together by sympathy and enthusiasm. There was, however, in the movement an element
of romantic vitalism which aroused the suspicion of the
ecclesiastical authorities. The *Sillon* won great external

[1] Cf. Chapter VI.
[2] Cf. H. Platz, *Geistige Kämpfe im modernen Frankreich* (1922),
p. 280 ff.

successes, it was a power in French public life, when Pius X., on the 25th of August 1910, in a letter to the archbishops and bishops of France, condemned it. One cannot be surprised. The Sillonists were, without doubt, quite loyal to the Catholic Church—indeed with one consent they bowed to the decision of the Church—but they had gone beyond the official doctrine of the Church in social and political matters. Without exactly intending it, but in actual fact, the *Sillon* identified the cause of democracy with that of the Catholic religion—just as the *Action française* identified it with Nationalism. In both instances, after a period of suspense lasting for years, the Pope finally pronounced his veto.

Nationalism arose as a political movement during the Dreyfus crisis. The question whether Captain Dreyfus— condemned in 1894, and a second time in 1897, for betraying military secrets—were innocent or not, caused an upheaval which stirred the whole of France to its depths. Extremely complicated opposing elements of general, political and social origin were summed up in the formula: *Justice*— or *Patrie?* Conservative France saw her army insulted, her national honour trodden under foot, her fatherland in danger. Radical France, however, fought for the preeminence of the moral idea, and for the ideals of the Enlightenment, of the Revolution, of Humanity. Both parties accused each other of self-interest and fanatical sectarianism. In 1899 the nationalistic tendency was organized into a movement by Henri Vaugeois as the *Action française*. Its intellectual leader was, and still is, Charles Maurras. He defined "integral" Nationalism as Royalism, and was able to revive the Monarchist idea in a very real way. An atheist himself, he admired the political and social system of the Catholic Church, and respected and honoured the ecclesiastical hierarchy. The *Action française* teaches that in the struggle against the disturbing forces of the modern world Nationalism and Catholicism ought to combine. This movement gained increasing interest and support among French Catholics. The Church is the "Ark of Refuge for society" because it is a Roman institution. Rome created Western civilization. Maurras has said, "Je suis Romain, je suis humain: deux propositions identiques", and "Le christianisme non catholique est odieux".

In 1926, after a long period of inaction, the Pope condemned the *Action française* in a series of pronouncements, and the French bishops supported the Papal decision. But Maurras and Léon Daudet would not submit. Their resistance caused a crisis within French Catholicism whose result is not yet clear. Will the old ferment of Gallicanism revive and drive one section of French Catholics into a rigid opposition to Rome? Or will the Papal condemnation mean the end of the *Action française* as it meant the end of the *Sillon*?

As we study the religious situation in France at the present time, the most important fact which emerges is this: there is a renaissance of Catholic faith and life, to an extent which would have been considered impossible twenty or thirty years ago.[1]

It is, of course, true that in the eighties and nineties of last century there was a "neo-Catholic" tendency in literature. More or less sensational conversions (Verlaine, Coppée, Bourget, Huysmans, Brunetière) attracted a good deal of attention. But in these movements there were many elements which were outside the sphere of religion: aestheticism on the one hand and social-conservative traditionalism on the other. The leaders among the intelligentsia were alien to or hostile towards the Church. Since 1910 this has changed very considerably. At the same time there was launched partly in the name of the philosophy of Bergson (Péguy), and partly in that of Thomism (Maritain), an offensive of Catholic intellectuals. No longer were they content to point to the emotional values of the liturgy, the group-experience of the Church, to charity and social reform, or to mystical poetry—they now carried the war into

[1] Cf. Georges Goyau, *L'Effort catholique dans la France d'aujourd'hui*, 1922.

the enemy's country and attacked him in his chief position: in philosophy and science. To-day French Catholicism numbers among its supporters and adherents a large *élite* of intellectuals in all professions, and it has a great following among the young.

In literature also Catholics take a leading position. Dramatists like Claudel and Ghéon, novelists like Mauriac and Bernanos, critics like Massis and Maritain and, finally, a versatile writer like Léon Daudet set their mark on the literature of present-day France.[1] In the *Revue des Jeunes* the Catholic movement has an excellent paper. Whereas formerly the literary productions of Catholic authors were mostly on the level of the dreary, stale art of the Salons and the Academy, to-day there are fruitful contacts between the most modern artistic experiments and Thomist aesthetics. It cannot be denied, however, that for some time past the Catholicism of the literary circles has often aroused misgivings among the ecclesiastical authorities. There have already been too many disappointing experiences. Only too often apologists for Catholicism in the camp of the intellectuals have confined their efforts to commending the Faith to others. Thibaudet has very aptly described this attitude of the "outsider" as a French peculiarity: "Depuis le *génie du Christianisme* il est facile de marquer une des voies les plus fréquentées, les plus pittoresques, et les plus singulières de la vie intellectuelle française: Le catholicisme du dehors, soit le catholicisme des autres. Quel beau livre un esprit indépendant et curieux écrirait sur cette série: Chateaubriand, le Sainte-Beuve de 'Port-Royal', Auguste Comte, Barbey d'Aurevilly, Barrès, Maurras, Péguy, Montherlant. Le catholicisme du dehors (que le catholicisme tout court a l'air de vouloir mettre en effet dehors) dans sa masse et ses incidents, est assez particulièrement français. Les étrangers le comprennent mal, s'indignent ou se moquent. Le clergé, après s'en être aidé, s'efforce de

[1] J. Calvet, *Le Renouveau catholique dans la littérature contemporaine*, 1927.

couper les liens avec lui. Il y aurait là un curieux sujet d'enquête."[1]

The religious psychology of France is indeed far more varied than the massive contrast between the two points of view would allow one to guess. In the old French bourgeoisie there exists a good deal of religious indifference combined with the external maintenance of tradition. A Liberal like Thiers could say: "Certes, je ne suis pas bigot, à peine religieux, mais je tiens, comme Français, à mon étiquette catholique, et je suis passionnément déiste."[2] And the conservative historian, Fustel de Coulanges, has explicitly stated his position thus: "Je désire un service conforme à l'usage des Français, c'est-à-dire un service à l'église. Je ne suis, à la vérité, ni pratiquant, ni croyant; mais je dois me souvenir que je suis né dans la religion catholique, et que ceux qui m'ont précédé dans la vie étaient aussi catholiques. Le patriotisme exige que si l'on ne pense pas comme les ancêtres, on respecte au moins ce qu'ils ont pensé."[3]

It would only be possible to express an opinion upon the religious psychology of the rural and industrial population in France on the basis of an extensive survey. Large masses of these classes, particularly in the South, have, indeed, fallen away from the Church. They have relapsed into a paganism which is not anti-Christian, but is rather outside it altogether, or pre-Christian. Those who wish to know about the obscure religious practices which are still carried on in remote peasant communities in the south of France should read Jean Giono.[4] So far as the psychology of the "faithful" in rural districts is concerned, or at least of "practising" Catholics, the statement of a country priest who was doing political work for the *Action française* may

[1] *Nouvelle Revue française*, January 1927, p. 108 ff.
[2] Juliette Adam, *Mes Sentiments et nos idées avant 1870* (1905) ; p. 322.
[3] E. Champion, *Les Idées politiques et religieuses de Fustel de Coulanges* (1903), p. 26.
[4] *La Colline*, 1928.

be taken as fairly near the truth: "Les Français," said M. Appert, "sont bons catholiques et mauvais chrétiens."[1]

In the intellectual life of Catholicism as a whole France occupies to-day the leading position. The works of the poets, philosophers and historians of Catholic France are also translated into German, and give rise to much discussion; German Catholics receive a great deal of intellectual stimulus from these French writers. Particularly in the Catholic Rhineland there is a great deal of understanding for, and interest in, the Roman spirit in Latin form, although the Nationalistic attitude of French Catholicism is definitely rejected.

To assert that France might rediscover her intellectual unity in the Catholic Faith would seem to be too audacious a suggestion. There is as much conflict as ever between the different points of view.[2] Two points, however, are clear: Catholicism in France has an unbroken vital power, and, all the religious energies of France are absorbed by Catholicism.

How often, since the revolution, has the decline of Catholicism been prophesied. Again and again it has arisen from the dust and has gained new life. This has not only disappointed its political opponents, but it has also given the lie to those philosophers and historians who expected that the progress of scientific criticism would cause the destruction of faith and dogma. A spiritual idealist like Jouffroy thought that he had proved, in his famous work of 1833, *comment les dogmes finissent*. The generations whose intellectual outlook was shaped by Taine and Renan believed that they were watching by the death-bed of Christianity. Many gloated with melancholy ecstasy over the purple twilight mood of this great act of dying. No one feels like this to-day. The conflict between religion and science,

[1] Dimier, *Vingt ans d'Action française* (1926), p. 97. The whole passage, however, should be read.
[2] Cf. the collection of testimonies to *La Renaissance religieuse*, published by Georges Guy-Grand in 1928.

which used to cause so much unrest, has ceased to be a problem. No longer are the faithful bewildered by the Biblical criticism of a man like Loisy. All forms of Catholic piety flourish in contemporary France. One need only visit one of the numerous places of pilgrimage and read the inscriptions on the votive offerings which thank the Saints for all kinds of "favours" (frequently for success in examinations), or study the specialized functions of the Saints (Saint Christopher protects those who travel by motor, and the *exposés sportifs*, Saint Expédit is *médiateur des procès* and *notre secours dans les affaires pressantes*), in order to gain a vivid impression of the naïve and practical piety which flourishes in many circles. The cult of the Saints constantly produces new devotions and new industries, of which the most recent, and the one which exercises the greatest attraction, is that of Sœur Thérèse de l'Enfant Jésus at Lisieux. Since the war her cult has spread throughout the Catholic world; it inspired Thérèse Neumann at Konnersreuth, and it has brought streams of money into the Carmel of Lisieux.

The sublimest mysticism is also represented in modern France. The *Journal Spirituel* of Lucie Christine[1] (1874–1908), the life of Madeleine Sémer[2] (1874–1921) are documents of a *vita spiritualis* with which it would be difficult to find anything to compare in the whole range of the life of the modern world.

Catholicism has made such a deep impression upon the soul of France that in many instances it survives loss of faith. The freethinker movement in France has its own orthodoxy, combined with the spirit of an order, a moral rigourism, and an almost monastic hostility to the world, which remind us of the Church. It is only in France that we find the phenomenon of "Catholic Atheism"; in France alone are there materialists like Jules Soury, who read the Liturgical Office, or romantic Nihilists like Barrès, who make

[1] Paris: Communauté de l'Adoration Réparatrice.
[2] Published by Abbé Félix Klein, Paris, Bloud et Gay, 1923. See also *Hochland*, March 1928, article by Guardini.

the pilgrimage to Lourdes. In France, when anyone tries to establish a new religion it is always expressed in the forms of Catholicism: the outstanding example of this statement is Auguste Comte's "religion of humanity". In France there is less diffused religiosity than in Germany, but it is clear that there is no less religion. The difference in religious experience lies in this, that in France the needs of the spirit are subordinated to the striving for order and fellowship, for a clearly defined form and for a settled standard.

It looks as though the period of controversy between Church and State were over, and as though a certain contentment had taken possession of the minds of men. The common experience of warfare has also had an equalizing influence in this respect, and has drawn the various "spiritual families" in France nearer to each other.[1] Many members of the French clergy who served in the foremost line at the Front gave heroic examples of fidelity to duty. It is well known that Marshal Foch was a strict Catholic. When Briand once went to visit him at Headquarters he found that, as was his daily custom, he was at Mass. The statesman of the secular Republic said that he was not to be disturbed, for, said he, "ça lui a trop bien réussi".

In the Catholic camp there are, it is true, those who would press for a revision of the law of Separation of Church and State. But most Catholic politicians would not ask for more than for individual modifications, and—this is the chief point—for freedom of education under the supervision of the State. The idea of overturning the present system is scarcely seriously entertained. If a leader were to adopt this position he would have to incur the odium of being regarded as a disturber of the peace, and he would meet with very strong opposition. The opposition between Catholic and "secular" France—apart from the extremists in both parties—has adjusted itself, so that France is no longer anti-clerical, though it is deeply laïque.

[1] Maurice Barrès, Les Diverses Familles spirituelles de la France, 1917.

The separation of Church and State has had a good effect on the religious forces of the country. It has spiritualized the religious ideal and made it more heroic. To the clergy it has brought an increase of moral energy and authority.

The situation in Alsace is menacing, it is true. The chief cause of the *malaise alsacien* is the fact that the majority of the inhabitants of Alsace possess a French political consciousness and a German race consciousness; the French cannot understand this, and the Germans can scarcely understand it either. To this we must add the fact that Alsace is peculiar from the religious point of view: whether Protestant or Catholic it stands out for the Concordat, the confessional elementary school, freedom to give religious instruction in the German tongue; it would regard the application of the *laïque* legislation as a menace to its most sacred possessions.[1] It remains to be seen whether French politicians will succeed in finding a solution which will satisfy the centralization policy of the Republic and the desires of Alsace, and will avoid a renewal of the conflict between Church and State.

[1] Cf. Georges Roux, *Divorce de l'Alsace?* Paris, 1929.

# VI

## THE EDUCATIONAL SYSTEM

IN order to understand the character and growth of the French system of education it is best to begin with the French University and the history of its development.

University education in France has a long and venerable tradition. In the Middle Ages the idea was widespread that *studium* was the privilege of France, just as the *imperium* was the privilege of Germany, and the *sacerdotium* of Rome. From the twelfth century the Paris University was the centre for the study of theology and philosophy for the whole of Christendom. Many German scholars studied there. They were united in the *nation d'Allemagne*, the *constantissima Germanorum natio*, which, with the three other "nations"—France, Picardy, Normandy—formed the corporation of the students of Paris. The poetry of the wandering scholars of the Middle Ages, of which our *Gaudeamus igitur* is a final echo, preserves the remembrance of these conditions. What a German student of those days hoped to find in France is expressed in this farewell song addressed to his student friends in the homeland:

> Hospita in Gallia nunc me vocant studia:
> Vadam ergo: flens a tergo socios relinquo.
> Plangite, discipuli, lugubris discidii[1] tempore propinquo.
> . . . . . . . . . .
> Vale, dulcis patria! suavis Suevorum Suevia!
> Salve, dilecta Francia, philosophorum curia!
> Suscipe discipulum in te peregrinum,
> Quem post dierum circulum remittes Socratinum.

The following Germans may be cited as instances of teachers or scholars who spent some time at the ancient University of Paris: Albert the Great, Otto von Freising, Conrad von Gelnhausen (the first Chancellor of the University of Heidelberg), Johannes Tauler, Agrippa von Nettesheim, Geiler von Kaysersberg, Reuchlin and Fischart.

---

[1] *Discidium* = farewell.

During the Renaissance the ancient glory of the Sorbonne became dim. The Sorbonne was hostile to the Humanist movement because it regarded it as an ally of Lutheranism. Petrus Ramus attempted to introduce a reform into the antiquated system of study. He failed, was forced to flee to Heidelberg, and then, having returned to Paris, at the suggestion of a reactionary colleague, he was murdered during the massacre of St. Bartholomew. Henry IV. succeeded in securing some amount of reform, but this did not prevent the Jesuits from competing successfully in their institutions with the University, which lessened the prestige of the latter.

The Sorbonne and the other old universities were bodies with four faculties: Theology, Law, Medicine, Arts. There were, however, universities with three, two, or even with only one faculty. In addition the *Collège Royal* (to-day *Collège de France*), with nineteen "lectors", fulfilled the functions of a college of university standing. At the close of the *Ancien Régime* the only faculty in the University of Paris which retained any life was the Arts faculty; this was due to the fact that this faculty alone had retained the collegiate constitution of the Middle Ages. It included sixteen *Collèges*, which were resident institutions, possessed their own teachers, and received boys as pupils from their ninth year. In the one institution the boys passed through their public school and university course. The Arts faculty formed the common preparation for the other faculties. It imparted that formal Humanistic culture which still forms the basis of French culture, with its unity of style, and its literary tradition.

The faculties were only connected by their privileges, and by the fact that they were under a common administration. There was no inward vital unity of a scientific or broadly intellectual kind. How, indeed, could one expect it? The German universities progressed under the influence of Humanism, Protestantism and the Enlightenment, but the French universities were almost untouched by these three forces. It is, of course, true, that the Enlightenment attained a more brilliant and vigorous development in France than in Germany, but this took place entirely outside the universities in literature and independent philosophy. The study of Descartes only entered into the universities of France in the year 1760. It is a paradox of history that, as we shall see shortly, during the nineteenth century the rationalism of the Enlightenment finally became the dominating element in the university life of France.

In the faculty of Arts the main subject of study was Latin, interpreted in the sense of ancient and medieval rhetoric. Verbal and written facility in Latin, as well as the composition of Latin verse, was the aim which was attained. *Rhétorique* and *Philosophie* both formed the highest stages in the system of instruction. Until far into the nineteenth century they remained the usual subjects studied in the lower and upper classes. In *Philosophie* a Latin Compendium of Logic, Metaphysics and Ethics (written by hand) was dictated by the professor to the scholars. In addition to rhetoric and philosophy there were mathematics and physics. Greek and French were little studied, and history and geography practically not at all. This system of education filled the mind with an abstract empty scholasticism. It formed the men who made the Revolution.

One exception ought to be noted: the University of Strassburg. Even under the rule of France its spirit and its life were that of a German university. At Strassburg the Arts Faculty was called the faculty of philosophy. The lectures dealt with all kinds of subjects of intellectual interest, as well as with natural science. The peculiar features of this university come out very clearly in a memorial presented by the Strassburg professors to the directorate in Paris. In it they say:

"La réunion de plusieurs nations et particulièrement de celles du Nord dans cette Université, y rendait l'enseignement dans les trois langues: latine, française et allemande, indispensable. Tous les professeurs devaient donc être au fait de ces trois langues. . . . Ce concours d'étrangers de différentes nations mettait également les professeurs dans la nécessité de se familiariser avec la littérature étrangère, de saisir toutes les nouvelles découvertes, et de tenir ainsi comme une marche égale avec le progrès des connaissances dont l'enseignement leur était confié. Ils s'y trouvaient d'ailleurs encouragés par cette parfaite liberté d'opinions qu'ils puisaient dans les principes mêmes du protestantisme. . . . Les dissertations imprimées et soutenues dans cette université ne ressemblaient nullement à ces thèses insignifiantes qu'on a vu paraître dans d'autres Universités."[1] Until the year 1870 the University of Strassburg held a unique position in the university life of France.

The decline of the French universities also became evident in the practice of bartering diplomas which crept in during the seventeenth century. All university degrees could be obtained for money. The expulsion of the Jesuits in 1762 might have served as an occasion for introducing reforms. The universities themselves, however, felt no need for reform at all, and they only reflected, on a smaller scale, the public opinion of the day.

It is, therefore, not at all surprising that the Revolution, which on principle could not tolerate any independent corporations in the State, abolished the universities. They regarded them as obsolete institutions.

The question then was: What should be put in their place? The French university system of the nineteenth century grew out of the intellectual movement of the Revolution. It betrays this origin even at the present time. The German universities also received their present tendencies from the intellectual forces which were operative at the beginning of the nineteenth century, to them also that period signified a distinct break in their history. But among us these forces took the form of political Liberalism and

[1] L. Liard, *Histoire de l'enseignement supérieur en France* (1888–94), i. 64.

idealistic philosophy. In France they took the form of the ideal of the centrality of the State and the positivist ideal of science. The contrast between these historical factors explains the great differences which exist between the universities of France and of Germany.

Revolutionary France recognized the urgent necessity of creating a new educational system. The leaders felt that education should be national in character, that it ought to be taken in hand by the State, which should see to it that the nation as a whole should be instructed in all positive knowledge; and, finally, it should be free. In their essence these leading ideas still hold good in the French system of education. Before we follow the course of their historical development any further let us examine their significance.

The idea that the State should claim the monopoly of education is a logical deduction from the principles of the Revolution. All the educational institutions were placed under one branch of the administration of the State, the elementary school (*enseignement primaire*), the secondary school (*enseignement secondaire*) and the universities (*enseignement supérieur*). This means that the medieval idea of the corporation had been renounced. Henceforth the aim of the whole system of education is to form citizens who will be loyal to the State. Hence in theoretical questions also it can receive direction from the State. When the civil authorities are in sympathy with the Church in these questions (as was the case under the second Empire), the clergy will have the upper hand. Under the Republic the educational system will be controlled by a rationalistic ideal of life, hostile to religion: the spirit of *laïcisme*, which will be discussed later.

Under the government of the Revolution practically nothing permanent was achieved for the renewal of the educational system. The debates on educational theory, however, which went on for years, were fruitful, and exercised a lasting influence. Opposing tendencies were in conflict with each other. Among the Girondins, and in the party of extremists known as "the Mountain", there were many adherents to the philosophy of the Enlightenment, who, faithful to the spirit of the *Encyclopaedia*, considered that the cultivation of the spirit of free research should be an honourable task of the Revolution. But alongside of them there was a strong party which regarded philosophy and science with suspicion. To some they were suspect as a source of atheism; others feared them as a danger to the ideal of equality, and a possible point of departure for the growth of a new aristocracy of culture. Thoroughgoing revolutionaries declared that it was not scholars who were needed but free men; that freedom is not the fruit of the arts and sciences: "Les sans-culottes ne sont pas des savants, et les savants ne sont pas des républicains". Instinctively those who were fanatics for equality scented hostility in science, art and intellect. A provisional reorganization was decreed by the Resolution of the Convention passed on the 15th of September 1793; the universities were abolished, and their place was to be taken by *lycées* and *instituts*.

In the course of the debates which had gone on for years, two leading conceptions of the ideal of the essence of a university had emerged: the universal and the specialist. It was felt one could envisage a university as a place where the system of education would be as wide and universal as the whole range of human knowledge—or as a place where each institution of university standing concentrates on some special task and sphere of knowledge. Both conceptions have been realized in France. Even to-day this two-fold idea is revealed by the fact that there exist side by side, on the one hand, the universities, and on the other, the so-called *grandes écoles*. Particularly at the outset, it was easier to establish schools for special purposes. Thus the Convention turned the former *Jardin du Roi* into a College for the study of natural science, which was named *Muséum d'Histoire naturelle* (1793). In addition it created: the *École Centrale des Travaux publics* (1794), which under the name of the *École polytechnique* soon became famous;

the *Conservatoire des Arts et Métiers* (1794); and, finally, the "Normal School" in Paris, which was intended to be a Training College for teachers; after four months, however, it was closed, because it was badly attended and its results were disappointing; at a later date it became a very important part of the French educational system. But all these establishments lacked cohesion and a synthetic organization. They did not yet meet the need for a systematic development of the national system of education, which was so often demanded.

An attempt was made to achieve this by setting up the *Institut National*, which was put in the place of the old Academies of the Monarchy, and was meant to represent the living unity of knowledge. On the 8th of August 1793 the Academies had been abolished, not out of hostility towards science, but on political grounds. Public opinion viewed them with suspicion as "schools of deceit and servility", as Mirabeau had described them in 1789. The *Institut National* was intended to replace them, and, like the other institutions of the new State, it formed an integral part of the republican constitution. Originally it was planned to be a teaching body and a universal university —Talleyrand and Condorcet had planned schemes which had this in view; ultimately, however, it became a Research Institute without a teaching staff.

With the Consulate came the reaction against the spirit of the Revolution. Everything was removed from the curriculum which bore any resemblance to the ideas of the Encyclopaedists. Formal rhetorical humanism again became the central element in the educational system. In each *Lycée* there were a certain number of free places which belonged to the Government. Twenty-nine "special schools" for higher education were scattered throughout France. The idea of the university with a universal aim was given up. Under Napoleon the centralization of education under the State was rigidly carried out. It reached its zenith in the *Université impériale* (1808). With this imperial institution all the plans and arrangements of the Revolution came to a head, even though not to a full development. Freedom of thought and of research were sacrificed to the supreme power of the State.

The Emperor was not satisfied with organizing the educational system as a branch of the administration; he made it into a hierarchical corporation, which was to obey a unified ideal prescribed by the State, endowed with its own property and financial privileges. He regarded the system of education as a moral support of the *régime*. His view is characteristically expressed in these words: "Il n'y a pas d'état politique fixe, s'il n'y a pas un corps enseignant avec des principes fixes. Tant qu'on n'apprendra pas dans l'enfance s'il faut être républicain ou monarchique, catholique ou irreligieux etc., l'État ne formera pas une nation: il reposera sur des bases incertaines ou vagues; il sera constamment exposé aux désordres et aux changements."

It was impossible to realize Napoleon's ideal in full. His university had to be constructed out of the institutions which were already there. But even though the *Université impériale* did not fulfil all the hopes of its founder, and although after an existence of forty years it had to make way for fresh educational schemes, still, essential elements of its spirit and of its administration have lasted down to the present day, and we can only understand the present *Université de France* if we understand the organization of the Napoleonic University.

The Law of the 10th of May 1806 defined the "Imperial University" as "un corps chargé exclusivement de l'enseignement et de l'éducation publique dans tout l'Empire". This means: the Napoleonic University included in the form of a corporate body the educational administration and also the teaching bodies of the colleges and universities throughout France as a whole. Every teacher or professor appointed by the State is a member of the *Université Impériale*. Their chief is at the same time Minister for

Education. The organization of the university was settled by a decree of the 17th of March 1808.

It was organized in administrative districts, which coincided with those of the judicial courts of appeal, and were called *Académies*. They were administered by the "recteurs d'académies". The public educational institutions were under the supervision of the "rectors", who were also responsible for the supervision of private institutions.

The public institutions were divided into *collèges communaux*, *lycées* and *facultés*. There were faculties of law, medicine, natural science, letters (*faculté des Lettres*—we would say, philosophical faculty), and theology. Yet they were not to be found in equal numbers everywhere. Further, even in the same town the different faculties were not combined to form a whole. They were united only by their common subordination to the central authority. For this reason alone they can scarcely be regarded as Universities. In Paris a *Pensionnat normal* was established, in which three hundred pupils were trained to be teachers in Middle Schools: the present *École Normale Supérieure* grew out of this institution. We cannot compare the faculties of the Imperial University with those of the medieval or modern universities. They scarcely rose above the level of Middle Schools, were badly endowed and the teaching staff was insufficient. Very often professors at the *Lycées* were also teachers in the Faculties. The great number of these can only be explained by the fact that they could confer the degrees which the State required from its officials. The Faculties had deteriorated into Examining Boards. The Napoleonic University perpetuated the old empty ideal of education. It had no vital intellectual and scientific impulse.

At the Restoration, after an initial period of hesitation, nothing essential was altered in the structure of the Imperial University. Here also the Government desired to have this instrument in its hands, in order that, in case of need, it could be used to increase the influence of the

Church. Each Bishop received the right to supervise the institutions of higher education in his diocese. In spite of this, however, the Paris University developed an important activity at that period. The youth of France was drawn into the current of a fruitful intellectual movement. Romanticism created a new poetry and a new school of painting; philosophy, history, criticism, revealed new points of view and opened up new spheres of study and knowledge. This movement would not allow itself to be permanently thwarted by the forces of political reaction. Cousin, the philosopher, and Guizot, the historian, were suspended for a time, it is true; eventually, however, they were restored to their posts, and along with the critic Villemain they formed an intellectual triumvirate which exercised a strong influence, both in politics and in other spheres, upon the life of the younger generation.

Under the July Monarchy the University rejoiced in a period of undisturbed development. The majority of the provincial faculties, however, led a wretched existence. But it was otherwise in Paris. Although the fame of the Sorbonne was somewhat dimmed, owing to the fact that Guizot, Cousin and Villemain had left the University for Parliament, the attraction exercised by the *Collège de France* was all the stronger, since it was there that Michelet, Quinet and Mickiewicz gave vent with fiery passion to their prophetic and rather Utopian ideas.

The February Revolution was hailed with enthusiasm by several representatives of the University. But after the events of July a reaction set in. The *bourgeoisie*, the Church and the Government were united in the endeavour to fight against the "anti-social forces" of proletarianism and Socialism. The Minister of Education, Count Falloux, was an ardent Catholic. But even Liberals like Cousin demanded a close association between the university and the clergy. Thiers declared that *démagogie* was an enemy, and made this statement: "La société vaut bien l'Université." It was under these circumstances that the "Loi Falloux" was passed in 1850. By this law the Napoleonic University was abolished: even the word *université* was effaced. A wealth of new privileges were created for the *enseignement libre*, that is, for the educational institutions of the Church and of the Religious Orders. The Empire, however, went even further. A Decree proposed by Fortoul, the Minister of Education, in 1852 proclaimed that all professors and teachers could be immediately dismissed. Guizot, Cousin, Michelet, Quinet, Mickiewicz, Jules Simon were the first victims of this decree. The absolutism of the Empire had made an alliance with the ecclesiastical idea of authority. Under such conditions scientific life could not prosper. Taine's Letters (written in his youth) give a vivid, though rather dark, picture of the academic situation at that time.

After the defeat of 1870 the reform of the educational system was regarded as an important element in the work of national reconstruction. The Third Republic believed that the spirit of positive science was its most valuable support, and in free research, and in reason, it envisaged the form of human idealism which suited it best. The universalist ideal of Higher Education was revived once more, aided by the example of the German universities. Slowly and deliberately the Republic carried through the reform of the Universities. First of all, the indispensable external equipment was either provided or renewed. A large number of new buildings and institutes were erected, and several new professional Chairs were instituted. Finally, by the law of the 10th of July 1896, the faculties were again formed into coherent independent bodies which received the ancient name of "universities".

Since that time the word *université* has possessed a double significance in France. The *Université de France* or *l'Université* still means the whole teaching staff appointed by the State ("corps enseignant choisi par l'État et chargé de donner en son nom l'enseignement primaire, secondaire, et supérieur"). In addition, the institutions of Higher Education under the State which are distinct and independent and are composed of Faculties, are called Universities. There are seventeen of them, corresponding to the division of the country into seventeen state educational districts (*académies*). These are: Paris, Aix, Algiers, Besançon, Bordeaux, Caen, Clermont-Ferrand, Dijon, Grenoble, Lille, Lyon, Montpellier, Nancy, Poitiers, Rennes, Strassburg, Toulouse. Each university is governed by a University Council whose president is the Rector. The Rector, however, is nominated by the Government, and he represents the State in the University. The number of Faculties oscillates between two and five. Strassburg is the only university which, as the heir of the German epoch, has a theological faculty. The teaching body includes the following categories: *professeurs titulaires, professeurs sans chaire, chargés de cours*, and *maîtres de conférences*. The professors must possess the degree of Doctor. They are proposed by the Faculty, and appointed after being examined by the "section permanente du Conseil supérieur de l'Instruction publique". The *Chargés de cours* and *Maîtres de conférences* are nominated by the Minister, according to a list drawn up by the *Comité consultatif de l'Enseignement supérieur. Habilitations*,[1] therefore, in our sense of the word, do not exist. Public lectures (*cours publics*) are open to all, without ticket and without charge. The *cours réservés*, and *exercices pratiques* are intended especially for students. The University year begins on the 1st of November and closes at the end of June. At Christmas there is a holiday of one week, and there is a fortnight's break at Easter. The academic degrees are divided into more grades, and are more rigidly defined than with us.

As a result of the political policy of centralization, which determines the whole educational system of France, the universities are far less independent than they are in Germany. They form an integral part of the administrative

[1] *I.e.* the formal admission of an academical lecturer into his faculty.—*Translator.*

system of *académies*. At the head of each academy there is a *recteur d'académie* with extensive powers. He is usually chosen from the teaching body of the universities, and proposed by the Minister for Education. He supervises the elementary, secondary and university education in his district. Every year he has to give a written report about every individual who is engaged in teaching under him. He sees that the curriculum is carried out. All time-tables, even those of the Faculties, must be approved by him.

In order to escape the dangers of this schematization the universities have been granted the right to manage their own finances. They are allowed to accept endowments. Thus, for instance, at the Sorbonne there is a Chair endowed by the City of Paris for the History of the French Revolution. In the Provinces also professorial Chairs have been set up in this way: in Bordeaux for Gascon; in Toulouse for Provençal and Spanish; in Nancy for the History of Eastern France. In this way it has become possible for the universities to make regional distinctions. This development is still going on.

None of the provincial universities can in any way compare in importance with Paris. The official description of the Paris University is *Université de Paris*, but the popular name, which is universally used, is *La Sorbonne*. Originally the two names did not coincide. The Sorbonne is younger than the University. It was founded by Robert de Sorbon (1201–74) the confessor of St. Louis, and for many centuries it was a *Collège* for theology. Gradually, however, the name *Sorbonne* came to be applied to the whole theological faculty at the University of Paris, and from the sixteenth century it has been applied to the University of Paris as a whole; this was due to the fact that in consequence of the decline of the other faculties the theological faculty and the university came to mean the same thing. In 1627 Richelieu replaced the old Sorbonne by a new building. This was inadequate for modern requirements, and it again had to make way for a new building which was put up by

Nénot in the official style of the Republic in the period between 1885 and 1901. To-day all that remains of Richelieu's building is the Church.

To-day, accordingly, the word Sorbonne is used in two meanings: on the one hand it covers the University of Paris as a whole; in the narrower sense, however, it is also used to describe the group of buildings which has just been mentioned. The Sorbonne as a building houses the administration of the university and two faculties: the philosophical faculty (*faculté des lettres*) and that of natural science (*faculté des Sciences*). The other faculties and institutes of the Paris University occupy other buildings outside the Sorbonne itself. Beside the faculties already mentioned, the Sorbonne includes the *Faculté du Droit*, the *Faculté des Lettres*, the *École Supérieure de Pharmacie*, and the *École Normale Supérieure*.

At the present time the total number of lecturers at the Paris University is more than 350; there are about 26,000 students, of whom 7000 are foreigners. (These are the statistics for 1927.)

The French system of Higher Education differs from that of Germany most of all in its examination system. In France examinations are more frequent and more difficult than in Germany. By means of a complicated system of reckoning by marks, the achievements of the candidates are reduced to a common denominator. As a rule, only a small percentage of the candidates are successful. The reason why the examinations are made so difficult is that a successful candidate has the right to a settled post under the State. Therefore every time there is an examination only so many candidates can pass as there are vacant positions for them. The number of vacancies in each faculty is communicated every year to the authorities. Examinations of this kind—with restricted admission—are called *concours*. The *agrégation* is a *concours*, but the doctorate is not.

When a person wishes to be appointed to an institution of Higher Education he must first of all gain his *Licence d'enseignement*, and later the final examination of the *Agréga-tion*, by which he receives the degree of *agrégé de l'Université*. The requirements are very high, and they are highly specialized. The examination takes place once a year. Each year the programme is made known in advance.[1]

[1] The programme of the *Agrégation d'Allemand* for 1924 will serve as an illustration:

### I. HISTOIRE DE LA CIVILISATION

(i)  La légende de Tristan en Allemagne au moyen âge.

*Texte*: Gottfried von Strassburg, Tristan und Isolde, chants 16, 17 et 27. Tous les candidats auront à traduire un passage de texte et à en faire le commentaire linguistique.

(ii)  Le rationalisme religieux, philosophique et moral dans la se-conde moitié du xviiie siècle.

*Textes*: Lessing, Gedanken über die Herrnhuter, Ernst und Falk, Die Erziehung des Menschengeschlechts; Lich-tenberg: Bemerkungen vermischten Inhalts. I. Philoso-phische Bemerkungen.

(iii)  Le relèvement de la Prusse après Iéna.

(*a*)  Les instigateurs du mouvement et leurs idées directrices.
(*b*)  Les réformes sociales, politiques, administratives, mili-taires et pédagogiques.

*Texte*: Fichte, Reden an die deutsche Nation, discours 4 à 8.

### II. HISTOIRE DE LA LITTÉRATURE

(iv)  Wilhelm Meister et le roman éducatif à la fin du xviiie siècle.

*Textes*: Wieland, Agathon, livre 16. Goethe, Wilhelm Meisters Lehrjahre, livres 6 et 8. Hölderlin, Hyperion, livre 4. Friedrich Schlegel, Lucinde, Lehrjahre der Männlich-keit. Novalis, Heinrich von Ofterdingen, Ire partie, chapitres 5 à 8.

(v)  Le théâtre de Hebbel et Otto Ludwig.

*Textes*: Hebbel, Mein Wort über das Drama; Maria Mag-dalena, actes 2 et 3; Gyges und sein Ring, actes 1, 4 et 5. Otto Ludwig, Der Erbförster, actes 1 et 5; Die Makkabäer, 1, 4 et 5.

(vi)  La poésie lyrique de 1890 à 1910.

*Textes*: Dehmel, Hundert ausgewählte Gedichte (S. Fischer Verlag, Berlin); An mein Volk, Bastard, Heimweh in die Welt, Bergpsalm, Der Arbeitsmann, Predigt an das

Examination programmes of this kind, of course, do not leave any scope for the intellectual individuality of the candidate. They must inevitably produce a specialistic conception of science.

The following statement gives some idea of the way in which the examinations are carried on.

In 1928, for the *Concours de l'agrégation d'histoire et de géographie* ninety-nine candidates entered for the examination, of whom seven were women. Only fifty-five of the candidates were students; the rest were already teachers, that is, they were persons who had already applied for permission to sit for the examination, and had been kept back. Of the ninety-nine candidates, first of all fifty-eight were excluded after a preliminary examination; the forty-one who remained were pronounced *sous-admissibles*. Their achievements were tabulated on the basis of a scheme of 40 marks; the best gained 30, the worst 18½ marks. In the course of the oral examination a further twelve were rejected. Of the twenty-nine who remained as *admissibles* twenty were "proposed for the title of *agrégé*". Among these the highest marks were 75 (gained by two persons), the lowest 49¼, and the highest of those who were not finally successful had 48.

Thus twenty out of ninety-nine were successful, or 20 per cent. This result was described as highly satisfactory. It was the best since 1919.[1]

The system of reckoning achievements by marks, even

Grossstadtvolk, Ein Heine-Denkmal, Die Harfe, Mein Trinklied. Hofmannstal, Der Tor und der Tod. Rainer Maria Rilke, Das Stundenbuch (Inselverlag, Leipzig). Drittes Buch; das Buch von der Armut und von dem Tode, depuis p. 89 Das letzte Zeichen lass an uns geschehen, jusqu'à la fin. Stefan George, Der siebente Ring (George Bondi, Berlin); Das Zeitgedicht, Goethe-Tag, Nietzsche, Böcklin, Porta Nigra, Franken, Die Gräber in Speier, Die Hüter des Vorhofs, Landschaft I, II und III, Der verwunschene Garten.

[1] According to the official report of Ch. Diehl in the *Revue Universitaire* (May 1929).

to the half and the quarter of a mark[1] (there are examinations for higher posts in the administration in which the reckoning is on a basis of 300 marks), represents a mechanical system which the French consider the natural and logical result of democracy. Its aim is to secure entire impartiality. This system of calculation makes it necessary to have an examination programme which is fixed to the very last detail, which breaks up the educational material into small sections. It means that all start equal. If we wish to read a criticism of this system we can turn to the pages of Renan.[2]

The development of the university system, and of the examination system which is connected with it, is not only the expression of French ideas of research and education; it is not only the final form of a long historico-political development; it is also of the highest importance for the understanding of French society, and of the methods by which it maintains its equilibrium. Not only through economic competition but also by way of academic selection the Frenchman can find his way into that class of society which is described as the *bourgeoisie* or the *classe moyenne*, which is the stabilizing force in the body corporate. When a man has acquired a "higher" or university education he becomes *bourgeois*. It is the ambition of the "lower" classes, of the manual labourer, the peasant, or the workman, to make his son a *Monsieur*. This is almost always possible if the boy is gifted in any direction. He can procure a free place in a *lycée*. If he is industrious he will leave the *lycée* as one of its most promising scholars, and he can offer himself as a candidate for the entrance examination to one of the higher special schools, and, if he is suc-

[1] Even the most vigorous method of marking does not entirely exclude the subjective factor. The same performance which one examiner will judge worthy of 10, will be estimated at 9 or 11 by another. Hence recently there has been a demand for a scientific method of reckoning marks! (*docimologie*). See the *Revue Universitaire* (June 1929), p. 65.

[2] *Questions contemporaines* 268.

cessful, he can then enjoy the privilege of an excellent scientific education at the cost of the State. If, again, he is successful in his final examination he can certainly count on a post as mining engineer, or professor at a *lycée*, or in some branch of the administration of the State. Through this mechanical system of free places, examinations and *concours*, he can rise out of the proletariat into the *bourgeoisie*. In the so-called *grandes écoles* the majority of the pupils come either from the "lower middle class", or from the "people". Thus, thanks to the educational laws and the scholarship system, in the Third Republic an ever larger percentage of the nation rises from the lower into the higher classes.

This applies in particular to the school and university course. Unlike Germany, both are closely connected; normally the university professors are drawn from the world of higher education. Those who belong to the *enseignement* are almost entirely drawn from the ranks of the *boursiers*, that is, of sons of poor families, who have prosecuted their studies at the expense of the State. Hence, as a whole, these professions represent a select body of "new men": an educated class which has risen from the ranks of the "people", whose roots are in the people; who, on the other hand, are closely bound to the democratic, political rationalistic ideology of the State, to which they owe their intellectual and social rise in the world.

The sons of well-to-do parents usually choose the professions of Law or Medicine. Contrasted with the *boursier* they represent another class: that of the *héritier*. Albert Thibaudet has shown very forcibly how this contrast works out in French sociology.[1] In the Republic, from the intellectual and political point of view, the *boursiers* represent the Left, while the *héritiers* are overwhelmingly conservative, or radicals of the Right: thus in the *milieu* provided by the Paris Faculties of Law and Medicine the agitation of the *Action Française* finds fruitful soil. The advantage of the

[1] Albert Thibaudet, *La République des Professeurs* (1927).

system of scholarships is that it opens "a free course to the virtuous"; its disadvantage is that official posts in the State are often filled by men whose strong points are simply memory, industry and ambition; such men often take positions away from those who are really gifted and creative, but whose talents do not enable them to shine in examinations. In France itself there is much controversy about the value of this system. But whatever may be one's views, the fact remains, that the French schools and universities do represent a social factor of selection. This corresponds to the rational feature in the French way of thinking: since the State requires the "best", and must have them in its service, and since the competition among these "best", in accordance with the requirements of the republican idea, should be conducted on the basis of strict equality, the only possible method of selection is that of a chain of successive examinations. These examinations give to the existence of the French student a character of oppressive coercion, and doubtless they hinder the development of many fruitful ideas and powers which can only flourish in freedom. It is also clear that, to a considerable extent, they limit academic freedom of movement. The exactly prescribed course of study and examination makes it more difficult for the French than for the German student to spend a term abroad.

Alongside of the universities the *grandes écoles*, the special institutions of Higher Education, play an important part in the intellectual life and the political administration of France.

The *École Normale Supérieure* deserves special mention.[1] It is true that at the present day it has lost its independence, and that since 1903 from the administrative point of view it forms part of the Sorbonne, but it still possesses its own special unique character, so that one can speak of the *esprit normalien*. This institution was founded during the

[1] On this point, cf. the article by Henri Jourdan in the *Deutsch-französischen Rundschau* (1929), 720 ff.

period of the Revolution. Its aim was to prepare a whole generation of teachers. In its first form, however, it was unable to maintain its existence. But, as has already been mentioned, it was renewed in 1808. It had its own teaching body for intellectual and natural sciences, and its body of students was most select, since the entrance examination was made very difficult. This still holds good to-day. On the other hand, to-day the *Normaliens* take part in the instruction offered by the Sorbonne. In the political and intellectual history of modern France the *École Normale* has played, and still plays, a great part. Cousin, Taine, Lachelier, Bergson, Boutroux, Fustel de Coulanges, and Lavisse all studied at the *École Normale*; among its students, however, there are also the names of politicians like Jaurès, Herriot, Léon Blum and Painlevé, and of writers and critics like Jules Lemaître, Péguy, Jules Romains and Jean Giraudoux.

The *Collège de France* likewise occupies a unique position. It owes its inception to the desire of Francis I. to provide a home for the new spirit of the Renaissance, to which the Sorbonne with its rigid Scholasticism had refused a welcome. On the advice of the Humanist Guillaume Budé, in 1530 the king appointed five "royal lecturers", who taught Greek, Hebrew and mathematics. From these beginnings there developed the corporation which in the seventeenth century received the name of the *Collegium regium Galliarum*. At the end of the eighteenth century it had developed into an independent institution of Higher Education, which bore on its coat of arms the motto *omnia docet*. The *Collège de France* is one of the few institutions of the *Ancien Régime* which the Revolution has preserved. In the nineteenth century it entered upon a period of fresh prosperity. It offers a home to research, where it can follow its own path without let or hindrance, free from the hampering restrictions of examinations and timetables. To this extent it may be compared with the institutes of the Kaiser-Wilhelm-Gesellschaft. Both by history and by tradition, however, its interests are mainly in humanistic studies. If one professorial chair falls vacant it is possible, if necessary, to instal a professor of another subject. The decision on this question lies in the hands of the teaching body as a whole, with reference to the actual scientific needs of the moment, and of the available candidates. Thanks to this organization the *Collège de France* has been able to introduce new elements into French science (such as Egyptology by Champollion, Indian studies by Burnouf, Biblical Criticism by Renan, and also several forms of Natural Science). In contrast with the eloquent and dazzling achievements of scientific popularization, which, for a long time, characterized the French universities, the *Collège de France* has always valued the quiet patient labour of research, and has done all in its power to further it. The professors of the *Collège* give lectures, it is true, but there is no official regulation about this. Each professor decides for himself the number of hours which he intends to devote to teaching during the university year. At the present time the effectiveness of the activity of the *Collège* is greatly restricted owing to its insufficient endowment, and the totally inadequate equipment of its laboratories.

Among the *grandes écoles*, in addition to the *École Normale*, are also reckoned the *École Polytechnique*,[1] the *École Centrale*, the *École des Mines*, the *École des Sciences Politiques*, the Military Academy of *Saint-Cyr*, the *École Navale*, the *École Coloniale* and the *École des Hautes Études*.

Each of these institutions has a clearly marked character of its own; each has its own special language, its own traditions, and in some, its own uniform. There is a "spirit" of the *Polytechnique*, just as there is an *esprit normalien* and even a *style normalien*. The former students of a particular *École* remain in touch with each other when they have entered the practical world of professional life, and they

[1] For this see Susini, *Deutsch-französische Rundschau* 1929, 471 ff.

transmit the spirit of their "school" to politics and to economic life. After the elections of the 11th of May 1924 a French statesman said: "Voilà l'École de Droit et l'École des Sciences politiques qui cèdent la place à l'École Normale."[1]

The organization of the French system of Higher Education closely resembles a State monopoly of education. The law permits "free" institutions of higher education, it is true, and these institutions, according to the size of their teaching staff and their system of organization, can earn the right to call themselves *facultés libres*, but they may never call themselves "universities".

From 1875 Catholic institutions of this kind have existed at Lille, Angers, Toulouse, Lyons and Paris. At the time that they were founded their model was the University of Louvain. The results, however, have not been very encouraging. In the year 1909 the five Catholic institutions, all told, had only 2200 students upon their books. The importance of these universities lies less in their direct influence upon youth, and upon students, than in their literary and scientific influence upon the Catholic intelligentsia of France.

Even to-day, the spirit of higher education in France is still strongly determined by the literary-Humanist tradition, which has existed in France for hundreds of years. This tradition, in spite of great differences in professional work, has set its mark, intellectually, upon the leading people in the nation, and has given to this class a certain intellectual unity. In France quotations from Roman poets are in the mouth of politicians and industrial magnates, and in the journals of biological specialists as well as in leading articles in general papers. At the present day, however, the existence of this Humanist tradition has certainly reached a critical stage. Among young Conservative students, and in nationalist literature, the blame for this is thrown on the Sorbonne. During the last few years before

---

[1] Thibaudet, *La République des Professeurs*, p. 12.

M

the War a spirited wordy warfare raged round this question.[1] Péguy accused the Sorbonne of having betrayed the *humanités*, and said that she had become a "maîtresse d'erreur et de barbarie". This conflict is still going on at the present time.

Since, as we have already seen, in France the typical expression of the national intellectual life is not science but literature, the criticism of the Sorbonne is clothed in literary and journalistic form. "A Paris," says Thibaudet, "les grandes corporations de l'intelligence sont l'Académie, l'Institut, la littérature, le journalisme, le barreau: l'Université ne vient qu'à la suite, et à un rang secondaire."[2] The French universities represent an essential section of the intelligence of France, but it is still only a section.

We can only understand controversies of this kind from the point of view of the political and sociological structure of the intellectual life of France. Since the Sorbonne supports the secularist ideal of the Republic, and does so by research of a positivist character, it also encounters the opposition of the Conservatives, and of the counter-revolutionary forces. What, however, actually is this *laïcisme* which has already been mentioned several times? Before we discuss the French system of schools we must devote a short section of this book to this specifically French phenomenon.

The expression *Laïcisme* and *idée laïque* have no literal equivalent in German. They are derived from *laïque* (lay), but the sense in which these words are used differs from that which they bear in our own language. In *laïque* or *laïcisme* a spirit is implied which is opposed to the "Catholic Church"; this again is used in a double sense—both philosophically and politically. *Laïcisme* opposes dogma: this is the point of view of Reason; and it opposes the world

---

[1] Agathon, *L'Esprit de la nouvelle Sorbonne* (1911). Pierre Lasserre, *La Doctrine officielle de l'Université*. Rene Benjamin, *La Farce de la Sorbonne* (1911).

[2] *La République des Professeurs*, 123.

domination of the Church: this is the point of view of the State without religion. It thus combines the philosophical rationalism of the Enlightenment with the political autonomy of the modern State. This peculiar blend of ideas could only arise in France. It is the result of the Revolution.

Under the *Ancien Régime* the State was a confessional State; the Catholic religion was the State religion. Through the Revolution the French State became a secular State. This was a fundamental change. It was already announced in the Declaration of Rights. The Concordat of 1801 only seemed to set the clock back. Napoleon himself had said to the Protestants: "Je ne décide point entre Rome et Genève". This conception, according to which the State as such is absolutely neutral towards the religious creed of its citizens, corresponds to the spirit, if not to the letter, of the "organic articles". The idea of the State which dominates modern France, and has evolved out of the Revolution, is in principle independent of the Church and the churches: "La loi est athée," Odilon Barrot proclaimed to the Ultramontanes of the Restoration. The principle that all citizens are equal in the eyes of the law, is in itself possible to combine with a policy of Concordats, which may be a measure based upon the interests of public order, as a convention between independent powers. Purely logically, it could also lead to separation between Church and State, and inevitably it did lead to this as soon as political Radicalism had grown strong enough to seize the reins of power. In France, however, this Radicalism is always supported by a certain conviction: by the faith that human reason is sufficient unto itself; by the spirit of the anti-clerical Enlightenment. Whenever this faith becomes politically active it is no longer content with the neutrality of the State in religious and moral questions. The *laïque* idea, by the urge of its own nature, must inevitably strive to fill the institutions of the State, and education above all, with a rationalistic metaphysic of the State. The fusion of the desire of the State for power (*Étatisme*) and anti-clerical Enlightenment has become a fact in the France of the Third Republic. But this was only attained after a long and stormy period of development.

The beginnings of anti-clerical propaganda go back to the July Monarchy. Michelet and Quinet opened a campaign against the Jesuits, attacked the confessional, declared that Christianity was conquered, and wanted to put Deism and Patriotism in its place. Proudhon taught that "L'homme est destiné à vivre sans religion".

Under the Second Empire, however, the Church increased greatly in power and influence, and the decade 1849–59 was the high watermark of this reaction. But about the same time the rationalism of the Enlightenment gained a powerful new ally in modern science. Through the Protestant Theological Faculty at Strassburg German Biblical criticism penetrated into France. The *Revue Germanique* (1858–65), which was founded by the Alsatians Dollfus and Nefftzer, spread the knowledge of German philosophy and humanism. In the hands of French publicists this became a weapon which they used against revealed religion. French science and philosophy on its side, led by Renan, Taine, Havet and Littré, shattered the foundations of faith. Positivism and materialism found support in the natural sciences, especially in the Darwinian doctrine of evolution. *Laïcisme* found another ally in Freemasonry. At that time the latter was very largely Deistic in outlook, but it included a left wing, which in 1867 attempted to alter the statutes in an atheistic sense. The Republican youth, which regarded Gambetta as its leader, was steeped in the teaching of Proudhon—that democracy could not be combined with the Church or with any "Deistic system" at all, for this was a logical impossibility.

The early years of the Republic (1871–75) were marked by a reaction in the conservative and ecclesiastical direction. At the same time, however, Renouvier created his philosophical system, which imparted his ideals to the new form of the State, and outlined a social and political programme. Even at that time Renouvier demanded separation between Church and State, and added, significantly, that the separation also means "l'organisation de l'État moral et enseignant". He believed, however, that an ethic which was based purely upon philosophy and reason would not suffice for the education of the nation. He felt that an appeal to feeling also was necessary. He suggested that this need might be met by Protestantism. The Republic, criticism and Protestantism ought to combine. The fight against the Church was also taken up by able journalists like Sarcey and About.

When the Republicans were actually in power they considered that it would be tactful to modify their anti-clerical programme, in order to avoid unsettling the masses of the electors. They initiated that policy which is known in the Parliamentary history of the Third Republic as Opportunism. This course was easier for them because at that time the Papal dignity was given to Leo XIII., whom Gambetta called an *opportuniste sacré*. The separation of Church and State was postponed as inopportune. The Radical Party, however, led by Clemenceau, were loud in their criticism. The newly-revived Freemasons, among whom were many Republicans, developed along radical freethinking lines. The General Assembly of France in the Far East, on the 10th of September 1877, erased from its statutes the formula "the Great Architect of the Universe", and in so doing it proclaimed the fact that Atheism had triumphed over Deism.

The moment had now arrived when the Republic was able to organize the state system of education from a purely secular point of view. After Sedan, as after Königgrätz, the word went round that the German victory was the work of the German schoolmaster. The new organization of the schools appeared to be an urgent patriotic duty.

Already under the Second Empire Jean Macé had outlined a scheme for the secular elementary school, and had tried to influence public opinion on these lines. In 1866 he founded his *Ligue de l'enseignement*. The Republic took over what he had begun. When, in 1879, Jules Grévy became president of the Republic in place of MacMahon, Jules Ferry became Minister of Education. He retained his portfolio through five changes of Government, and was thus able to carry through the reforms which he had planned; he was supported by Paul Bert in the Chamber in matters connected with educational legislation. Ferry's starting point was this: the "principles of 1789" are the foundation of modern society in France, and ought therefore to be taught in the schools by the State. Hence the need to fight against Clericalism, whose strongest bulwark was the Religious Orders, and, above all, the Order of the Jesuits. It *must* be opposed; in so doing France would only be following an old tradition: that of the royal and parliamentary Gallicanism which had firmly opposed the ecclesiastical claim to dominate the State. Yet Ferry abstained from attacking Catholicism. He claimed that the French nation wished the Church to have a free hand in her own sphere, and only desired her not to meddle with politics. Ferry's hope was that the *laïque* elementary school, the cornerstone of the Republic, would represent a "fraternité supérieure à tous les dogmes".

On the 29th of March 1882 the Education Bill proposed by Ferry became law. Since this law was passed the French elementary school has been in existence. The amendment of the idealistic philosopher Jules Simon, who wished the curriculum to include instruction in "duties towards God and the Fatherland", was not carried. Henceforth Victor Hugo's vision of the future which he saw in 1835 was to be fulfilled:

> Chaque village aura, dans un temple rustique
> Dans la lumière, au lieu du magister antique,
> Trop noir pour que jamais le jour y pénétrat,
> L'instituteur lucide et grave, magistrat
> Du progrès, médecin de l'ignorance, et prêtre

De l'idée: et dans l'ombre on verra disparaître
L'éternel écolier et l'éternel pédant.[1]

Within the limits of this chapter it is impossible to attempt to describe the French system of popular education,
to give a sociological study of the *primaire* and the *primaire
supérieur*. Charles-Louis Philippe gives a good description
of the spirit of this educational system in his book, *La Mère
et l'Enfant*, from which I take this characteristic passage:
"Les lectures parlent des mœurs des castors, de l'oisiveté
qui ronge l'homme comme la rouille ronge le fer, et du
petit Jean qui cause avec le vieux Thomas sur les bienfaits
de la 3ᵉ République. Nous avons appris que le grandpère
du riche châtelain était serf au temps des seigneurs, et cela
prouve qu'en notre siècle on peut arriver à la fortune et
aux honneurs par le moyen du travail et de la probité".

René Goblet, Ferry's successor, went a step further in the
secularization of the State schools. In 1886 he promulgated
a decree according to which the members of the Religious
Orders were entirely excluded from all the State schools as
teachers. This law was imbued with the spirit of Paul
Bert's motto: *paix au curé, guerre au moine.*

In the years that followed an opportunistic policy mod-
erated the pace of this conflict between Church and State.
But at the election of 1893, for the first time, Socialism
gained some political influence. After the Commune had
been suppressed the public had forgotten its existence.
Meanwhile, in quietness, it had been gaining strength, and
now it emerged as a political party and revealed itself at
once as the enemy of the Church.

This was the situation when the Dreyfus affair broke out.
The simple question whether there had been a miscarriage
of justice was transformed, under these circumstances, into
a passionate controversy between opposing parties in
Church and State. Protestants, Jews and Freethinkers
fought for a revision of the trial; the Catholics opposed
them. The struggle between the two parties filled the whole

[1] "A propos d'Horace" (*Les Contemplations*).

country with passionate excitement. "Dreyfusard" meant anti-clerical, and "anti-dreyfusard" meant clerical. Catholicism and Secularism thus came again into conflict, and with renewed intensity. Various groups combined their forces in order to prosecute the struggle with greater vigour: the secular clergy and the members of the Religious Orders, the army and the conservative bourgeoisie were on the one side, and on the other were Republicans and Socialists, intellectuals and working-men. In 1899 Waldeck-Rousseau, a disciple of the ideas of Gambetta and of Jules Ferry, became Prime Minister. His policy was aimed first and foremost against the Religious Orders. The elections of 1902 were a victory for the Government. After Waldeck-Rousseau had voluntarily resigned, Combes carried on an energetic struggle against clericalism. The ideas of *laïcisme* were vigorously propagated by the recently founded People's High Schools (*Universités populaires*) and by Youth Associations (*Jeunesses laïques*). Leading politicians (Clemenceau), authors (Anatole France), and scholars (Ernest Lavisse), placed themselves at the service of these ideas. Lavisse formulated their content thus: "Être laïque, ce n'est pas limiter à l'horizon visible la pensée humaine, ni interdire à l'homme le rêve, et la perpétuelle recherche de Dieu: c'est revendiquer pour la vie présente l'effort du devoir. Ce n'est pas vouloir violenter, ce n'est pas mépriser les consciences encore détenues dans le charme des vieilles croyances: c'est refuser aux religions qui passent le droit de gouverner l'humanité qui dure. Ce n'est point haïr telle ou telle église ou toutes les églises ensemble; c'est combattre l'esprit de haine qui souffle des religions, et qui fut cause de violences, de tueries et de ruines. Être laïque, c'est ne point consentir la soumission de la raison au dogme immuable, ni l'abdication de l'esprit humain devant l'incompréhensible; c'est ne prendre son parti d'aucune ignorance. . . ."

The second Congress of *Jeunesses laïques* (1903) was ardently in favour of Socialism and anti-militarism. Upon the agenda there was the problem of secular morality. The following resolution was carried unanimously. "La morale laïque doit être scientifique, sociale, humaine. Elle s'appuie sur la raison et sur l'expérience: (1) pour garantir et développer la liberté individuelle; (2) pour assurer la justice sociale par la solidarité nationale et internationale des individus et des peuples." From 1901 the Freethinkers had their own paper: *La Raison*. One of its favourite topics was the "bloody history of the Church". It controlled the religious position of the officials of the State, and made public the names of Radical politicians who allowed their children to make their First Communion. An "Association nationale des libres penseurs de France" was founded, and international congresses for Freethinkers were held. Ferdinand Buisson formulated the principles of the Freethinkers' Movement, and Anatole France fed the flames of the anti-clerical temper with fuel. There was difference of opinion on this point however: does Clericalism mean Catholicism as a whole? and if so, does that mean that religion itself is to be attacked? All this propaganda of *Laïcisme* prepared the way for the Separation Law of 1905, and its acceptance constituted a great victory for *Laïcisme*.

In the France of the present day it is possible to distinguish various modes of *laïque* thought. Many scholars of a rationalistic turn of mind regard the "religious phenomenon" as a subject of objective scientific research. Thus Théodule Ribot and Delacroix have founded a psychology of religion, and Durckheim and his colleagues a religious sociology. Other philosophers, like Boutroux, have sought to bring freedom of research into harmony with religious feeling. Alfred Fouillée, for his part, does not attack the Church, but he defends the *idée laïque*, and lays stress on the fact that France does not represent Catholicism, but "certain principles of universal law and universal brotherhood, which foreign countries like to ridicule, but whose greatness they still acknowledge". One of the earliest propagandists of the *laïque* idea was Gabriel Séailles. He proclaimed that both the metaphysic and the ethic of Christianity had been finally overcome. Some Catholic priests like Marcel Hébert (d. 1916), Houtin and Loisy passed from Modernism to a kind of Free Thought tinctured with religion.

Félix Pécaut and Ferdinand Buisson laid down the main lines of policy for the secularization of the elementary schools, the former as Director of the Teachers' Training College at Fontenay, the second as Divisional Director in the Ministry of Education. Formerly both these men had been Protestant pastors, and then had drifted away from Christianity. The central point of their life-work was the development of a *morale laïque*, and its incorporation in the elementary school.[1] In his book *La foi laïque* (1918) Buisson proclaims: "Il n'est pas vrai qu'il y ait deux Frances,[2] qu'il y ait deux peuples en ce peuple. Il n'est pas vrai que la patrie, notre mère, ait enfanté deux races irréconciliables. L'école fera la lumière: dès que la lumière aura lieu, les fantômes disparaîtront, nous nous apercevrons qu'il n'y a en France que des Français, aujourd'hui tous égaux, et demain, quoiqu'on fasse, tous frères." Buisson's final aim in his scheme was so to fashion the secular moral instruction that it would become capable of effecting that deepening and ennobling of the spiritual life which the genuine believer owes to religion; this effort may be described as a religiosity without God.

To-day *Laicïsme* has lost its aggressive spirit. The leading intellectuals of France have turned away from it. Even in university circles its influence is declining.[3] In party politics, however, its influence is stronger than ever. It represents the ideals of the Cartel of the Left. Since the War this

[1] Cf. the chapter entitled, "Art und Wirksamkeit der weltlichen Schule und ihres Moralunterrichts" in Platz, *Geistige Kämpfe im modernen Frankreich*, p. 434 ff.

[2] An allusion to *Les deux Frances*, by Paul Seippel, 1905.

[3] Its outstanding champion to-day is Alain, the philosopher. In the *Europäische Revue*, March 1928, there is an argument by Alain in favour of *Laïcisme* which ends with the words: "Der Geist ist Laizismus".

group has enriched the *Laïque* programme with a new re-
quirement. This is the idea of the "unity-school". This
ideal, if it is carried out, will also affect the system of
secondary education (*enseignement secondaire*). Now, therefore, I will give an historical survey of this system.[1]

The present form of secondary education in France goes
back to the Jesuit Colleges of the seventeeth and eighteenth
centuries. This system had two main characteristics: the
predominance of Latin (Greek was scarcely studied at all),
and subordination to the ecclesiastical authority. The goal
of the training was the *clericus*[2] or *litteratus*. In essentials this
type of secondary school education was unaltered until
1880. It produced a formal humanism: facility in all forms
of literary expression. But it imparted as little of the spirit
of antiquity and of scientific methods of research as it did
of historical knowledge or natural science. As a rule the
pupil read the Latin poets merely in order to seek for epi-
thets which he could use in the Latin speeches and poems
which he had to compose. Thus Renan, as he tells us in his
memories of his youth, composed a hymn for the Crusades
with the refrain "Sternite Turcas!" ("solution brève et
tranchante de la question d'Orient").

After 1870 on all sides[3] this type of education was
severely criticized. In vain Jules Simon, as Minister of Education, tried to introduce reforms. It was only after the
Republic had been consolidated, that is—after 1879, that
this could be done. Since that date the conflict over the
predominance of Latin, and experiments in educational
reform have not ceased in France.

The last reform of the curriculum dated from 1902. For

[1] Based on Georges Weill, *Histoire de l'enseignement secondaire en
France* (1921). Cf. also Gastinel, *L'Enseignement secondaire en France* (1919).
P. Frieden, *Das französische Bildungswesen* (1927). O. Voelker, *Das Bil-
dungswesen in Frankreich* (1927).

[2] The word *clerc* is still used in the medieval sense at the present
day, meaning "intellectual". Cf. Benda, *La Trahison des clercs*.

[3] Cf. especially Michel Bréal, *Quelques mots sur l'instruction publique
en France*.

the first time it created a school-leaving examination without Latin. It includes four types of courses in the public
schools: A (Latin-Greek) B (Latin-living languages), C
(Latin-science), D (science-living languages). All four
paths lead to the *baccalauréat*. Almost everywhere this reform was unfavourably received. All the reproaches which
people felt they must cast at the programme of 1902 were
crystallized in the controversy about the so-called "crisis
in French". The paper entitled *L'Enseignement secondaire*,
which was edited by men who championed the cause of
the humanistic subjects, gave a large number of instances
of amusing and yet shocking offences against orthography,
syntax and language, which were said to have taken place
in French public schools after 1902. Protests were so
numerous that in 1909 an additional hour's instruction
in French was introduced. In spite of this, however, the
so-called *crise du français* still remained one of the main
subjects of discussion in the Press. It became the fashion
to argue that the study of Latin and French was insepar-
able. Public discussion on these questions was thoroughly
coloured by party politics.

The influence of the World War was revealed by
the fact that German vanished suddenly, and almost
entirely, from the school curriculum, while humanistic
culture gained a new halo, because it was supposed
to be this which distinguished the Latins from the
Germans.

Since the War the controversy over the curriculum has
broken out as hotly as ever. It has gained in intensity
through the Radical-Socialist propaganda for the "unity-
school". This political programme is also, in part, an
indirect result of the War: "La guerre égalitaire avait
inspiré le vœu d'une école égalitaire" (de Monzie). But it
also arose out of the need felt by the Left to make their
party programme more distinctive and vigorous. Herriot,
who from 1920–23 was Minister for Public Instruction,
borrowed from English reform proposals, as well as

from the Weimar Constitution, the principle of the *école unitaire* (Report of 1920), which was soon afterwards called *école unique* (Report of 1921). The *école unitaire* was the main plank in the Radical platform of 1924, and it is sure to appear again as soon as France has a Government composed of politicians of the Left.

The programme of the *école unitaire* signifies nothing less than a fundamental transformation of the whole public educational system of France. In place of the State elementary schools and the lower classes in the *Lycées* there would be a uniform obligatory course for all children from the age of six to that of twelve (*enseignement du premier degré*). No hint or suggestion is given of what would happen to the Church schools which still exist (*enseignement libre*).

At the age of twelve pupils would be obliged to enter for an examination, and according to their capacity they would be apportioned to the various courses of the *enseignement du second degré* (*lycées, collèges* and also to technical and trade schools). The selection for the *enseignement du troisième degré* (university education) would be made in the same way. The whole system of education for all scholars and in all stages would be free.

This is logical, authoritative and anti-liberal democracy. The parents are left no choice in the matter of schools, and the teachers would have their last remnant of freedom in the formation of the curriculum taken from them.[1] The whole programme betrays an illusory over-estimate of the schools—and also the danger, which is also realized in Germany, of over-pressure at school. It intensifies the defect in the French system of education which now exists in the shape of over-development of the system of examinations and of reckoning by marks, which cramps the effort to acquire culture within the narrow bounds of a super-refined system of reckoning, and thus becomes a mere competition. Finally, the *école unique* would probably mean

[1] Cf. P. Dufrenne, *L'École unique* (Cahiers du Cercle Fustel de Coulanges, 157 Boulevard Saint-Germain, Paris, mai 1929).

injury to Humanistic studies, and the ceaseless endeavour to carry out a State monopoly of education: the triumph of the *État moral et enseignant*.

The Radicals and Radical-Socialists need the programme of the *école unique* because their older programmes of reform (Income Tax and the separation between Church and State) have been carried out, and are therefore finished.[1] Since the close of the Dreyfus affair and the Separation Laws, that is, since about 1906, the ardour of the parties of the Left has declined. The programme of the *école unitaire* is addressed to the feeling for social justice, which forms part of the best traditions of French democracy. But it will provoke other and older traditions of France to resist it.

[1] Thibaudet, *La République des professeurs* (1927), 181 f.

# VII

## PARIS

ANCIENT Rome and modern Paris are both unique examples of the fact that the political capital of a great State can become the central point of the whole of its national and intellectual life, and that it can also gain world-wide importance as a cosmopolitan centre of culture.

Neither London, Vienna nor Berlin can make this claim.

Only in Paris does one have the sense, as in Rome, "of being surrounded by something as universal as humanity": the historian of Rome, Ferdinand Gregorovius, coined this formula in his Paris Journals, and it expresses, very clearly, an essential feature of Paris.

The significance and the spirit of both cities, however, are entirely different. It has been well said by an English critic: "It is not Roman dominion or power any more than it is Roman permanence which Paris means. Its universality is a later thing in history; it is the Latin spirit expressing itself as Taste in a world already civilized, and conquering, not with man's will, but with feminine attraction. Paris will be the metropolis of modern civilization as long as culture appreciates elegance, as energy attains refinements, and as glory finds its complement in pleasure."[1]

To France Paris signifies the epitome of the national existence; at the same time it is also an intellectual *caput orbis*. To the extent in which the intellectual predominance of Rome in the West has been diminished by ecclesiastical divisions, and by the influence of the Enlightenment, the world significance of Paris has increased. Though it may be wrong to say that to know Paris is to know France, still, Paris is the heart and brain of the nation, and this can be said of no other capital city in the world, not even of Rome. Here all the fibres of the whole organism meet. The

[1] "The City of Paris"—anonymous leading article in the *Times Literary Supplement* for 25th July 1929.

foreigner in Paris is conscious not only of the majestic history of a thousand years, as in Rome, nor of the energy of the contemporary development of power, as in Berlin: the phenomenon which rivets his attention is the fact that the past is indissolubly interwoven with the living present. Here he still finds some of the earliest traces of the influence of Rome; here he finds a glorious testimony to that medieval Christianity which built the cathedrals of Northern Europe, and kindled the faith which achieved the Crusades. Here the glory of royal and imperial France created its great monuments. And all these worlds of history are not shut away from view in the mouldy atmosphere of museums, but are surrounded by a sea of vital experience, by that mystery of life itself, into which no one has peered so deeply as Balzac, and in which all the fever of pleasure and of ambition, all desires and all renunciations are gathered up and raised to their highest pitch. On a bright summer evening as one walks along the beautiful slope of the Champs-Élysées it almost seems as though an ocean of pleasure must extend beyond the Arc de Triomphe. Yet under this Arch there burns the everlasting flame in the remembrance of the dead. It is in this close proximity of life and death that one catches a fugitive glimpse of the external aspect of Paris. Paris is rich in contrasts of this kind. Above the pleasure resorts of Montmartre there rises in hallowed glory the white dome of the church of the Sacré-Cœur. A few hundred steps from the roar of the traffic of the great capital ancient trees offer an inviting shade, monastery bells are ringing, and quiet little provincial alleys suggest a place for calm and tranquil reflection. All these contrasts, however, are touched with a unity of atmosphere and spirit, in which the grace of gay gardens, the naïve and homely life of the streets, the arches of the bridges over the Seine, the grey waters of the mighty stream, the mathematical precision of the residential quarters, the widely differing quality of the various regions of the city form a symphony. Paris is not only a town, it is also a landscape, with water, trees, lawns; even the sky of Paris has a special quality of its own, and its delicate colours tone in with the pale grey and buff of the houses.

How has Paris attained her predominant position? The reply is often given: through her geographical position; and the older geographers expended much acuteness in the endeavour to prove this thesis. They conceived the "Paris Basin" as the predetermined, natural point of attraction for the population, for trade, and for the political authority. The science of the present day, however, has destroyed these theories. The Paris Basin is not a clearly demarcated geographical unity. Neither from the geological nor from the agricultural point of view is it homogeneous. It includes rich grain-bearing districts, but also unfruitful regions like the Sologne, and the *Champagne pouilleuse*. Its unity lies in its network of communications, but this is due to historical causes, it is not a geographical fact. The predominance of Paris may have been assisted by Nature, but if history had taken another course, Paris would not have gained this position. The geographical conditions which facilitated the rise of the city lie in the conjunction of the valleys of the Seine, the Marne and the Oise; in the nearness of extensive tablelands useful for roads and for agriculture; in the presence of stone, which was useful for building houses. These conditions, however, as a modern geographer has said, explain Lutetia;[1] they do not explain Paris.

The first settlements, made before the historical epoch had begun, were not in the marshy valley of the Seine, but on the neighbouring heights: Charonne, Ménilmontant, Belleville in the East; Montmartre in the North; Chaillot in the West; the Mount of St. Geneviève in the South.

The Gallic Lutetia was the modest capital of the Parisii. It was situated upon the island known to-day as La Cité.

[1] Camille Vallaux, quoted by Lucien Dubech and Pierre d'Espezel in their excellent *Histoire de Paris* (Paris, Payot 1926), which I follow in this chapter.

This island was the best spot for crossing the Seine. The two most important Roman imperial roads which crossed Gaul, and connected it with Rome on the one hand and with Britain on the other, did not touch Lutetia. The network of Roman roads radiated from Lyons, and was so constructed that one of its main arteries which followed the valley of the Rhone was connected crosswise both with the ocean and with the valley of the Rhine: in the ancient world Gaul served as a link between Italy and the ocean. A comparison between a Roman road map and one of the *Ancien Régime*[1] shows with convincing clearness that it was not until the Capet Monarchy was established that Paris became the centre of the country.

In the year 53, for a short time, Caesar made Lutetia his headquarters: *concilium Lutetiam Parisiorum transfert* (*De bello Gallico* iv. 3)—this is the first time the Parisians are mentioned. Under the Romans Lutetia became an important centre of river traffic. It was the seat of a sailors' corporation (*nautae Parisiaci*), which, under Tiberius, erected an altar to the Emperor and to Jupiter. In 1711 this was discovered under Notre-Dame; (to-day it is in the Cluny Museum). At the point where the Pont Notre-Dame to-day spans the river, there was a wooden bridge which connected the Cité with the right bank of the Seine; as far as Montmartre, however, the slope was almost entirely empty of human life. Gradually Roman buildings arose. The earliest of these buildings (which date from the second half of the second century) are the so-called *Thermes*; it is still impossible to determine the purpose for which they were used; the situation seems too small for a public bath; (relics may be seen to-day in the Cluny Museum). Camille Jullian has suggested that the building may have served as the headquarters of the nautical guild which I have already mentioned. If that were so, then the nautical design

[1] Cf. both the maps in Vidal de la Blache, *Tableau de la géographie de la France* (vol. i. of the *Histoire de France*, by Lavisse), pp. 378 and 379.

on two of the pillars in the main hall might be regarded as
a foreshadowing of the Paris coat of arms—the ship with
the inscription, *fluctuat nec mergitur*, the oft-renewed allegorical and poetical symbol of the city,[1] which appears from
the twelfth century upon the municipal seal of Paris. In any
case, in all probability we may regard the *nautae Parisiaci* of
the Imperial period as more or less directly the ancestors
of the medieval Paris *Hanse* (*mercatores aquae Parisiaci*). In
the middle of the thirteenth century, the master of this
guild received the title of *prévôt des marchands*; in this capacity he was the head of the administration of the town of
Paris until the central power of the Monarchy destroyed
his authority. Thus the oldest monuments of Gallo-Roman
Lutetia foreshadow the later history of Paris.

In addition to the *Thermes* Paris contains another important relic of Roman times: an arena (*Arènes de Lutèce*),
which was only discovered in 1869 in the rue Monge; recent excavations have made it possible to see it more
clearly in its setting. Other Roman buildings also exist.
Roman Paris, however, could never compare with the
Rome of the South. She still retained a pronounced Gallic
character. Very early she had to suffer from the German
invasions. The southern town, on the left bank, seems to
have been the victim of a conflagration about the year 280.
The people left it, and went to live on the *Île de la Cité*. The
deserted district was used as a quarry, and for viticulture.
The Cité became a military town. Julian (who later became Emperor), lived there in 358. In his *Misopogon* he
gives a delightful description of Lutetia, with her vineyards
and fig orchards.

When Julian speaks of the town as "Lutetia" he is using
the traditional term, which was still in vogue, although
officially it had already been discarded. Caracalla's edict

---

[1] Cf. for example the three sonnets by Charles Péguy, "Paris vais-
seau de charge", "Paris double galère", "Paris vaisseau de guerre".
For coats of arms and mottoes of Paris cf. Coetlogon-Tisserand, *Les
Armoiries de la ville de Paris* (Paris, Imprimerie nationale, 1874).

of 212, which granted to all free inhabitants of the provinces the right of Roman citizenship, led to the re-naming of the municipalities of Gaul. The chief town of each tribe, and of the territory which belonged to it, was henceforward called by the same name, and in the struggle between the name of the town and the name of the tribe the latter conquered. Thus Avaricum was replaced by Bituriges (Bourges), Augusta by Treveri (Trier), and Lutetia by Parisii.[1]

The adoption of Christianity as the national religion furthered the development of the city. Her first bishop was St. Denis, whom medieval legend loved to regard as the same as Dionysius the Areopagite; in the old French epics he is celebrated as the patron saint of the French. About 250 he seems to have founded the Church of Paris. The real patroness of Paris is St. Geneviève. There seems good ground for the belief that her life (419–512) and work are historical. She saved the city from the invasion of the Huns. The beautiful frescoes of Puvis de Chavannes in the Panthéon keep her memory green.

Under the Merovingians Paris did not play any great part; under the Carolingians, who gave their chief attention to the eastern part of the country, she was still less important. In spite of this, however, the city grew. It was a steady, gradual process. New communications were opened up. The city and abbey of St. Denis gained in importance through King Dagobert. To him is attributed the foundation of the annual Fair of St. Denis, which became of such great importance in the ecclesiastical, economic and intellectual life of the early Middle Ages. Pilgrims, merchants, strolling players, and other travellers filled the streets of Paris leading to St. Denis with life.[2] The result was that the main interest of the Île de la Cité moved towards the West. A new bridge over the Seine was erected

[1] First used in an inscription about 305. Cf. Jullian, *Histoire de la Gaule*, iv. 525 ff.

[2] For the relations between Paris and St. Denis cf. L. Olschki, *Der ideale Mittelpunkt Frankreichs im Mittelalter* (1913).

at the spot where the Pont-au-Change stands to-day.
Charles the Bald strengthened its position on both sides of
the river with two towers of defence, known, later on, as the
Grand and Petit Châtelet. The northern building (Grand
Châtelet), also called *Porta Parisiaca*, formed the most important outwork in the defence of the city against the Normans. The rue St. Denis started at that point, as it does
to-day. At Châtelet it crossed an ancient route—going east
and west—which led from the older Seine Bridge (Grand
Pont, Pont Notre-Dame) to St. Germain-l'Auxerrois; to-
day this corresponds roughly to the direction of the rue
St. Antoine and the rue de Rivoli. In the Middle Ages
these cross-roads were *la croisée de Paris*. It still constitutes
the main point at which the two great axes of the traffic of
Paris cross each other. The north to south axis is to-day
bounded by the line of the Boulevard de Strasbourg and
the Boulevard St. Michel, which has taken over the
function of the old streets of St. Jacques and St. Denis.
This route is the one most used for traffic connected with
business and commerce. The east to west route (especially
in the direction of the rue de Rivoli and the Champs-
Elysées) in present-day Paris is the great main traffic
artery of luxury and elegance. At the point where both
routes intersect each other stand the great shops and market buildings in a compact mass. Thus to-day the life of
the great metropolis still flows on along the pattern traced
by the ancient *Croisée de Paris*.

The ecclesiastical foundations furthered the development
of Paris. In the absence of the king it was possible to extend the episcopal power. The struggle for predominance
took place between him and the Count of Paris. Then the
star of the Capets arose. They resided in Paris; it seems
clear that this is the main reason why Paris became the
capital of the country.[1] So far as population and wealth

[1] Robert Michels, however, argues that Paris became great owing
to the power of her citizens. ("Zur Soziologie von Paris", *Zeitschrift für
Völkerpsychologie*, 1925, 233.)

were concerned, at that time cities like Laon, Compiègne or Soissons were just as important as Paris. The second Capet, Robert, actually considered making Orléans the capital. But from the time of Philip I., Paris, and in Paris the Palais de la Cité, became the permanent residence of the king. Philip Augustus (Philip II.) did a great deal for the development of the city. In 1204 he began to build the Louvre, and he erected a belt of walls and towers of which traces can still be seen at the present time: this was the first of the four encirclements of the city which the history of Paris displays. He had the streets paved, set the administration of the town in order, founded the university, or at least established it firmly by granting it a charter which secured its privileges (1200). At the same period, thanks to the energetic Bishop Maurice de Sully, the Cathedral of Notre-Dame was erected (1163–96). Several Religious Orders settled in Paris. In 1217 came the Dominicans. Their monastery in the rue St. Jacques was near the hospice set aside for the use of pilgrims to Santiago de Compostella. They thus received the name of "Jacobins", which became so famous later on. A few years later the Franciscans (Cordeliers) also settled in the city. The Austin Friars established themselves on the bank of the Seine, which is still called the Quai des Grands-Augustins. From the year 1147 the Templars had a kind of fortress-settlement, *Le Temple*, whose growth was closely connected with that of Paris itself.

The twelfth and the thirteenth centuries were a time of prosperity for France, for its monarchy, its culture, and its capital.[1] The writers of the period call Paris *locus deliciarum* and *letitia populi*. St. Louis adorned the city with the masterpiece of the Sainte Chapelle (1246–48). Its glorious windows gave rise to a proverb which compared a good wine with the colour of this glass. Paris now became the chief theatre of events in the history of France, and the intel-

---

[1] Cf. Anton Springer, *Paris im dreizehnten Jahrhundert* (1856). Contemporary descriptions of medieval Paris can also be found in Budinsky, *Die Universität Paris im Mittelalter* (1876).

lectual centre of Europe. The University accommodated
fifteen thousand students, who were divided into four
"nations" (France, Picardy, Normandy and Germany).
Foreigners had special financial and legal rights, possessed
their own "colleges", and could even appoint the Rector.

The Hundred Years War was a serious set-back. Only
under the rule of Charles V. (known as "the Wise", 1364–
1380) was Paris again able to develop in a favourable
atmosphere. The king did a great deal for the capital,
which he scarcely ever left. The wall built by Philip
Augustus on the right bank had become insufficient.
Charles V. set in hand the bu'lding of a new line of fortifications on that side of the city. Paris had grown to such
an extent that the king begged the Pope to make it into an
Archbishopric; Gregory XI. would not grant this request,
because he feared that it might offend the Archbishop of
Sens under whose jurisdiction Paris lay at that time.
Charles V. also greatly enlarged and strengthened the
Louvre, and he designed the Bastille; both these enter-
prises were designed to strengthen the power of the Crown.

But under his successor Charles VI., who inherited the
throne at the age of twelve, and became mad at the age of
twenty-four, the work of the wise king fell to pieces. Paris
also suffered much from the various troubles which fell
upon the country as a whole, through the enemies who
assailed it, both within and without its borders. The worst
disasters occurred in the thirties of the fifteenth century.
Plague carried off tens of thousands. Famine and bitter
cold did the rest. Wolves crept over the frozen Seine into
the deserted city. It was the lowest point in her history.
France did not recover until the reign of Louis XI. (1461–
1483). Then security and well-being returned once more.
Two beautiful non-ecclesiastical buildings of this epoch have
remained in Paris: the Hotel de Cluny and the Hotel de Sens
(rue du Figuier), the Paris residence of the Archbishops
of Sens. Paris was still a simple episcopal town; only in
1622 did it become the seat of an independent bishopric.

A new era of prosperity opened with the Renaissance. In the architectural history of Paris it was the period when the monarchs took a more active and personal interest in the city from the architectural point of view; this period also witnessed the growth of a new taste in art which aimed at symmetry and perspective. When the bridge of Notre-Dame was restored, between 1500 and 1510, it was adorned on each side with four and thirty houses all built in the same style; it was also decreed that the street which led to the bridge should have houses "equal in height and style" erected along it. This is the first piece of evidence we possess of the new spirit in architecture.

The French kings had brought back a new taste in art from their campaigns in Italy. This new spirit was revealed first of all on the Loire. Louis XI. had lived there, and his immediate successors remained loyal to the neighbourhood. Amboise, Blois, Chambord were the residences of Charles VII., Louis XII. and Francis I. It was only after the defeat at Pavia and the Spanish imprisonment that Francis I. moved to Paris. The conflict with the Hapsburgs made him think it would be desirable to change his place of abode; he needed the support of the people of Paris; he needed to finance himself with the money of the *bourgeoisie* of the capital; for military reasons, also, he dared not live too far away from the open Northern frontier. This move made it necessary to restore the Louvre. In place of the old fortress-like tower which faced the Seine there arose the new Louvre, which Pierre Lescot began in 1546. Francis I. acquired for his mother the ground on the western side, where until that time there had been tile-fields (*tuileries*). Francis I. sold the numerous royal dwelling-houses which were out of date, and thus gained sufficient means to beautify the capital, and to erect new buildings. He loved court festivals. When Charles V. was his guest he arranged for him to be welcomed with great pomp. At the Porte St. Antoine an *Arc de Triomphe* was erected, and the pomp and circumstance was increased by the production of allegorical representations; in all this the spirit of the Renaissance is evident.

For the entry of Henry II. the Porte St. Antoine was turned into an *Arc de Triomphe*; it became the model for arches of this kind, in the Roman style, which were to re-appear frequently in the classical urban architecture of France during the following centuries right down to the *Arc de l'Étoile*.

The Renaissance kings did not intend to leave the ex-tension of the city to chance. They were afraid of over-population, and of its attendant problems: the difficulty of feeding large numbers, and the problem of adequate police supervision. So as early as 1548 Henry II. issued an edict forbidding the building of houses in the suburbs. Ten decrees of the same kind followed until 1576, and this policy continued till the end of the *Ancien Régime*. It was not until the Revolution that the rural population were free to enter the city and settle there.

The new taste of the Renaissance affected secular build-ings more speedily than ecclesiastical architecture. Here late Gothic still predominated. One example of this is St. Severin, which was completed in 1540. The "Hotels" of the nobility, on the other hand, were built in the Renaissance style. For the President de Ligneris Pierre Lescot and Jean Goujon built the present Hotel Carnavalet. Under the guidance of Philbert Delorme, the Tuileries were begun in 1564 for Marie de Medici. In other directions, however, building activity was hindered by the Wars of Religion. When Henry IV. ascended the throne a new epoch of pros-perity and order began for the whole of France. This was also to the advantage of Paris, and its development. The king himself "took delight in buildings", as a contemporary says. He appointed his minister Sully "Grand-Voyer de France", and at the same time handed over to him the control of the public works in Paris. From 1550 a new means of transport appeared in the capital: the *carrosses*. It was then discovered—just as to-day with the influx of

motor traffic—that the streets were too narrow. A widening
of the streets was planned, which could only gradually be
carried out. It was a block in the traffic on the 14th of
May 1610 which made it possible for the fanatical mad-
man Ravaillac to stab the king as he sat in his carriage in
the rue de la Ferronerie.

Under Henry IV. and Louis XIII. new districts of the
city were opened up: the Marais in the east, St. Honoré
in the west, the Île St. Louis in the centre. In 1603 the Pont
Neuf was built: the first modern bridge, unencumbered by
houses, and with a foot-path for pedestrians. A water tower
was added. It was adorned with a bas-relief which represented the Samaritan woman giving water to our Lord.
The building of the *Samaritaine* was one of the sights of
Paris until the end of the eighteenth century, and its name
still lives to-day. In 1607 the rue Dauphine was laid out.
The king had designed the plans, and he gave orders that
the householders "y fissent le devant de leurs maisons tout
d'un même ordre, car ce serait d'un bel ornement d'avoir
au bout du dit pont cette rue toute d'une même façade".
Another creation of Henry IV. is the Place Royale (to-day
the Place des Vosges). Here also the king made the plans:
"Maisons ayant la muraille de devant de pierres de taille
et de briques, ouvertes en arcades, et des galeries en des-
sous avec des boutiques toutes bâties d'une même symétrie
pour la décoration". This design for laying out a square
dates back to the days of Vitruv. The Place Royale became an aristocratic residential quarter, and a fashionable
meeting place; this comes out, for instance, in the comedies
of Corneille, among others.

The Île St. Louis is a creation of Louis XIII. It consisted originally of two islands, which were now joined;
roads were made along the bank, and bridges were built.
Magnificent palaces for the nobility were erected there.
Many of them still stand to-day. Few parts of Paris have
conserved to the present day so much of the tranquil splen-
dour of the *Ancien Régime*. The peace of the Île St. Louis

has always attracted poets and thinkers. On the Quai d'Anjou, in the glorious old Hôtel Lauzun, Gautier and Baudelaire used to live, and in his preface to the *Fleurs du Mal* Gautier has preserved the memory of this place. In the house at the corner of the rue Budé and the Quai d'Orléans Félix Arvers was born, the poet who wrote that sonnet to *une Inconnue*, which has made his name immortal. To-day the peaceful beauty of the tree-bordered island is disturbed by the opening of new streets and the building of new bridges, which will soon sacrifice this solitude to the roar of the traffic of the great city.

The present Palace of the Luxembourg also dates from the period of Louis XIII. Marie de Médicis had it built in 1615, in the new classical style, by Salomon de Brosse, and in 1620 it was adorned with the series of pictures in which Rubens extolled the story of the Queen. At first it was called the Palais d'Orléans. The present name owes its origin to a house in the neighbourhood which belonged to the Duke of Luxembourg. The Gardens of the Luxembourg, whose shady alleys, flowers and artificial waters have formed a tranquil oasis for so many generations of students in the Latin Quarter, for conversation and for reading, were also laid out at that time. Somewhat later Richelieu built the Palais Cardinal (to-day the Palais-Royal). To him also Paris owes the Church of the Sorbonne, in which he is buried. The life of the city was developing in a modern direction; in 1612 the first posters appeared, in 1617 a tariff was established for the hire of sedan chairs, followed in 1623 by a similar regulation for hired carriages. In 1631 Théophrast Renaudot founded the first newspaper, the *Gazette de France*, which lived until 1914.

In his youth Louis XIV. had passed through the agitating upheaval of the Fronde. This occurred in Paris, and these impressions affected him for the rest of his life. They made him out of love with Paris. He lived at St. Germain, and later he built Versailles. After 1666 he only spent three winters in Paris: in 1667, 1668 and 1670. Between

1700 and 1715 he only visited the capital four times. In spite of this, however, the foundations of modern Paris were laid during his reign. This was the work of Colbert, whom the king appointed *surintendant des bâtiments*, and of the lieutenant of police, Nicolas de la Reynie. During the disorders of the Fronde the cleanliness and order of the capital had greatly suffered; Boileau's satire, *Les Embarras de Paris* (1660), gives an amusing picture of the state of affairs. La Reynie looked after the lighting of the streets and their cleaning, attended to the paving of the roads and to all that affected public security. Colbert, on his side, had grandiose plans for the beautification of the city, which were only partially realized. Nevertheless, even to-day a number of splendid buildings still testify to the magnificence of the Roi Soleil. We only need to recall the colonnade of the Louvre by Claude Perrault; the north façade on the same building which faces the rue de Rivoli; the Galérie d'Apollon by Le Brun; the gates of St. Denis and St. Martin; the Place des Victoires (by Mansart); the Pont Royal; Hôtel and Dôme des Invalides (Hardouin-Mansart); the Observatoire (Claude Perrault). The Champs-Élysées were begun by Le Nôtre. During the reign of Louis XIV. one hundred and twenty-three new streets were constructed. At that time the population of the capital was estimated at 560,000.

Under the Regency the Palais d'Élysée was built. It was begun in 1718 by Mollet for Count Évraux; later it was used by Madame de Pompadour, Murat, Joséphine, Napoleon, Alexander I. Napoleon III. lived there as Prince-President. In the rue de Varennes the former wigmaker Peyrenc, who was Controller of Taxes, and ennobled under the name of Peyrenc de Moras, ordered Gabriel and Aubert, in 1728, to put up the wonderfully proportioned building which to-day contains the Musée Rodin. Under Louis XV., likewise under the guidance of Gabriel, the present Place de la Concorde was laid out; to the north it was hemmed in by two palaces, one of which has housed the offices of the Admiralty since 1792, while the other has remained a private dwelling (Hotel Crillon).

The mighty tide of development had long since over-flowed the previous boundaries of the city walls. Walls and towers gradually disappeared. The result of this was that the Tax Controllers, whose business it was to collect the *Octroi*, had to throw wooden barriers across the most important thoroughfares. In 1785 they received permission to build a new series of walls (the third circle). This followed the course of the outer ring of boulevards, and was not pierced by gates but by elegant *Octroi* Pavilions, of which some still remain (at the Parc Monceau, in the Place Denfert-Rochereau, and at the Place de la Nation). The people of Paris were not pleased with the innovation. It was at that time that there arose the famous couplet:

*Le mur murant Paris rend Paris murmurant.*

Constant changes were made in the Louvre. When it was no longer used as a royal residence it was used by Academies and other learned bodies. The first Art Exhibitions were held in the Salon Carré, hence they received the name of the *Salon*. After 1750 the king opened part of his collection of pictures in the Luxembourg to the public. This was the origin of the Paris Museum. The Panthéon, St. Sulpice and the Odéon belong to the close of the *Ancien Régime*. The central point of the life of Paris was the Palais Royal. In the period between 1782 and 1784, Philippe-Égalité had the galleries erected in which shops, coffee-houses and gaming rooms were opened. For fifty years this pleasure resort was a chief centre of attraction in Paris. In April and May 1814 Field-Marshal Blücher visited it every day, as Varnhagen von Ense tells us. From 1776 the *Journal de Paris* appeared daily with news of politics, society, the theatre, exhibitions, concerts, races and the rate of exchange. In addition there appeared in Paris twenty-six other French papers, and fourteen in foreign languages. Paris was a cosmopolitan centre. The population had risen to 600,000.

During the Revolution Paris was the centre of the political movement. So far as building was concerned these years were years of stagnation and destruction. Many buildings were violently destroyed, like the Bastille for instance. Other buildings fell down. The churches suffered greatly. Many of them became so insecure that under the Empire they had to be demolished. The chapels of Notre-Dame were used as shelters for prostitutes, and archives were stored in the Sainte Chapelle. The Convention tried to create some new buildings; finally, however, the net result was that several places were renamed or adapted. In this connexion we ought to mention the transformation of the Louvre into a National Museum (1793).

Napoleon's attitude towards Paris was twofold. He called Paris the curse of France, but at the same time he wished to make her the most beautiful of cities. He was only able to carry out a few of his plans, but even these have greatly affected the appearance of Paris at the present time. He created the rue de Rivoli and the network of streets which connects it with the Boulevards (rue des Pyramides, de Castiglione, de la Paix, etc.). The Empire gave special attention to everything which was of public utility, such as market places, fountains, quays, bridges. Decorative buildings of this period are: the façade of the Palais Bourbon; the new sections of the Louvre; the triumphal arch of the Carrousel and of the Étoile (only completed under Louis Philippe); the Exchange; the pillar of the Vendôme, the Madeleine. Most of these buildings are characterized by a cool and moderate classicism.

The Restoration and the July Monarchy did not greatly affect the development of Paris. Notre-Dame de Lorette and St. Vincent de Paul (this was the work of the architect Hittorf of Cologne who also built the Gare du Nord) are churches of an intimate beauty and peculiar charm, which, however, do not fit into the picture of the city as a whole because they lie off the main line of communication. The municipal authorities gave their main attention to the chief streets. In 1814 the gas installation was put in; in 1828 the first omnibus line was established (from the Bastille to the Madeleine). The wall set up by the Tax Controllers was pulled down in 1823. But its line still formed the boundary of the town. At that date the Champs-Élysées was a disreputable region with few houses. Flocks of sheep used to feed in the rue de Clichy, and the Quartier de l'Europe was arable land. The centre of Paris consisted of a medley of narrow alleys which could swiftly be closed by barricades. They made it easy for the street fighting and rioting during the period of the July Monarchy. In 1840, at the suggestion of Thiers, a new line of fortifications was planned, which was to encircle the city (finished in 1845): this was the fourth and last time that a wall was built round Paris. The first railway line—from Paris to St. Germain—was opened in 1837, but the significance of the new means of transport was not yet understood. In 1838 the Chamber of Deputies rejected a Bill providing for railway lines to Belgium, Bordeaux and Le Havre. In the forties the first railway stations were built. In 1846 Paris had a million inhabitants. At this period the Boulevards were the scene of fashionable life. In 1836 the public gaming houses were closed. This meant that life ebbed away from the Palais-Royal. The first large shop, or department store, was opened in 1834, in the rue Montmartre, under the name of La Ville de Paris.

Under the Second Empire, as I have already said, Paris was changed more than in the preceding fifteen centuries. A new principle entered into her development: that of systematic rational enlargement and transformation—urbanisme, as the French call it. Until then the changes had only been due to the exigencies of natural development. Now for the first time the process of development was deliberately organized. The Emperor himself set the example. The plans were carried out under the guidance of Baron

Haussmann, who from 1853 to the beginning of 1870 (when his fall from power was brought about by Jules Ferry), was Prefect of the Seine. His aim was to make Paris the capital of the civilized world, by means of a system of extensive modernization. The example of London also gave a certain stimulus; the idea of laying out new parks and squares was borrowed from this source.

The result of Haussmann's activity was the final destruction of old Paris. He says himself in his *Mémoires*: "C'etait l'effondrement du vieux Paris, du quartier des émeutes, des barricades". Artists and poets mourned the annihilation of the beauty of so many centuries. Baudelaire complained:

> Le vieux Paris n'est plus: la forme d'une ville
> Change plus vite, hélas! que le cœur d'un mortel.

His contemporary, the great draughtsman Méryon, has preserved some of the moods and aspects of this ancient Paris in her period of decline in drawings full of vision and power.

Haussmann's arrangement of streets, and the way they cut across existing roads was dictated partly by reasons of strategy. He was also actuated by ambition, which caused him to include some of the outlying districts; there was also a natural expansion of the city towards the West. These changes took place, unfortunately, during a period when taste was decadent. The style of the "Second Empire" is a hybrid blend of many historical periods of architecture; it is overloaded and inwardly insincere. A characteristic example of this is the Grand Opera of Charles Garnier (1861–75). New streets of the period are: the Boulevard St. Germain; the twelve avenues which radiate from the Étoile; the Avenue de l'Opéra; the Boulevard Haussmann, the rue Lafayette and several others. A reasonable planning of the railway-lines was overlooked. The present railway stations of Paris date mainly from the time of Louis Philippe. Great shops like the Louvre and the Bon-Marché also date from this period. The enlargement and modernization of the city was absolutely necessary, but the manner in which Haussmann carried it out has been much criticized, and with good reason. His perfectly straight streets caused too much unnecessary destruction. They are non-organic. The principle of arranging for several wide thoroughfares to meet at a certain point (as at the Place de l'Opéra and the Place de l'Étoile) has proved itself unpractical. It endangers and hinders the traffic. From the practical, as well as from the aesthetic, point of view, to-day the system of Haussmann stands condemned.

Haussmann himself believed that he had beautified the city, and at that time the taste of the public was with him. To-day no one would admire the monotony of a Boulevard Sebastopol or of a rue Monge. One of the lesser results of Haussmann's system, which was not intended and is often overlooked, is the fact that the visitor to Paris usually remains within the network of wide modern streets, and thus he often never sees the beauties and sights of ancient Paris which may be only a few steps away. How many of the thousands who call themselves lovers of Paris know the rue Brise-Miche, which seems to have scarcely changed at all since the fourteenth century, or the giant pillar of the former Hôtel de Soissons, with its cabbalistic symbols, which served Catherine of Medici and her Court Astrologer as an observatory.

Under the Commune Paris suffered greatly. The Tuileries and Cour des Comptes were wholly destroyed, including the staircase which Chasseriau had decorated with marvellous frescoes (a few scanty relics are now preserved in the Louvre). Under the Third Republic Paris has never been the subject of systematic and generous consideration. The one great monument of this period, which occupies a large place in the picture of the city as a whole, is the Church of the Sacré-Cœur on Montmartre. The building of this Church was decided by the National Assembly in 1873; it was begun in 1875 under Abadie, completed in 1912, and consecrated in 1919. It has been much criticized.

And yet it must be confessed that the white shimmering sanctuary, so happily proportioned in its main outline, makes a strong impression of majesty and mystery, which all forms part of the spirit of the Paris of the present day.

To Paris as a city the close of the World War meant the beginning of a new epoch. Great changes are now being planned. The most important factor in these transformations is the destruction of the belt of fortifications of 1844, with which a beginning has been made. The aim is to provide a belt of parks, gardens and playing fields around the city. At the same time the consequences of the War have greatly increased the value of the land in the neighbourhood of Paris, and this, together with the violent upheavals in the financial fortunes of many people, has led to the breaking-up of property, and to an increase of speculation in property which has created social and political problems which are not yet solved.[1]

Within the city, too, the years after the War have brought considerable changes, which are still taking place. New streets have been cut in the Quartier de la Monnaie, in the Île St. Louis, and by the Pont-Neuf. More far-reaching plans are being considered. People have even talked of pulling down the Palais-Royal. All this causes the liveliest apprehension to the true lovers of ancient Paris.[2] This is all the more intelligible when we remember that the leading public places in Paris, as in France as a whole, render homage to an academic official tradition of taste which runs clean counter to all sane feeling for art. During the last decades this official taste has led to much disfigurement in Paris, and the newspaper *Les Marges* sent out a questionnaire in 1919 with great success with the main query: "Quel est le monument le plus laid de Paris et quelle est la statue la plus laide?" The largest number voted for the

[1] Cf. Wladmir d'Ormesson, "Le Problème des lotissements", in the paper *Politique*, 15th September 1927.

[2] Louis Dimier, "Les Rues et monuments de Paris et leur avenir" (in the volume *Faits et Idees de l'histoire des Arts*, 1923).

Grand Palais, the Trocadéro and the Gambetta monument. Particularly from the point of view of sculpture
Paris has made many mistakes. From an amusing and instructive collection of statistics we learn that there are
nine hundred statues in Paris.[1] The following callings are
represented among them: two gardeners, three mathema-
ticians, "three victims of religious passions", five revolutionaries, five kings, twelve politicians, thirteen chemists,
thirty-seven writers and fifty poets. We miss the generals.

Happily, public opinion is becoming increasingly aware
of the need for a solution of the problem presented by the
development of Paris which will be modern, technical, and
both socially and aesthetically satisfying. At the request of
the *Redressement Français*, a non-party body of students
which seeks to renew the life of France in the social,
economic and regional sphere, Le Corbusier has worked
out a comprehensive programme "for a modern Paris".[2]

Each year, indeed nearly each month, brings with it
fresh discussions and proposals. More and more it is evident
that the opinion is gaining ground that the planning of
Greater Paris is a political and economic problem of primary importance for France. Looking at Paris and the *région
parisienne* as a unity, we find that it includes four *Départements*, with almost seven million inhabitants. Thus more
than one-sixth of the whole population lives in an area
which does not even make up the fiftieth part of the whole
surface area of France. This means a concentration unknown in any other capital in the world. The bad conditions of housing, transport and hygiene of this Greater
Paris are a source of perpetual discontent and unrest, which
could easily develop into a social danger. It is not an accident that the *Banlieue* of Paris is the one district in France
in which, for the past ten years, Communistic propaganda
has been making progress.

In order to improve these conditions the first necessity is

[1] Marius Boisson, *Coins et recoins de Paris*, 1927, p. 195 ff.
[2] Accessible in German in the *Europäische Revue*, March 1928.

to reform the administration. The city of Paris, three or four departments, and a whole host of communes, would need to be united into an administrative unity as the *Région parisienne*. In March 1928 a "Comité Supérieur d'aménagement de la Région parisienne" was created. But so far it is only an advisory body which stands behind the Minister for the Interior. This is the point at which legislation should be introduced.

The history of Paris, like that of Rome, forms part of world history. To learn to know Paris is a study which needs months and years, and is one which offers the mind inexhaustible nourishment. One can take a longitudinal section of Paris from the point of view of its historical development, or a cross-section of its life at the present day—and in both ways one will discover such a wealth of differing pictures that they seem to cover the whole of human existence.

The impression of Paris as a whole is not dominated by one epoch, one style or one mood, but it is composed of an almost inexhaustible number of characteristic and unique aspects. Paris is as manifold as France itself. Each quarter of the city has its own physiognomy, and its special function in the life of the whole. The specializing of these functions extends both to the economic and to the intellectual sphere, and appears to be carried out most logically. On the Quai Malaquais are the art antiquaries, on the Quai de la Mégisserie there is the trade in flowers, plants and animals; in the rue St. Antoine furniture predominates, in the Champ-Élysées motor cars. Montparnasse belongs to the artists, the Boulevard St. Michel and the neighbourhood of the Panthéon to the students. Here we are in the "Latin Quarter": *le pays latin, le quartier latin*; this meant originally the space which was formerly occupied by the University (between the Seine, rue de Bac, Montagne Sainte-Geneviève and rue du Cardinal Lemoine).

> Non loin des bords de la Seine,
> Paris ne connaît qu'à peine
> Un quartier sombre et lointain,

Qui sur le coteau s'élève,
Devers Saint-Geneviève;
C'est le vieux quartier latin.

Thus sang the popular Chansonnier of the Second Empire,
Gustave Nadaud, at a time when the confusing medley
of lanes and alleys of the ancient *quartier* was not yet
disturbed by the Boulevard St. Michel (1857–62). But
these verses were written upon the right bank of the
Seine; they are conceived in the spacious and spiritually
remote atmosphere of the Boulevards; right and left
bank: these are two different worlds, which do not know
each other, and regard each other with some contempt.
For a Suarès[1] the left bank is "la bonne rive: . . . je passe les
ponts, et je les romps derrière moi. Voici que je retrouve la
ville des livres et des maisons studieuses, des savants et des
prêtres et de l'amour pensif qui défend les lieux sacrés de
l'occident contre les Barbares: Sainte-Geneviève sur sa
colline penche un visage de reine toujours jeune sur le
miroir de la Seine. Là, du moins, entre Notre-Dame et la
Parnasse, il est encore un air respirable pour les hautes
pensées. On peut sortir de l'impure mêlée; On peut se
promener parfois dans les rues silencieuses, et marcher à
pas lents, le matin dans le Jardin du Luxembourg, fleuri
de rêves et d'amants. Tout, ici, n'est pas une foire aux
plaisirs, dans l'arène des gros sous. Ici, il est permis de
croire encore à la volupté secrète qui ne se passe, dans l'âme
et dans la chair, ni de loisir ni de retraite. Me voilà de retour sur la Bonne Rive."

Romain Rolland also, in his *Jean-Christophe*, has
contrasted the noisy "fair" of the right bank with the
dignified, tranquil intellectual atmosphere of the left bank.
And recently Albert Thibaudet has thus described the intellectual atmosphere of this region of Paris: "La rive
gauche c'est la province de Paris, et elle est le côté du

[1] On this point compare my book, *Die literarischen Wegbereiter des
modernen Frankreich.*

cœur, le cœur est ici. De jeunes provinciaux abordent Paris non comme Rastignac par Montmartre, mais par la Montagne Saint-Geneviève, ses lycées, ses grandes écoles, sa Sorbonne (naguère Saint-Sulpice, ce Luxembourg clérical). Ils y apportent, pour la circulation et la lumière, les réserves d'économie provinciale, de substance terrienne et de durée française. Stendhal vient du Dauphiné, Taine arrive des Ardennes, Renan débarque de Bretagne, Barrès descend du train de Nancy. Quand les 'Déracinés' paraissaient, en 1897, dans la 'Revue de Paris' j'avais ma tablée d'étudiants chez un marchand de vins de la rue Monsieur-le-Prince. Barrèsien depuis le lycée, où je lisais fiévreusement *Un homme libre* pendant la classe de math., ce renouvellement de Barrès, cette prise de contact direct et ardente avec l'âme de la jeunesse française, m'émerveillaient; quelques camarades de table partageaient mon goût.''

The contrast between the two banks of the river Seine is mingled with many other factors which belong to the sociology of Paris. The specialization of callings sometimes agrees with that of the various provinces. Coal merchants and hotel-keepers come from Auvergne; plumbers and painters from Limousin; coachmen and chauffeurs from Corrèze. All preserve their own distinctive quality and hold together. Thus, for instance, in Paris before the War the people from the Nivernais possessed seven friendly societies and insurance clubs; those from Morvan had three, one of which was founded only for those who were *Originaires de Moux*—Moux is a tiny place with a population of fifteen hundred souls! From the days of Napoleon the speciality of Morvan has been nurses and roadsweepers. Those who come from the department of Lot meet each other at the "Dîner du Calel", those from Reims in the "Société amicale de la Marne"; the Savoyards (who are no longer chimney-sweeps, but who evince a preference for the bronze industry of the Marais) meet at the "Banquet du Matafan," while people from Nantes

meet at the Café "Aux Enfants de la Loire-Inférieure";
the Drôme provides some of the most famous chefs for the
restaurants of Paris—these are only a few indications of
the variety of the population of Paris.[1]

Nearly two-thirds[2] of the population of Paris consists of
people who have come from the provinces. Often they tend
to settle in certain districts; those who come from Alsace-
Lorraine are often found in the north and north-east of
the city (*i.e.* the 18th, 19th, 10th and 11th Arrondissement; Savoyards live in the centre and on the right bank
(2nd and 3rd Arrondissement); Bretons on the south-
west (6th and 15th Arrondissement).[3]

Paris conceals a number of small *patries*. But also apart
from this specialization according to calling and origin each
quarter of the city forms a town in itself, and fills its inhabitants with local patriotism. To the genuine Parisian of
the old stamp we may apply the saying of Dumas *père*:
"Quand on est né dans une grande ville comme Paris, on
n'a pas de patrie, on a une rue." This feeling of love for
one's home can develop into a very deep kind of patriotism: this is shown by the memorial on the birthplace of
the poet G. T. Franconi, who fell in 1918: "tué . . . pour
défendre contre l'envahisseur sa maison, sa rue et la place
Saint Sulpice" (13, rue des Canettes).

The street is the smallest community in the life of Paris;
next in order comes the *quartier*. In the broad sense this
word has always been used to denote a district within a
town whose inhabitants feel it to be a unity. This explains
expressions like the following: "faire les visites du Quartier", that is: "faire visite aux personnes qu'on veut voir
parmi celles qui demeurent dans le quartier où l'on
vient s'établir". It is said of Fontenelle (1657–1757) that
he held social intercourse only with the inhabitants of his
own *quartier*. In old Paris the *Quartier* was really a small

---

[1] I follow Pierre Bonardi, *De quoi se compose Paris* (1927).
[2] According to R. Michels, 63 per cent.
[3] Jean Brunhès, *Géographie humaine de la France*, 2, 47.

town within the larger one, in which all the inhabitants knew each other. This meaning of the word still holds good at the present day; but since the Revolution another new technical meaning has been added: the *Quartier* is an administrative subdivision of the *Arrondissements*.

By the constitution of the year III. of the Republic Paris was divided into twelve *Arrondissements* for every four *Quartiers*. By the Consular Constitution it was further decreed (28 Pluviose VIII.-17 February 1800) that the general council of the Department of the Seine should take over the functions of the municipal council of Paris, and the Prefect of the Seine the duties of the Mayor of Paris. This regulation is still in force. Each *Arrondissement* of Paris has its *maire*, but there is no *maire* of Paris as a whole. The *Arrondissements* of Paris are not sub-prefectures, like those of the provincial Departments, although, like these, they form voting districts for the general elections. The Paris *Arrondissement*, moreover, forms a spiritual unity which expresses itself in various ways. Books have been written which give the history of particular *Arrondissements* during the Great War.[1] The following may be adduced as instances of the local pride of the Parisian municipal districts: the monument at Buttes-Chaumont which is dedicated to the 19th Arrondissement; a detailed and able description of this occurs in the *Paysan de Paris* (1926), by Louis Aragon. The 2nd Arrondissement has found its chronicler in André Salmon (*Les Panathénées du 2e arrondissement*), Belleville in Robert Garric (*Scènes de la vie populaire*), Montmartre in Francis Carco (*Jésus-la-Caillé and others*) . . . and the list could easily be extended.[2]

It is a significant fact that even the municipal history of Paris is written from the "regionalist" standpoint. Its organs are called: *Le Centre de Paris* (Ier et IIe arr.); *La*

---

[1] Docteur Philippe Maréchal, *Un Arrondissement de Paris pendant la guerre*. Avant-Propos de M. Raymond Poincaré. Paris, Fasquelle, 1921.

[2] Cf. Otto Grautoff, "Paris bei Tag und bei Nacht" (*Deutsch-französische Rundschau*, 1928, 697 ff.).

*Cité, revue historique et archéologique des IIIe et IVe arr.; La Montagne Sainte-Geneviève et ses abords* (Ve, XIIIe et XIVe arr.); *La Société historique du VIe arrondissement; Le Bulletin de la Société historique d'Auteuil; Le Bulletin de l'Association des Parisiens de Paris; Le Vieux Montmartre*, etc.

In addition, of course, there are also scientific societies and publications which cover the whole of the municipality of Paris. There is a "Bibliothèque Historique de la Ville de Paris" in the old Hôtel Le Peletier de St. Fargeau (29 rue de Sévigné), which also contains, in the same building, the "Institut d'Histoire de Géographie et d'Économie urbaines". Finally there is also the splendid "Musée historique de la Ville de Paris", which is better known under the name of the Musée Carnavalet.

The study of Paris, of its geography, history, economics and culture, has become a far-reaching special science, whose origins extend back into the sixteenth century, with its own bibliographies and its own journals.

The way in which Paris is reflected in the best literature provides an inexhaustible theme of great charm. Even the medieval heroic epic offers a good many instances.[1] Poetry about Paris begins about 1300 with the ballad-minstrels, with the *Dit des rues de Paris* by the Parisian Guillot, and the *Crieries de Paris* of Guillaume de Villeneuve. Since then the *Cris de Paris*, that is, the crying up of their wares by wandering street-vendors, have always been rendered into verse, or otherwise used in some literary way.[2] The most recent example is that of Marcel Proust, who has woven this *motif* into the composition of his great work of fiction.

If Zola has described the "stomach" of Paris, Hugo, Michelet, Balzac, Baudelaire and Verlaine have unveiled to us her soul. But we ought to name many others—and not only Frenchmen: Herman Bang's *Michael* is one of the tenderest and most intimate poems about Paris. The finest

---

[1] L. Olschki, *Paris nach den altfranzösischen nationalen Epen* (1913).

[2] Also in music: see, for example, de Jannequin (d. 1560).

evidence of love which a poet of our day has given to Paris is "Paris de France" by Valéry Larbaud.[1] Here knowledge and wisdom, intelligence and play of spirit are combined— and through the whole there sounds the solemn melody of life and death.

What Paris has meant to the leading personalities in the spiritual and intellectual world of Germany is summed up in the period which lies between the cosmopolitan *adhortatio* of the aged Goethe to Eckermann (Gespräch vom 3 Mai 1827) and the tribute of gratitude paid by Georg:

> Und in der heitren anmut stadt · der gärten
> Wehmütigem reiz · bei nachtbestrahlten türmen
> Verzauberten gewölbs umgab mich jugend
> Im taumel aller dinge die mir teuer—
> Da schirmten held und sänger das geheimnis:
> VILLIERS sich hoch genug für einen thron.
> VERLAINE in fall und busse fromm und kindlich
> Und für sein denkbild blutend: MALLARMÉ.
>
> Mag traum und ferne uns als speise stärken—
> Luft die wir atmen bringt nur der Lebendige.
> So dank ich freunde euch die dort noch singen
> Und väter die ich seit zur gruft geleitet. . . .
> Wie oft noch spät da ich schon grund gewonnen
> In trüber heimat streitend und des sieges
> Noch ungewiss · lieh neue Kraft dies flüstern:
> RETURNENT FRANC EN FRANCE DULCE TERRE.

[1] In the volume *Jaune Bleu Blanc* (1927). German translation by Max Rychner, *Lob von Paris* (Zürich 1929).

# VIII

## THE MAIN ELEMENTS

In literature—French as well as foreign—and in educated public opinion, we find a great number of more or less pregnant conceptions of the essence of the French nature, a formidable series of definitions of the French "character", of the French "spirit", of the "French" pure and simple. In France itself, writers, critics, psychologists, and scholars have tried again and again to create a definition of this kind. Writers and others construct an "ideal Frenchman", or a "normal Frenchman", or a "consistent Frenchman". This Frenchman is just as abstract, just as unreal, as the "man" who figured so prominently in the philosophy of the eighteenth century. To reduce the French spirit to a definition is a more or less (mostly less) amusing literary pastime; and when it has been done, little has been achieved for real knowledge. Indeed, this theorizing is not merely futile, it can have a very harmful and illusory effect. When it is used as a standard it makes it impossible to gain any spontaneous apprehension of French realism. Someone meets a French writer or artist who does not fit into this theory, and at once he draws the conclusion that this person is "un-French"—instead of saying the opposite: "This Frenchman forces me to correct and broaden my conception of the French character". In France itself this conception of what is "un-French" is also used; but this is simply a mixture of mental laziness and prejudice.

Must we, then, entirely renounce the attempt to analyse and describe the psychology of the French? It is obvious that this too, would be a mistake. We *must* make this attempt; and in every period it will be repeated; and both from the historical and from the psychological point of view it will be constantly necessary, and indeed, inevitable. Of course it will always only represent a personal point of

view, but there are causes of error which can be avoided,
and methods which are out-of-date.

It might seem a safe method to collect what the French
have said about themselves, and then to prepare a description based on these observations. There are, however, two
objections to this method. First: these statements will vary
so greatly that it will be impossible to bring them into any
kind of unity; secondly, the most illuminating characteristic of an individual, or a group, is precisely that element
of which the individual or the group is quite unconscious.
If an individual describes himself, inevitably he overlooks
these psychical *A prioris*. Psychological self-evidence therefore often conceals the distinctive elements. These only
become visible when they are compared with other psychological structures. What the French say about themselves
affords a valuable indication of their conscious tendencies
and value-judgments, but it needs to be completed by
something from outside.

Therefore we can learn most from those French people
(not very numerous) who have passed through the experience of a foreign civilization, and from the small group of
foreigners who have really entered into the French way
of life, and who understand them from the human point
of view. I think, for example, of the American Brownell,
the author of *French Traits*, of the Spaniard Salvador de
Madariaga,[1] or of the Englishman Harold Nicolson, whose
able criticism of the French character I give below: "Of
all civilised races the French are perhaps the most gifted,
as they are certainly the most charming; but they have one
basic defect: they have no sense of infinity. They possess
indeed, every quality of the brain and soul; but they possess these qualities in so vivid, so self-realised, so precise a
manner that there is no scope for expansion: there are no
gradations. Thus they have patriotism but no public spirit,
foresight but no vision, wit but no humour, personality but

[1] Author of *Englishmen, Frenchmen, Spaniards* (Oxford University
Press, 1928).

no individualism, discipline but no order. . . . They have none of our cheerful and blundering intuition. . . . In practical and objective affairs, such as the great European War, this peculiar adaptation of the French genius works admirably. In more subjective businesses, such as literature and politics, it is apt to be conventional and short-sighted. Above all these secondary aspects of national temperament rises the essential quality of French genius—as a glacier, arrogant, lucid and cold. The French mind is, above all, architectural in character: it is deliberate, cautious, balanced and terribly intent upon the proportions, the stability and the meaning of the business in hand. It repudiates the improvised. . . ."[1]

Descriptions of this kind are steeped in personal observation, and are therefore more instructive than psychological theories. A living view of the French character is something quite different from a knowledge of French history, French customs or French literature. In France the intellect is so strongly socialized that we gain a false picture of French literature if we have no experience of the national and social way of life which the tradition of this literature bears and carries forward. French literature is not a mirror of society. Literary expression can intensify certain traits of cultural reality; others it can ignore, and some it can oppose. Literature transforms life. Often it accentuates difficulties which are smoothed out in real life. A psychology of the nations based upon literature only incurs the risk of producing artificial and illusory results.

The usual analysis of the French character begins by ascribing to it certain qualities which are piled up one on top of another like building blocks. Thus the list may include "clarity", "order", "moderation", "*sociabilité*"— (one of the oldest clichés of French criticism); "pleasantness", "rhetoric", "scepticism" may be added. The list can be made longer if desired. But the total impression of a

[1] Harold Nicolson, *Paul Verlaine* (London, Constable, 1921), pp. 225-6.

person can never be understood as the sum of his qualities, and the personality of a nation can be understood just as little from this point of view. Further, the psychology of nations should include the ways in which nations function, their peculiar forms of national life, and the laws which result from these, instead of artificially isolated qualities.

If we regard French civilization from the point of view of its particular kind of experience, the first thing which strikes us is this: it is a late civilization. It begins with the assimilation of the late Roman civilization. The importance of the Roman element must be rated very high in French civilization, in spite of the objections of scholars like Jullian who exaggerate the Celtic element. The most important of these structural peculiarities is that which may be described as the secondary character of French civilization. The experience which determined the form and direction of the whole psychical experience of France, which stands at the beginning of its growth, is not an original primitive experience, but an experience of culture: the acceptance and assimilation of a foreign, mature, ancient civilization. The Germans have had a primitive elemental experience: the wandering of the tribes and the founding of states, the source of our heroic epics. The Romanized Gauls, on the contrary, assimilated a finished civilization. Hence their civilization bears traces of its secondary or derivative character. It is not a primitive creation (*Urschöpfung*), indeed, the French language cannot easily find an equivalent for our prefix *ur-*. We must, however, remind ourselves that Roman civilization itself was also secondary: it arose through the assimilation of the Greek world of intellect, and its adaptation to the popular life of Italy. Thus the civilization of France is derivative also in a secondary sense. This is revealed in the literature of France, but it comes out also in customs, in national feeling and in faith. This derivative character may be regarded differently, according to the personal standpoint of the individual. Those who value originality will think that it is a pity, or they will depreciate it. Those who have a strong sense of the value of tradition, on the other hand, regard this as an advantage.

In any case this secondary character means a great deal for France. Within herself she contains the spirit of Rome and of the ancient world. The traveller in Provence who visits beautiful Nîmes, the Nemausus of the Gauls, finds in the central square of the town a well-preserved Roman Temple, known in popular speech as *la maison carrée*. Close by is the magnificent amphitheatre, which is now used for bull-fights and also for magic lantern shows. In the public gardens there stands a monument to the Emperor Antoninus Pius: he was a child of this town, and the town seems to value the connexion, for the statue was erected in 1874 by the Town Council. The chief park of the town, the Jardin de la Fontaine, is a perfect example of the classical *jardin à la française*, a masterpiece of Le Nôtre, the landscape gardener of Louis XIV. But at its highest point there rises a ruined Roman tower, the *Tour magne*, that is, *Turris magna* or "great tower". Finally, some miles outside the city there is one of the greatest monuments of Roman architecture: the Pont du Gard, a three-tiered bridge and aqueduct over the Gard, whose yellow-brown freestone and mighty arches display in the most impressive manner the monumental and permanent character of Roman architecture and thought. Similar sights can be seen at Arles, Orange, Vienne, and in many other small towns in Provence: these buildings help us to understand the indestructible Latin character of south-eastern France. The tradition of Rome is more impressively displayed here than in many parts of Italy, and it is not confined to the Roman province of Narbonensis. Even Paris still has its ancient theatre, the Arena of the Roman Lutetia. Thus Rome still towers visibly above the scene of the France of the present day, and is actually incorporated into her life; France feels herself to be the daughter and the heiress of Rome; for that very reason her feeling about the Rome of Italy differs entirely from ours. Because France contains so much of ancient Rome within her own borders she needs modern Rome less than we do. In our intellectual history we come again and again upon the type of the German-Roman: Winckelmann, Goethe, Marées, Feuerbach, Gregorovius. To these men Rome became their true home. Of great Frenchmen of this type I suppose Claude Lorraine is the only one who felt like this.

The French Monarchy of Louis XIV. felt itself Roman in spirit. The intellectual and artistic flowering of the seventeenth century seemed to be a renewal of the Augustan Age. The Revolution too was full of the spirit of ancient Rome. The historical pictures of David are a speaking expression of this fact. The Empire of Napoleon also was Roman in sentiment. The Emperor renewed the world dominion of Rome, and he named his son and heir King of Rome. The French sense of justice is Roman. The written law and the formal written agreement possess an inviolable authority in France. French Crown lawyers played an important part in the history of the Monarchy, especially in the days of Philip the Fair and in those of Louis XIV. The creation of the *Code Napoléon* is one of the glories of the imperial era. Even from the point of view of style and language it is a masterly achievement: it is well known that Stendhal made it a habit to read this law book in order to prepare himself for his literary work. It is to its legal discipline that the French language owes much of its clarity and definiteness. But the spirit of the Roman law has also formed the ethos of France. In France if any doubt arises about the justice of a legal sentence, at once popular feeling becomes agitated. Revisions of sentences form an essential part of the history of France. It was certainly no merely dynastic interest which caused Charles VII., in 1456, to have the Process against Jeanne d'Arc re-examined, and the sentence of 1431 reversed as irregular. Not a little of the lasting fame of Voltaire is due to the fact that he championed innocent people who had been condemned or persecuted. A hundred and fifty years later Émile Zola played this part in the Dreyfus affair. We can still remember the passionate conflicts which raged round the question whether Captain Dreyfus were guilty or innocent. A generation ago they plunged France into a state of inward civil war. It is clear that this would have been impossible were it not for the loud echo which is evoked whenever the least doubt arises about the justice of any legal sentence.

Justice is no merely theoretical virtue in France. It wields authority over the spirit and temper of the people. Whoever appeals to this element can be certain of having the sympathy, the temperament and the practical energy of the nation on his side. Politicians of all parties know this. It is impossible to rouse the French people for a cause unless it can be described as a "just cause". Military discipline also appeals to this feeling. Generals of the Third Republic speak thus to their troops: "Vous ferez respecter la Justice, parce que tel est le premier devoir de tout honnête homme et que la Justice—plus encore la Liberté, l'Égalité et la Fraternité, qu'elle résume en un mot et contient à elle seule—est la chose du monde à laquelle les Français tiennent par-dessus tout."[1]

This high sense of the value of law and justice also explains the high esteem enjoyed by the representatives of the Law in France. The French advocate holds an honoured position, and he often becomes a leading politician. Gambetta was a lawyer, and he leapt into fame through a speech he made at a political trial under the Second Empire. Among the some six hundred deputies to the Chamber of 1914 there were 142 advocates. The notary also belongs to the class which represents the law. He plays an important part in French life, especially in the provinces, as every reader of Balzac is aware. He is the confidential friend of the family, administers its income, advises it in important affairs, is indispensable for marriage settlements and in the making of wills. And then the Judge! In France the profes-

[1] Général Tanant, *L'Officier de France* (1927).

P

sion of the Judge incorporates a form of public ethics similar to that which exists in the Prussian official class. The magistracy preserves a traditional sentiment which belongs to the far distant past of ancient France. The Judge applies the laws and satisfies the desire for security of justice. During the period of the Revolution the Law was the sole source of justice, and the system of legislation was represented as the formulation of pure reason, but during the course of the nineteenth century a change has taken place: the science of Law has taken on, in addition, the task of adapting the law to the social conditions and the spirit of the age; in cases where the law has not already created a precedent it tries to create one itself. Thus in the course of the last hundred years French jurisprudence has achieved a great deal for the ideal of social and legal progress, just as the codified law preserves the ideal of stability.

The fact that the whole outlook of the French people is impregnated with the juridical spirit may be definitely assigned to the abiding influence of the Roman system of law. This juridical spirit also expresses itself in the following ways: in respect for institutions, in the conception of society as a collective body of free persons; and, above all, in the individualistic legal metaphysic with which the *Code civil* has permeated the life of France. Civil freedom, the sacredness of private property, and the institutional nature of the family[1] loom more largely in the national consciousness of France than they do among us. The State is regarded as "la grande famille française", and Utopian dreamers speak with enthusiasm of the "grande famille humaine" conceived as based on a legal constitution. This insistence upon "pure justice" often reveals a certain greatness. More often, however, it has hindered the progress of the nation; one of the causes of the Revolution was the rigidity with which the Parliaments clung to their privi-

[1] For the cult of the Family cf. Albert Chével, *La Famille française. Pages choisies de nos bons écrivains de 843 à 1924*, 3 volumes. In modern French painting Carrière represents the Ethos of the Family.

leges. The "Declaration of the Rights of Men and of Citizens" became the manifesto of the upheaval. When the mere idea of justice has been severed from the ideas of order, authority and the common good, it has always had a destructive effect. But in France the bare ideal of Justice can always appeal to the Roman tradition.

The influence of Rome is woven into the whole texture of the life of France, yet Rome is only one of the elements which compose the substance of France. Hence the French constantly feel the need to reinterpret the significance of the Latin element. During the last two hundred years there have been periods in which the spirit of France felt the need to break through the fence of the Latin tradition, and to assimilate the spirit of the Germanic peoples, or even to look back to its Gallic origin. But equally regularly a reaction would always follow. Very naturally the World War has strengthened the Latin element. In the gardens of the Palais-Royal there is a statue, the ideal figure of a naked youth; according to the inscription on the base it is supposed to represent the Latin Genius, and during the War it was presented to the city of Paris by the Latin nations. After the War the so-called "Latin idea" was ardently discussed. The question was raised whether France could form a unified Latin civilization in union with Spain, Portugal and the Latin-American peoples. Thoughtful observers, however, have made it clear that this Latin idealism is mingled with a good deal of unreality. The linguistic relationship is of course a very close one. From the point of view of language the ideal is that of a unified, clearly-defined *Romania*. But from the intellectual and cultural point of view there is no unity. From the intellectual and literary point of view France has a far closer connexion with England than with Spain. She likes to choose Minerva from the ancient gods of Olympus as her patron deity, but France is not completely absorbed in the Latin idea. Perhaps one of the reasons for this is the fact that upon her own soil France contains the contrast between the North and

the South. The strongest impulses to the renewal and exclusive importance of the Latin idea usually come from
the South, from Provence, Languedoc and the districts
round the Pyrenees. Characteristically the Latin idea is
there claimed by some as the support for the ideals of the
Republic, and by others for those of the Monarchy. It is
indeed just as easy to call the ideas of reason and civic
freedom "Latin", as those of order and authority. In the
last thirty years the South of France has produced the
great theorists of "integral Nationalism" (that is, Royalism), the school of the *Action Française*. But the mass of the
electors, and thus the actual political power, belong precisely in the South to the parties of the Left.

Rome is the revered ancestress of France. But the Roman
spirit has been blended so closely with Gallic and Germanic blood that the result of this fusion has become a
new and unified race-personality. Even where French
civilization perpetuates Roman features, she transforms
and adapts them to her own organic law which cannot be
ascribed to any foreign element. One thing, however, remains true: by the acceptance of the Roman tradition
during the period of her development, France received
the inheritance of a thousand years. And this inheritance
gives to French civilization a peculiar imprint of age and
maturity. But in the external sense France is not old;
it is her habit of thought and her outlook which are
mature.

The French regard time in a sense which differs wholly
from the German point of view. The French live more
deeply in remembrance and in the past than we do. For
us the past is the story of a growth, for the French it is the
vivid and vital realization of a tradition. Compared with
the German spirit—and all that has been said is naturally
to be applied within this relationship—the French spirit
is non-historical. Her historical form of thought is not one
of development but of permanence. There is depth in the
statement of Rivarol: "Il faut que la France conserve et

qu'elle soit conservée; ce qui la distingue de tous les peoples anciens et modernes." The same sentiment is thus expressed by Péguy: "Il faut que France, il faut que Chré- tienté se continue".

In France whenever anything has become a historical reality it retains its value. The past is not made to give way to the present, nor the old to the new. When a French- man reads Montaigne or La Bruyère he does not regard these authors as the expression of the outlook of their own day, nor as examples of a definite stage in history, but as timeless valid voices which express the human spirit. In France every great book, every historical epoch of the nation, can be sure that it will always find a number of lovers and admirers who will settle down comfortably in it and study it with antiquarian interest.

This sense of belonging to an ancient civilization is also expressed in the French national consciousness. Fustel de Coulanges has said that true patriotism is the love of the past, and Barrès has coined this motto for his ideal of nationalism: *La terre et les morts*. The cult of the dead is a striking feature in the character of France. It preserves a peculiar religious reference even where the faith of the Church has vanished. Among the most impressive sights of Paris are the graveyards: Montparnasse, Montmartre, and above all, Père-Lachaise. There the dead repose, not under green mounds but in stone houses, which are often built in the form of a temple, or a chapel, and are sur- rounded by iron railings. Many of these graves bear the inscription: "Concession à perpétuité". This graveyard is a second city, a stone city of death, set in the midst of the living "City of Light". There rest, alongside of one an- other, Molière and La Fontaine, there the most eminent names of the nineteenth century: Musset and Chopin, Balzac and Ingres, Delacroix and Comte. . . . And their graves are decorated, they are visited by admirers, many of whom come from far. The atmosphere of this quiet city of tombs is so impressive that one could almost believe, like the men of old, that the spirits of the dead are hovering over their graves.

But in Paris there are other great monuments of this cult of the dead: the *Panthéon*, in which the nation buries her great men; *les Invalides*, where the sarcophagus of Napoleon reposes so solemnly; the *Arc de Triomphe*, where the "unknown soldier" lies buried. In the midst of the roar of the traffic the tiny flame over his grave is a reminder of those who died in the Great War; at the same time it also symbolizes that deep reverence for the dead which is so deeply ingrained in the consciousness of France.

The French reverence for the past is not a Romanticism which simply gazes back at the past—this is a typically youthful way of feeling—it is an instinct which is close to reality, and shapes both the present and the future. We Germans issued from the War with the intoxicating sense that everything must become new. At the same time it made no difference to us whether we were thinking of a new national life or a new humanity. In France it was the other way round: the instinct of the nation rallied after the disturbance and upheaval of the War to the renewal of the old, of that which lasts. "Our old world still exists"— this was the prevalent feeling. From the literary point of view it was expressed in war books like Thibaudet's *La Guerre avec Thucydide* or Cazin's *L'Humaniste à la guerre*: the humanist tradition was constant and fruitful enough to preserve itself in the lower ranks of society; it served as a rallying point in the midst of a bewildering and unprecedented chaos to people like the corporal in his blue uniform whose real life was that of an intellectual. The same sense of consciousness of permanence, interspersed however with humour and with melancholy, inspired the gentle lyrical poet, Jean Pellerin, to write his *Romance du retour*, a poem which describes the soldier home from the front in his contact with Paris:

> Paris, milliers de promesses,
> Appels de taxis inviteurs,

Aveux de nocturnes prouesses
Dans les corbeilles des facteurs,
Milliers de maisons, de femmes,
Sarabande d'hommes infames,
Tournois de mauvaises raisons!
Le ciné donne Forfaiture.
La marchande, sur sa voiture,
N'a pas plus de quatre saisons.

\*   \*   \*   \*   \*

J'ai pleuré par les nuits livides
Et de chaudes nuits m'ont pleuré.
J'ai pleuré sur des hommes vides
A jamais d'un nom préféré.
Froides horreurs que rien n'efface!
La terre écarte de sa face
Ses longs cheveux indifférents,
Notre vieux monde persévère,
Douze sous pour un petit verre!
Combien va-t-on payer les grands?

But this same desire to perpetuate a situation which has once existed has also been displayed in the political attitude of France after the War. She wished to restore everything to its pre-war condition. Many a district in France has a history which stretches back beyond the Roman, and perhaps even beyond the Celtic period, and France wished to preserve the rights and forms of the past even down to the technical problems of the rebuilding of the ruined *Départements*.

In 1921 Rathenau mentioned this at the Economic Council of the Reich. He said: "The task of rebuilding is more complicated than we usually imagine it to be. We tend to think that new towns can be built, with new streets running in new directions, with houses of a new type. This is not the case in France. French law forbids it. French law requires, and the inhabitants of the town desire, that each individual house should be built up again on the old foundations, without any special consideration for questions of economy or uniformity."

This element in French civilization also accounts for the fact that in France mature age is preferred to youth. France does not possess, like Hellas or Germany, an ideal picture of youth. It is unyouthful in the manner of ancient Rome. "La France méprise la jeunesse," writes Jean Cocteau, "sauf quand elle s'immole pour sauvegarder la vieillesse. Mourir est un acte de vieux. Aussi chez nous la mort seule donne du poids aux jeunes. Un jeune qui rentre de la guerre a vite perdu son prestige. Il redevient suspect." Even the language has no special word for "youth"; it has to do the best it can with the somewhat unsatisfactory expression: *jeune homme*. The word "adolescent" is often used in a joking sense; ("se dit surtout des garçons, et alors souvent en plaisantant". *Littré*) this comes out still more strongly in the word *jouvenceau*. When Taine wrote his beautiful essay about the youths of Plato he had to use the circumlocution *Les jeunes gens de Platon*—which to us seems to convey a loss of something specific. Thus also there is no word which quite corresponds to the German *mädchen* or the English "girl". *Fille*, if it is not more precisely defined, may mean "daughter", or "unmarried woman", or "prostitute". A girl must be described as a *jeune fille*. In France there are no Youth Movements in our sense of the word. In France the young, in the perplexities and storms of the period of growth, can count upon sympathetic understanding less than in other countries. The young Frenchman sees in himself the man of the future more than the young German does. He calls his comrade *mon vieux*. Even schoolboys are treated as though they were grown-up, and are addressed as *Vous*. The children learn their own language from the *Fables of La Fontaine* with their worldly wisdom. The literature for children in France is poor. In literature and art to-day it is true that *les jeunes* are noticed a good deal, and are commercially exploited, but this movement only began at the end of the nineteenth century. In the early years after the War it reached its highest point. Until that time *les jeunes* were always referred to the *revues d'avant-*

*garde* when they wished to say anything. To-day the great newspapers and publishing houses are ready to use their material. It remains to be seen whether this new tendency will be permanent.

French literature is a literature for mature people. The values which French civilization prefer are the values of age. Such values are completeness (in the double sense of something which is finished and perfect), taste, the quality of a connoisseur, realism.

The French are *un peuple de finisseurs*. The reason why luxury trades (that is, trades whose value depends upon finely graded quality, the spirit of invention and taste) play such a large part in the economic life of France, is not only economic and social but psychological. In them the old spirit of French handicraft is perpetuated. This is the spirit which breeds the specifically French conception of perfection. The word *maître*, with which the disciples of an artist or a thinker honour their teacher, comes from this stage of the tradition, as well as the conception of a master-piece, which was originally the test-piece of work required from an apprentice, and which formed the most important part of the examination for the right to become a master (in Paris this appears for the first time in the Statute of the Embroiderers of 1316). This is the real meaning of the word *chef-d'œuvre*, and something of this is retained in the way in which the word is employed at the present time. It is the artistic spirit of the craftsman, which Boileau recommends to the poets, when he tells them:

> Vingt fois sur le métier remettez votre ouvrage:
> Polissez-le sans cesse et le repolissez.

Even though here *métier* does not mean handicraft, but the workman's bench, the suggestion that constant and assiduous polishing will produce a perfect work represents the craftsman's point of view.

From the French point of view art and handicraft are closely related. Ingres, when his friends urged him to finish his works more quickly, used to say: "If my works have any value it is because I have worked over them twenty times and have improved them with the greatest care". Not inspiration, but mastery of handicraft, long practice, continual polishing, have stamped upon his painting, as upon the poetry of Racine, or the prose of Flaubert, the mark of perfection.

This careful, patient work of the artist on his material requires a mastery of all its processes, and a sure and disciplined power of selection. The finished work must please, must satisfy the taste of the connoisseur. The French artist works for a public of admirers and connoisseurs. The connoisseur-capacity—expressed as the concentrated experience and refinement of feeling, as the capacity for making fine distinctions, as the discipline of the senses carried to a very high degree—occupies that place in the development of French civilization which we would give to the capacity for being stirred by greatness or beauty in any form.

In all matters of art, intellect and social life, the standard of French taste is not the strength of the impression, but the fine quality and the very subtle gradations which the work displays. French civilization is a civilization of connoisseurs, which is only another way of expressing an ancient and late culture. To be a connoisseur means to be able to distinguish, compare and estimate achievements and differences of quality in the spheres of intellect as well as of sense. To be a connoisseur in France means something which is both psychological and physiological, at one and the same time. It concerns both the intelligence and the tongue. It is exercised both in gastronomy and in criticism. Criticism, as the work of the connoisseur, is the power of making distinctions, the power of analysis, and it belongs to the noblest function of the French mind. The capacity to detect *nuances*, to savour the finest differences, characterizes both the French intellect and the French use of the senses. Both the intellect and the sense-life are fused in the typical experiences of French life into a unity which is described by the use of the word "taste". The connoisseur is a typical product of French civilization neither known nor desired elsewhere. In Germany the Faustian urge towards knowledge corresponds to this connoisseur quality in France. Between *erkennen* (to seek knowledge) and *Kenner* (the connoisseur, the knower) there lies the whole difference which is expressed by the use of the German prefix *er-*. It is akin to the prefix *ur-* and from the linguistic point of view it is simply the unstressed variant of that *ur-* which, as Fr. Kluge says in his *Etymologisches Wörterbuch der deutschen Sprache*, "has no fixed relations in the other Indo-Germanic languages".

The values of maturity are also expressed in the moral standards of French conventions. The *sagesse française* is a favourite theme for rhetorical exercises. The wisdom that is meant is nothing of a religious or metaphysical kind, but rather a wisdom of life gained through experience and knowledge of the world. The French often praise this virtue in their classic writers, in their moralists, in their statesmen. It has often something restrained and calculating about it, and it borders on *bon sens*; frequently it also contains, however, an admixture of scepticism and contempt for humanity. This is the spirit which warns, counsels prudence, which criticizes, and waits to see how things will turn out. It easily leads to mistrust, and it can be combined with the tendency to seek security, which finds its explanation in the history of a people which preserves as a racial memory the remembrance of the Roman Conquest, the attacks of the Germanic tribes, the Hundred Years' War, and which constantly feels that its existence is threatened by the "Barbarians". Buckle considers that one essential feature of the French is the "protective spirit". This desire for security brings with it the fear of risks. We know to how large an extent this determines the family life of France. It is generally admitted that careful calculation plays a part in making a contract of marriage, in the choice of a vocation, in the procreation and education of children. As far as possible the parents seek to diminish the risks of the future for their children. For long years the parents will save for the daughter's dowry, for the professional training of the son. Great foresight is exercised. The decline in the population is connected with this spirit which always looks ahead and fears to take risks. "La cause de la dépopulation est claire", says Paul Valéry, "C'est la présence d'esprit." And he adds: "Une somme d'époux prévoyants de l'avenir constitue un peuple insoucieux de l'avenir. Il faut perdre la tête ou perdre sa race." Careful calculation, waiting for opportunity, a slow moving forward, a step at a time, characterized the national expansion of France from the early Capetians down to Louis XIV. France admires this political wisdom in kings like Louis XI.

The dangers to which this old and cautious point of view are prone are these: loss of power to adapt to new circumstances, the instinctive rejection of the new, a blunting of sensibility through the force of habit and the attempt to imitate. "Les morts eux-mêmes", says Jean Finot, "ne cessent d'être nos hypnotiseurs. Nous les imitons sans y penser, de même que nous subissons l'action des siècles passés. Plus notre habitude d'imiter vieillit, plus la force, ou plutôt la facilité de l'appliquer grandit. Nous imitons encore plus facilement que nos ancêtres d'il y a quelques siècles." It is perhaps no accident that it is France which has presented to modern social science a classic work on *The Laws of Imitation* (by G. Tarde), that the French novel —(Balzac and Proust)—has represented the deformation of the soul through slavery to habit, and that French philosophy pays special attention to the nature of memory. Bergson, it is true, has reopened the way for the recognition of the creative factor in evolution. But Bergson's argument still confirms the importance of habit in French thought. He expends much skill on trying to prove that there really is something new in the world, and he warns his readers against ascribing this element to something which is already familiar and ready-made (*tout fait*).

That all life is change and new birth is of course just as true for the historical and present life of France as it is for other nations. All that is specifically French is the attitude which the consciousness brings to the new, and the form in which the new is received.[1] Psychical changes take place more slowly among the French than among us. This must be remembered in all attempts to bring about a better understanding between the French and the Germans. Jean Schlumberger gives a psychological explanation of this phenomenon which is full of a delicate insight: "If the French have gained a reputation for being a versatile and light-hearted people the reason is this: in Germany people have not understood how to distinguish between the qualities which appear on the surface and those which lie at a deeper level. Few nations are more faithful to their feelings, and are therefore less able to adapt themselves to a swift process of development than the French. Without doubt this is connected with a certain maturity of feeling and independence of character, which has a great objection to contradicting itself. Whatever the cause may be, this is the fact: in Germany and in France feelings cannot be changed at the same rate of progression. This is the greatest psychological obstacle which must be taken into account. We are often in danger of thinking there is discord, when at bottom all that is wrong is simply the different rate of movement in thought and feeling in the two countries. Our slowness often looks like hopeless rigidity when it is really honesty towards ourselves. But when this obstacle is clearly seen and recognized it can be overcome and conquered through patience. This is my deepest conviction."

Even when a Frenchman takes up the rôle of a reformer he is often dependent on the past. Tarde has shown that

---

[1] "Le Français ne croit pas au changement, ou il y croit trop tard. Alors, il se rattrappe comme il peut, d'ailleurs très adroitement. . . . L'esprit nouveau fleurira en France comme partout, mais quand? Question angoissante, que peu de Français se posent." Jacques Moreau, *Perspectives* (1929), 291.

there are two kinds of imitation: "faire exactement comme son modèle, ou faire exactement le contraire". Even the "contre-imitation" is an imitation. Determination of behaviour by the presentation of an example—in one sense or the other—is a frequent phenomenon in France. Critics still argue to-day about the nature of French Romanticism. But whatever it may be, the one thing that is sure is that it is an anti-Classical phenomenon. The school of 1830 did that which the school of 1660 forbade. It abrogated the laws of the latter: laws of metre, hierarchy of vocabulary, separation of species. When Victor Hugo writes poetry he writes against Racine, against Boileau. The bond which unites the literary schools in France is the need to make things "different" from the accepted form of the literature of the day. When Valéry analyses the idea of originality he discovers that: "Il est des gens, j'en ai connu, qui veulent préserver leur originalité. Ils imitent par là. Ils obéissent à ceux qui les ont fait croire à la valeur de l'originalité."

We must not, however, fall into the error of regarding the feature of age in French civilization as a defect or weakness, as so frequently happens in Germany. Here also, it is true that every stage in life has its own advantage. The advantage of mature age is that of heightened self-consciousness. Intensity of the illumination of consciousness is one of the chief characteristics of the French habit of mind. French maturity is a conscious maturity. Since it knows itself, it is also conscious of the dangers of which we have spoken, and it knows how to meet them. France knows that its danger is that of becoming rigidly confined within the influences of the past. For that very reason she strives deliberately to adapt and adjust herself to the new, which time brings with it. Thus she gains a certain elasticity which should not be undervalued.

But we must guard against making a picture of France which is artificially simplified. The quality of traditionalism is no more characteristic of the French habit of mind than is its opposite: radicalism. One who knows his own

nation very well, Émile Montégut, has once said: "La
vérité est que la France, pays des contradictions, est à la
fois novatrice avec audace et conservatrice avec entête-
ment, révolutionnaire et traditionnelle, utopiste et routi-
nière. . . . C'est un pays révolutionnaire et traditionnel pour
qui sait bien voir: révolutionnaire, parce que les métamorphoses y ont été plus nombreuses qu'ailleurs; traditionnel,
parce que sous toutes ses métamorphoses brille le même
esprit méconnaissable en apparence." [1]

If we describe the revolutionary tendency of the French
spirit as "radicalism", this word must be understood in its
most general psychological sense, and not in connexion
with any definite system of politics. Political radicalism
(which, again, must not be held to be the same as the
present-day Radical, or Radical-Socialist parties) is only a
special form of the radicalism of France. This radicalism
belongs to the basic group of French characteristics, and
cannot be traced back any further. We find it even in the
days of the Romans, when Caesar described the Gauls as
"seekers of novelties" *novarum rerum cupidi*. French radicalism is a blend of emotionalism and logic, which feels im-
pelled to deny the past radically, to break wholly with
tradition, and instead of the historic tradition to erect a
completely new structure based upon abstract principles.
The radical spirit has no reverence; it tends to fanaticism,
or in any case to the rigid onesidedness of a doctrine, a
programme, or a system.

Its most important expression in the history of France
was in the Jacobins. Only since that time, since the great
Revolution, has it become a political factor in the public
life of France. We might even go further and say: only
through the combination of the Gallic temperament with
the Rationalism of the last centuries has it come into its full
extent and influence. It feels the need to make *tabula rasa*.
We can detect this feature even in the father of modern
philosophy, Descartes. Since then it has become increas-

---

[1] *Les Libres Opinions morales et historiques* (1858).

ingly significant. Politically the radicalism which came from the Revolution has changed greatly during the past fifty years. The "ideas of 1789" are, it is true, still to-day a catch-word which orators like to use in platform speeches, —but they have themselves become an integral part of the national tradition. In the Third Republic the Revolution is something which has been actually attained. The French voter of the Left or the popular orator glorifies the Revolution, and sees in it an imperishable claim to the fame of his nation. But he is a citizen, and on no account does he desire to make another revolution: that lies behind him. This radicalism also determines the views of the average Frenchmen about foreign countries and the policy of foreign states. To the masses of the French people the fact that there are still Monarchies in Europe seemed unintelligible and foolish. And to popular French radicalism it seems to-day just as suspicious and foolish that the Germans have made a revolution without exiling their princes and turning everything upside down. Such a revolution cannot be a real revolution. Such a Republic can only be an object of suspicion.

The radicalism of France, however, expresses itself also in purely intellectual matters; we only need to think of the Cubists in painting, of the literary movement of the *Surréalistes*, and of similar movements. New initiative, new artistic experiments, radical constructions of the intellect will always find a welcome in Paris.

From the psychological point of view, however, how can we explain the fact that traditionalism and radicalism are so closely connected and yet so clearly differentiated in the French habit of mind? First of all we must remember that both have certain elements in common, to some extent they influence each other. The stronger the power of tradition and the cult of the past the stronger also must be the counter-pressure which will shake off this burden. There is also a second point. When I said that French traditionalism lacks the historical sense, and that it does not think in the categories of growth and evolution, this is equally true of radicalism. The chimerical illusion that everything can be made new and better overnight, displays the same lack of the historical sense which appears in the habit of mind which conceives the past not as past but as present. Thus it might be possible to describe these apparently extreme opposites as different forms of expression of an identical feeling for time. It is, however, possible that these opposites correspond to different racial elements in the French people which, either alternately, or at the same time, come into action, and which certainly are not accessible to an exact analysis. There are no methods by which such complicated processes can be examined. We can only make guesses at the truth.

To the German who feels in France mainly the power of tradition, France may seem non-modern and reactionary, but if the German retains this opinion his point of view is naïve, especially if in great complacency he lays much stress on it. He forgets the capacity of France to endure, and he overlooks her vital power. For a long time we have allowed the idea of the decadence of France to dominate our thinking. For a short time France herself believed it too. But the French feeling of decadence of the nineteenth century, and especially of the end of the century, was the result of certain conditions which belonged to the period, whose effect ceased many years ago. Its causes were political, literary and general. It arose as a reaction from that optimism about the future which flourished in the thirties and forties. The result of the February Revolution, its transformation into the Caesarism of Napoleon III., meant a deep disappointment for the Utopian Messianism of the spirit of the day. The opposition, which gradually increased in strength, prophesied evil and decline. Thus from the beginning the decadence-idea was coloured by political agitation. It grew in intensity under the Third Republic. The Conservative-Clerical party saw France nationally humiliated, and within her borders under the

Q

sway of a government hostile to religion. It laid the blame at the door of the Revolution. At the same time the remembrance of the decline of the Roman Empire was also operative. Without the example of Roman decadence the French sense of decadence would never have been able to grow. The defeat of the Italians in Abyssinia (1896), and of the Spaniards in Cuba (1898), was interpreted as a sign of the decline of the "Latin races". The atmosphere of the *fin de siècle* favoured a mood of decline and decay, a fatalistic spirit of resignation. At the same time poets and literary men discovered the morbid attraction of a decaying civilization. Thus in addition to the politicians and moralists there were the aesthetes of the sense of decadence. But the decade before the World War brought about a very thorough change. Both from the military and from the political point of view France felt herself stronger; people talked a good deal about a *réveil national*; philosophy turned away from Determinism; literature overcame the weary aestheticism of the Symbolists; youth hardened its muscles in sport; new powers of faith awakened and strengthened the idealism of the intellect, and also the life of Catholicism. The idea of decadence was interpreted as a transitional crisis, and that was the end of it.[1]

To-day faith in the decadence of France means as much or as little as that in the "decline of the West". If France is an ancient land we must remember that Europe too is an ancient quarter of the globe. To the extent in which the features and values of age are developed in the civilization of Europe—and precisely to that extent—can the French spirit fulfil an essential function within Europe.

In spite of all her variety, contradictions and inner crises, France and her civilization display a unity which can only be created by a long slow historical experience. In France Freethinkers and devout Catholics are chips of the same block, rebels use the same rhetoric as conserva-

[1] Compare my article on the problem of French decadence in the *Internationale Monatsschrift* xx. (1921), vols. i. and ii.

tives, intellectuals mingle with politicians, and leaders in the economic sphere understand the language of the artists. All classes of the nation seem to have a common vocabulary of feelings, the same register of sentiments and of the requirements of life. France as a whole has attained unity of personality. She thinks of herself as of a person, and she thinks of her history in personal terms. To the geographer the French soil is *un personnage historique*; to the historian France is either the personal creation of its kings, if his way of thinking is Conservative; or the creation of the people, if he, like Michelet, is connected with the spirit of the Revolution. The personification of France has become part of the general consciousness. "La France est la plus grande personne morale qui ait jamais existé réellement ——". Statements like these occur frequently in popular writings. This feeling is alive in the whole nation. Marcel Proust speaks in *Le Temps retrouvé* of the "immense être humain appelé France", and contrasts it with the "conglomerate of individuals which makes up Germany".

The name *La France* permits a personification of the fatherland which the word Germany does not allow. To us the figure of Germania is not something alive; she is an artistic creation. But *La France* lives in the consciousness of France as a heroic or magical feminine figure. She is a fiction, which through turns of speech and through artistic representations on stamps, pictures and monuments has become real. A speaker of the Opposition during the July Monarchy gave this warning to the Government: "La France s'ennuie", and Marshal Joffre in 1914, when he entered the little town of Thann in Upper Alsace, was able to declare: "Je vous apporte le baiser de la France."

As a woman *La France* is capricious and coquettish. She desires to be treated with gallantry. Even her moods and faults are charming. She demands and she receives the homage of the French. She has been made a goddess. The *Dea Roma* corresponds to the *Déesse France* whom André Chénier honoured, and upon whose altar Maurras celebrates the rite of "integral nationalism". The cry "Vive la France" is not raised in honour of a State, a nation, or a country, but in praise of that mythical being whom millions of human beings nourish with their hearts' blood, their spirit and their will. That France has been able to create this myth of her own being has given her, at all periods in her history, and especially to the one which began in 1789, such a great power over the hearts of men, and explains the fact that the civilization of France has developed into a cult.

# INDEX